KT-104-339

Public Management and Modernisation in Britain

CONTEMPORARY POLITICAL STUDIES SERIES

Series Editor: John Benyon, *University of Leicester*

Public Management and Modernisation in Britain

Andrew Massey

and

Robert Pyper

First published in 2005 by
PALGRAVE MACMILLAN
Houndmills, Basingstoke, Hampshire RG21 6XS and
175 Fifth Avenue, New York, N.Y. 10010
Companies and representatives throughout the world.

PALGRAVE MACMILLAN is the global academic imprint of the Palgrave Macmillan division of St. Martin's Press, LLC and of Palgrave Macmillan Ltd. Macmillan® is a registered trademark in the United States, United Kingdom and other countries. Palgrave is a registered trademark in the European Union and other countries.

ISBN-13: 9780–333–73919–8 hardback
ISBN-10: 0–333–73919–1 hardback
ISBN-13: 9780–333–73920–4 paperback
ISBN-10: 0–333–73920–5 paperback

This book is printed on paper suitable for recycling and made from fully managed and sustained forest sources.

A catalogue record for this book is available from the British Library.

Library of Congress Cataloging-in-Publication Data

Massey, Andrew, 1958–
    Public management and modernisation in Britain /
Andrew Massey and Robert Pyper.
        p. cm. – (Contemporary political studies series)
    Includes bibliographical references and index.
    ISBN 0–333–73919–1 (cloth)
        1. Public administration – Great Britain. 2. Administrative
agencies – Great Britain – Management. 3. Organizational
change – Great Britain. I. Pyper, Robert. II. Title. III. Contemporary
political studies (Palgrave Macmillan (Firm))

JN318.M28 2005
351.41—dc22   2004062716

10 9 8 7 6 5 4 3 2 1
14 13 12 11 10 09 08 07 06 05

Printed and bound in China

Contents

List of Boxes

Acknowledgements

The authors and publishers would like to thank the following who have kindly given permission to reproduce copyright material:

The Controller of HMSO (under click licence number CO1W0000276) for the right to reproduce Boxes 5.1 and 6.2.

Every effort has been made to contact all the copyright-holders, but if any have been inadvertently omitted the publishers will be pleased to make the necessary arrangement at the earliest opportunity.

1

Introduction

In the United Kingdom, the United States of America and much of Western Europe, the majority of the population have never been so wealthy, so healthy or so well-educated. For many of us living in these societies, we are living in a golden age; an age of opulence that previous generations strove for, but could hardly imagine would ever exist. Certainly, pockets of deprivation and ignorance stubbornly remain and are the subject of governments' attention, but on the whole, the majority of us live longer and possess healthier and more enriched lives than at any time in history. There are many explanations for this situation and many attempts to interpret the developments in our societies as they take place and to predict how we shall develop, indeed whether this affluence will continue or for how long.

Marxists and other economic determinists tell us our wealth and our political systems reflect the economic structures in society and that these contain within themselves the seeds for their own destruction (Bloch, 2004). Other perspectives have a cultural, political or anthropological explanation or part-explanation of these developments. Some would argue the material wealth has been obtained at the expense of less tangible, but nonetheless important religious and cultural richness, as well as at great environmental cost (Bernstein, 2001; Bloch, 2004; Gray, 2004). Technological change is an important element in the accumulation of societies' wealth. Developments in science, engineering, and medicine provide many of the material benefits, but it is important to remember that they take place within a political, social, cultural and economic context. By this we mean, that the money to conduct research and develop products needs to be available; and the social and cultural dynamics that inform research and enquiry need to be in place. The legal and political framework are important – for example, if certain types of research, such as that on stem cells, nano-technology, atomic energy or the human genome are favoured with tax incentives or proscribed by law, then this will affect their development. This has been true throughout the modern age; it is safe to assume the torture and prosecution of Galileo set back astronomy and astro-physics by a few years, just as the development of rocket technology and radio-telescopes, funded by governments, advanced these fields of study.

There are many ways of analysing the changes that have taken place over the last generation; these may be sociological, philosophical, or anthropological in nature. Our perspective, adopted for the purpose of this book, is to argue that an important key to understanding these developments lies in an understanding of the nature of the relationship of the state to civil society; how do societies organise and govern themselves for economic success and social harmony? What works in aiding this? Do these successful structures alter over time and place? We are seeking to understand politics and, more specifically, public administration and public sector management. It is through the public administration of goods and services that societies (as represented by their governments) decide how to order, reward, punish and structure the interaction and relations between the state and individuals, interest groups, professions, regions, big issues and the day-to-day realities of life. We don't seek to discover definitive answers to these questions; indeed, we close this book with a further set of questions. What we do seek to do is to provide factual coverage and analysis of the key managerial developments which have impacted upon British government in recent years. These developments in the machinery of government, its rules and procedures, represent attempts by successive governments to modernise their structures and organisations. They have sought to move from a Westminster model to something different in order to continue to develop the United Kingdom's economy in ways which allow continued social advances and access to the provision of goods and services for an increasing proportion of the citizenry. Throughout this process, there have been redefinitions of the role of the state, its proper size and function, as well as the rights and duties of ordinary citizens.

Issues of public administration, or, to use the more recent label, of public management are not particularly new in the context of government and politics. The Fabians and Syndicalists were already debating these same issues in the aftermath of the First World War (Smith, 1979). The expectations of a wealthy and well-educated populace have dramatically changed, though, as has the ability of governments to structure the production and delivery of a complex range of goods and services. It is the pace and nature of contemporary managerial change, coupled with its impact on systems of governance at all levels, that makes it a subject worthy of detailed consideration. Students of British government and politics require a firm grasp of the complex changes which saw traditional forms of public administration engulfed by waves of managerialism, from the 1970s onwards, the further evolution of these approaches into a 'new public management' by the late 1980s and 1990s, and the emergence of an all-embracing 'modernisation' agenda in the early years of the new millennium.

While most of the books in this sphere tend to adopt a post-introductory approach (assuming a considerable amount of prior knowledge and understanding), or offer introductory coverage, but from a socioeconomic or managerial outlook, we aim to provide a distinctive form of analysis, which combines introductory perspectives with a clear 'politics' viewpoint. This is reflected in the structure of the book.

First, in this chapter, we introduce what is understood by the terms 'public administration' and 'public sector management'. This is necessarily a brief introduction as a more detailed explanation is provided in Chapter 2. We then introduce the reader to the main aspects of changes in the British system over the last twenty years, discussing the move from the 'Westminster model' and on into 'New Public Management'. This is designed to prepare the reader for the chapters that follow.

Defining some terms: public administration and new public management

We can begin to understand what is meant by 'public administration' when we list its traits, or rather view a list of headings provided by Caiden *et al.* (1983) to describe what constitutes the discipline:

1. the ideological roots of public institutions, including social contract, federalism, the separation of powers, representative government and civil rights;
2. theories of public administration and administrative norms;
3. contextual influences on public administration in society;
4. the functions of administration;
5. the role of public administration in society;
6. the history of the public sector;
7. institutional arrangements of public service delivery, forms and structures, administrative organisations;
8. public administrative law, public controls and administrative discretion;

9. behaviour of government organisations and government officials, codes of conduct;
10. relationship between public organisations and between them and other social organisations;
11. relations between public officials and the people;
12. citizens' images and opinions of the public sector and officials' attitudes towards the public;
13. public sector productivity and performance, measurement and evaluation;
14. public planning and forecasting;
15. policy formulation and implementation;
16. management of government organisations, including leadership and supervision;
17. public finance and budgeting, accounting and auditing;
18. public personnel management and labour relations;
19. professional development: education and training for the civil service (and others in the public sector);
20. public enterprise;
21. comparative public administration;
22. the anthology and sociology of the field;
23. biographies of civil servants;
24. research methods;
25. Public information, accessibility. (1983: xiv–xv, quoted in Massey, 1993: 9–10)

To this list must be added European Union directives, laws and administrative structures.

We can see, therefore, that public administration is multidisciplinary, its study belongs in political science, business and management, economics, sociology, accountancy, law and statistics (Farnham and Horton, 1999; Massey, 2004). The study of public administration is the study of how things actually work, how governments make decisions and apply, or enforce those decisions. Traditional public administration concentrated upon the great bureaucracies and nationalised industries of the old welfare state, as well as the machinery of government and the study of local government, topics explored in more detail in subsequent chapters. But in recent years with a greater concern for leadership, organisational incentives and motivation, delivery and ethics (what in Britain has become known as 'public standards') in the public sector, we have moved back towards a more encompassing (or holistic) view of what we mean by public administration.

By contrast, public sector management, and what has become known as new public management (NPM), sought to move away from traditional public administration, its advocates viewing the latter as rather old-fashioned and limited in terms of its practical applicability. There are several core elements to public sector management, especially NPM, but essentially it is an attempt to modernise government (and the study of government) from the perspective of the individual and individualism, in particular an economic view of the individual. It grew out of what became known as the 'Public Choice' school of US academia, especially academics working in the Universities of Virginia and Chicago (see Chapter 2 below). It is a perspective that:

1. calls for attempts to peg back the growth of government;
2. recognises and incorporates the internationalisation of aspects of public administration and government and the provision of goods and services;
3. embraces privatisation;
4. embraces marketisation (that is the tendering of public services out to the lowest, or best-value bidder);
5. explores and embraces the delivery of public services based on greater efficiency, effectiveness and economy;
6. often leads to the breaking up of large bureaucracies into discreet, single-purpose agencies, sometimes in preparation for their privatisation;
7. concentrates on the role of the individual citizen as a consumer of services and seeks to deliver greater value, choice and accountability to the individual citizen;
8. it therefore seeks to empower citizens as individuals, but not as 'a collectivity';
9. explores new structures of government and service delivery based on the best practice of the private sector and involves the private sector wherever possible. (see Hood, 1990, 1998; Greenwood, Pyper and Wilson, 2002; Massey, 1993; Parsons, 1995)

Public sector management generally, and NPM in particular, is a managerialist perspective on the delivery of public services, indeed of the role and purpose of government generally. It looks to the role of government as the administration of things. It sees the key professional group as managers, able to oversee and deliver services to a set of clear and measurable targets.

In a sense, therefore, NPM – in conjunction with globalisation, privatisation, devolution, marketisation and the general hollowing out of the state – has led at least one influential academic to refer to modern government as 'governing without government', seeing the state as contracting out of its traditional responsibilities and obligations to others (Rhodes, 1994). Whatever the reality of these concerns, it is the case that the term 'public administration', although enjoying something of a comeback, at least with the international community, is still perceived by many who work within the public sector in Britain as somewhat old-fashioned. The great tranche of reforms and deep-seated changes that have taken place may be seen as essentially management-centred and often management-led. As such, within Britain at least, public sector management, a narrower and more focused term than that identified above for public administration, remains the preferred term for practitioners.

A connected definitional issue concerns the terms 'governance' and 'core executive'. Readers will encounter these terms in conjunction with work on public sector management and it is useful at this point to provide a very short introduction to them. The core executive is an entity which academics and practitioners began to refer to as the large-scale reforms began to take effect. With privatisation and other 'hollowing-out' activities, it became necessary to explore the nature of the executive as it laboured under the transformative dynamic of NPM. Partly this was also in response to the perceived weaknesses of the Westminster model as a tool of analysis of British politics, a model it should be noted that probably never fully existed in the 'reality' of day-to-day politics or indeed much beyond the pages of rather old fashioned political science textbooks.

The Westminster model is seen by most academics as an 'organising perspective' that defines the area of study and limits the kind of questions that can be asked, being built on the assumption that:

> There is parliamentary sovereignty: all decisions are made within Parliament and there is no higher authority. Legitimacy and democracy are maintained because ministers are answerable to Parliament and the House of Commons is elected by the people. Decisions are taken by the Cabinet and implemented by a neutral civil service ... This model is also perceived as providing for the best system of government. (Smith, 1999: 9–10)

It is largely a straw man, since its weaknesses are fairly obvious. There tends to be an overemphasis on particular institutions and the powerful individuals who dominate them (Smith, 1999: 11–13). It is an overly simplistic model that fails to place the prime minister, Cabinet and civil service in a broader political and socioeconomic context.

Rhodes, by contrast, emphasises the role of the core executive and policy networks: that is groups of individuals and institutions that coalesce around discreet issues and programmes. His definition of the core executive argues:

> The term 'core executive' refers to all those organisations and procedures which coordinate central government, and act as final arbiters of conflict between different parts of the government machine, covering the complex web of institutions, networks and practices surrounding the prime minister, cabinet, cabinet committees and their official counterparts, less formalised ministerial 'clubs' or meetings, bilateral negotiations and interdepartmental committees. It also includes coordinating departments chiefly the Cabinet Office, the Treasury, the Foreign Office, the law officers, and security and intelligence services. The label 'cabinet government' was the overarching term for (some of) these institutions and practices but it is inadequate and confusing because it does not describe accurately the effective mechanisms for achieving coordination. At best it is contentious, and at worst seriously misleading, to assert the primacy of the cabinet among organisations and mechanisms at the heart of the machine. (Rhodes, 1994: 12, quoted in Smith, 1999: 5)

In other words, to properly understand what we mean by the core executive, its structures, role, organisation and importance to understanding public administration, we need to ensure we view it and its activities in the broader context of the network of organisations, procedures and motivations of the political system and society generally.

These issues are returned to and more fully explored in the chapters that follow. In particular we implicitly explore changes in public sector management that impact on governing and governance, where governing may be seen to be:

> The totality of interactions, in which public as well as private actors participate, aimed at solving societal problems or creating societal opportunities; attending to the institutions as contexts for these governing interactions; and establishing a normative foundation for all those activities. (Kooiman, 2003: 4)

Kooiman adds that governance may be seen 'as the totality of theoretical conceptions on governing' (2003: 4), but it may also be defined as:

> A descriptive label that is used to highlight the changing nature of the policy process in recent decades. In particular it sensitises us to the ever-increasing variety of terrains and actors involved in the making of public policy. Thus, governance demands that we consider all the actors and locations beyond the 'core executive' involved in the policy-making process. (Richards and Smith, 2002: 15)

'Governance', therefore, means the inclusion of civil society and the economic and social interests into the networks of government policy formulation and service delivery.

Just prior to its election in 1997, New Labour wrestled with some of these issues by borrowing from the work of the sociologist Anthony Giddens and his book *The Third Way* (in Richards and Smith, 2002: 235). In this perspective, problems of governance arose from the way in which the old hierarchical public sector in the post-war welfare state no longer adequately addressed the problems, or met the needs of an increasingly mixed, multicultural, pluralist democracy in Britain. Neither did the great Thatcherite experiment, argued New Labour, with its overemphasis on markets, competition, managerialism and individualism. The result was an attempt by New Labour to accept some of the key reforms introduced by Thatcherism, while not turning its back altogether on the benefits of the welfare state that attempts to redistribute the wealth of the better-off members of society to those who were clearly less well-off, and to perform this neat conjuring trick while not appearing to embrace socialism or 'Old Labour'-style class-based politics. Consequently, as later chapters seek to demonstrate and discuss, the 'Third Way' in practice has ensured the Labour government has:

> attempted to resolve problems of social order, family breakdown, welfare dependence, education and health through mechanisms that involve many of the instruments of the Conservative era. Consequently, they have tried to involve the private and voluntary sectors as well as the public sector. They have also been concerned with some of the issues raised through managerial perspectives and thus have focused on changing incentive structures ... the importance they have attached to the Private Finance Initiative (PFI) or Public–Private Partnership illustrates the new types of relationship that have been developed between the public and private sector and the new ways in which

Labour is thinking about state intervention. (Richards and Smith, 2002: 236)

As Labour drew close to completing its second term of office, less was heard of the term the 'Third Way', but the approach to the issues of governance and the problems of delivering services to a sophisticated and affluent electorate remained constant. These important issues and the practical impact they have had on public administration are explored throughout the rest of this book.

The following chapters

Chapter 2 examines the main theories and debates surrounding issues of public management and modernisation, charting the historical context of many of the concepts of accountability and legitimacy in public administration that we now take for granted. The paradigm shift from public administration to public management and beyond, to the modernisation agenda, is clearly set out and discussed. The roots of the new managerialism are examined, and an analysis is offered of the extent to which it represented a departure from the fundamental principles of traditional public administration. The shift to managerialism is considered in the context of a consideration of the strengths and weaknesses of the public administration model. Additionally, attention is given to the debates about the appropriateness and applicability of private sector disciplines and procedures in the context of public sector service delivery. The tendency of the new public management to spawn its own bureaucracies will also be considered.

In order to make sense of the political aspects of new public management and modernisation, it is important to chart the response of the main parties to these public sector reform agendas. Chapter 3 seeks to do this by setting out the manner in which the Conservative Party established the basis for the introduction of the new public management. The rhetoric and policies of the Labour Party and the Liberal Democrats are then examined in order to establish their developing positions in relation to the key managerial themes and issues. To some extent, the emergence of a new consensus around the Conservative agenda saw the new public management occupy a pivotal position in the move way from 'big', interventionist government, although aspects of New Labour's 'Third Way' approach to managerialism and modernisation involved a reassertion of a (revised) role for the state.

In Chapter 4 we examine a core element of public management: its links to issues of economic and financial management. An account is offered of the changing framework of macroeconomic policy occasioned by the flight from Keynesianism, and the general impact this has had on UK public administration and management. We go on to examine some of the key features and aspects of the developing new public management in this sphere, including some discussion of the impact of the new Labour Government on the nature and character of public finance and economics.

No account of the impact of the new public management and modernisation upon British government would be complete without an awareness of the implications for the structure of our systems of governance. These can be seen at all levels: within and across central government departments and agencies, in the emergence of the devolved administrations, in local government and the National Health Service. In Chapter 5 we examine the structural effects of managerialism and modernisation.

Chapter 6 sets out the key service delivery and policy implementation issues which flow from the new public management and modernisation, in the context of an analysis of competition, markets and consumerism. We examine the way in which the disciplines of the marketplace have been introduced into the realm of public service delivery, while considering the array of mechanisms and devices which have been developed, including competitive tendering, market testing, and internal markets. Also considered, as part of this developing reform agenda, is the advent of a consumerist ethos, epitomised by 'charterism' and its offshoots.

Underlying the entire managerialist approach has been the perceived need for greater attention to be paid to the performance of the public sector. In Chapter 7 we analyse the introduction of mechanisms geared towards the attainment of greater economy, efficiency, and effectiveness in public sector provision and the way in which these have necessitated the advent of procedures through which performance can be measured. The regulatory role of bodies including the National Audit Office and the Audit Commission are given consideration in this context.

In Chapter 8 we turn our attention to the broad impact of the new public management and modernisation on the keystone of the system of government: accountability systems and processes. We conclude with some general observations about the nature of change and the future of public administration in Chapter 9.

2

Public Management and Modernisation: Theories and Debates

The study of government can be a dangerous occupation. His examination of the principles and theories of modern government led Colonel Algernon Sidney to the executioner's block in London on 7 December 1683. He had spent nearly all of his adult life engaged in fighting and in politics and argued that 'Implicit Faith belongs to Fools, and the Truth is comprehended by examining Principles' (Sidney, *c. 1683*, 1996: 12). In other words, students of government, indeed citizens everywhere, should constantly question the way in which government works. Furthermore, Sidney argued that 'God leaves to Man the Choice of Forms in Government; and those who constitute one Form, may abrogate it' (Sidney, *c. 1683*, 1996: 20). By which he meant, in a democratic country a sovereign people may choose to change the way in which they are governed. This is as true of electors in the Islamic state of Iran, as it is of those in the United Kingdom and the United States. In the modern world organisations as diverse as the fundamentalist Christian Right in the United States and Al Qaeda groups committed to a new Islamic order would question this approach, but it is the triumph of liberal democratic values that has set the current agenda for western governments.

While in some states of the world it remains dangerous to question the authority and nature of the state, in many western nations the purpose of the social sciences is to gain an understanding of the workings of society through fundamental questioning. The Nobel prize-winning economist, James Buchanan, argued

> I seek to emulate: the willingness to question anything, and anybody, on any subject anytime; the categorical refusal to accept anything as sacred; the genuine openness to all ideas; and finally, the basic conviction that most ideas peddled about are nonsense or worse when examined critically. (Buchanan, 1999: 15)

11

It is this search for reason and questioning of fundamental laws and truths that is intrinsic to much western political thought since the sixteenth and seventeenth centuries. It is a freedom that was not easily won or maintained. Public administration and public sector management is an important element of this study because it is the analysis of how government actually works, it is what one commentator has called, 'the seamy side of politics' (Price, 1983).

Sidney, the second son of the earl of Leicester, was a parliamentary hero, a devout Protestant, a soldier, a diplomat and a scholar. He died as he had lived, praying to God, defending democratic republican principles and defying a tyrant king. Following his death, many of the ideals he fought for became part of mainstream politics; indeed, they are the foundation of what may be called modern representative liberal democracy. A contemporary of John Locke and a member of the same conspiracy against Charles II, Sidney was never afraid to take up arms to overthrow unjust government. Indeed, he is credited with originating the phrase, 'God helps those who help themselves', when discussing his earlier combat during the English Civil War (West (in Sidney) 1996: xxiii). Alongside Locke, he provided a theoretical grounding for the rights of ordinary citizens to overthrow a tyrannical government, arguing such a course of action was not only a right, but also a duty. As an illustration of this, the inscription he placed in the visitors' book at the University of Copenhagen reads:

Manus baec inimica tyrannis,

Einse petit placidam cum libertate quietem.

(This hand, enemy to tyrants,

By the sword seeks calm peacefulness with liberty.)

The sentence faithfully represents the spirit of the Founders of the American Republic and resonated with their own experience of authoritarian government; it remains the official motto of the state of Massachusetts (West (in Sidney) 1996: xvi). The work of Sidney combined with that of Locke to influence and structure the principles adopted by Thomas Jefferson and John Adams, and through them (and the other Founders) to construct the foundations of American government and governance (Ellis, 2000). As such, the walk to the scaffold taken by many early liberal democrats in the seventeenth century was not the end of their journey, but the beginning of the march of modern politics.

Posthumously pardoned following the Glorious Revolution of 1688, Sidney's ideas were influential in Whig politics for over a century and included his unshakeable belief in the essential equality of individuals. This combined with his view that from the explicit consent of the people (and only from that consent) arose all legitimacy for the authority of government. Such revolutionary democratic republican notions crossed the Atlantic along with his Quaker friend and ally, William Penn, and formed the foundation for the US approach to governance; the belief that power and authority must be rooted in the consent of the people and accountable to them through democratic processes. Furthermore, from this also stems the egalitarian principle that the incumbency of public office must be based upon merit and ability, rather than inheritance or nepotism. This is in direct contrast to the Continental European tradition of authority flowing down to the people from a High Authority (in the personage of a leader, king, emperor, or Pope) in the form of devolution or principles of subsidiarity (Price, 1983; Massey, 1993). In this American inversion of the principles of authority and legitimacy may be seen the root of many of the differences between the Continental European and Anglo-American approaches to public administration and its contemporary manifestation as public sector management. It certainly runs through a significant number of the issues inherent to the debates on modernisation and the model of public management preferred by different cohorts of modernisers.

It may be argued reasonably that the continental European basis for the existence of public administration is one that sees it as emanating from reasons of state, it is a legalistic deductive approach (Stillman, 1999: 258). Whereas the US and much of the traditional British approach induces the state from public administration, it is a more institutional and institutionalist approach than the European one. For the British and Americans – that is those who eschew a Marxist analysis – the concept of *the state* is itself problematic. They tend instead to discuss and analyse institutions, and *government* or, more recently, *governance*, rather than *the state*. For continental Europeans, however, public administration and its constituent institutions are the result of state *diktat*, invented to implement the will of the political leadership. It is a product of the state and its activities are prescribed by (and located within) a corpus of administrative law (Stillman, 1999: 247–59; Massey, 1993; Price, 1983). In other words, the British and US traditions see 'the state' as a necessary evil, something to be controlled and constrained. There is a need to constantly question the structures of government, as well as to seek ways to make it accountable and responsive.

A strong note of caution needs to be inserted at this juncture. For the US tradition of public administration, this deductive perspective is based upon sound empirical observation and American political theory

(Aberbach and Rockman, 2000; Price, 1983). For the British, however, no matter how pragmatic many observers may consider them to be (Beer, 1965), the fact remains that one of the most powerful non-elected governmental institutions in terms of its day-to-day influence on policy is the central civil service. This organisation is the creation not of statute, but of feudal Crown Prerogative (Massey, 2002) and as such officials must consider themselves to have no interest or legal existence separate from that of the minister they serve (Wicks, 2002). They are, to all intents, cyphers, established in post to do their minister's bidding, no less mute than their European neighbours, but lacking in the statutory protection afforded those continental colleagues. If there is such a thing as *the British State*, then they constitute a significant part of it, and they serve the ministers who are legally and constitutionally part of – indeed indivisible from – the Crown. In Britain, therefore, not everything is as at first it seems. Nonetheless, for Britain, its Trans-Atlantic links have remained at least as important and influential as its cross-Channel connections and this is reflected in the tensions over what public sector management and modernisation means to people. The populism and individualism of the American Republic has provided the dynamic for many of the ideas that have remade British public administration.

In this current age of globalisation and (for those in Europe) increased Europeanisation, it is essential that we retain a healthy scepticism about those who peddle 'new' ideas. This chapter seeks to show two things. First, that few ideas are new; many of the debates now taking place in politics and academia are very similar to those that raged in the seventeenth century. They include a pursuit of the answers to questions as fundamental as: What is the limit to government? What is the role of government? What is sovereignty? Linked to this is a second point, a nod towards the debate on globalisation. Globalisation is partly an economic phenomenon, but it also signals the triumph of a set of ideals and ideas. The Enlightenment of the sixteenth and seventeenth centuries swept the world. It had many sources and dynamics, not least of which was the puritanical protestant aversion to authority and conservatism. It swept through Western Europe and via the Scottish Enlightenment and the influence of the Kirk (Herman, 2002), through the United Kingdom, the United States and beyond. New public management (NPM) can trace some of its roots back through James Buchanan and the University of Virginia, through to his Scottish ancestors and their cussed refusal to accept the authority of kings and bishops over an individual's right to conduct business and politics according to their own conscience and interests.

What is public administration?

Later parts of this chapter explain the theories behind administration in more detail, but the work of early twentieth-century writers such as Haldane in Britain, Wilson in the United States and Weber in Germany set out the modern reasons for structuring the executive, or administrative parts of the state in what became known as the bureaucratic model. In this model:

- There should be a clear separation between politics and administration and distinct roles for political leaders (normally elected) and state officials (normally appointed);
- Administration should be continuous and predictable, operating on the basis of written, unambiguous rules;
- Administrators should be recruited on the basis of qualification, and should be trained professionals;
- Organization should reflect a functional division of labour, and a hierarchical arrangement of tasks and people;
- Resources should belong to the organization, not to individuals working in the organization;
- The principal motivation should be a sense of duty, of public interest, which should override organisational or private interests. (Minogue, in McCourt and Minogue, 2001: 3–4)

We return to discuss this in more detail later in this chapter. The use of the term *public administration* then is more than simply a description of how the public sector, especially the central civil service and much of local government is, or was, organised. The term also makes a statement about *how* they should be organised. The notion of public administration suggests a clear division between elected and appointed officials with the former making strategic policy decisions based upon their election manifesto, while the latter, the bureaucrats, administer those decisions in a disinterested way, according to clear public interest rules and procedures. Its principle organising mode is through hierarchically organised bureau, or bureaucracy.

What is public management?

Criticism of the old public administration model grew throughout the last quarter of the twentieth century. The reasons for and nature of those criticisms forms a constant theme through the succeeding chapters, it is sufficient here to note the main characteristics of public management, often called new public management, before explaining why it is important.

Public management is characterised by:

- A separation of strategic policy from operational management, something that occurred in public administration, but which is re-emphasised in public management;
- A concern with results rather than process and procedure;
- An orientation to the needs of citizens rather than the interests of the organisation or bureaucrats;
- A withdrawal from direct service provision in favour of a steering or enabling role;
- A changed, entrepreneurial management culture (Minogue, in McCourt and Minogue, 2001: 21).

This new model was established through restructuring the public sector via:

- Privatisation;
- Reorganising and slimming down central civil services;
- Introducing competition into remaining public services, especially through internal markets, and the contracting of public services provision to the public sector;
- Improving efficiency and obtaining 'value for money' through performance management and auditing, especially against key performance indicators (Minogue in McCourt and Minogue, 2001: 21).

One of the ironies of the processes used to implement the cultural change is that through the establishment of 'quality' regulators and other inspectorates throughout the public sector, a fetish for process over product grew. A 'tick-box mentality' evolved that negated some of the rhetorical goals of public management as the pursuit of performance indicators became routinised, turning the gaze of public servants away from their more strategic goals. The growth of inspectorates and regulators such as the Quality Assurance Agency for Higher Education, and OFSTED in schools, led to professionals having to alter their activities to conform to the demands of these agencies. There is very little evidence that it improved services, but it did lead to a massive increase in the costs of complying with the new regimes, money that could have been spent on front-line policing, educating and health care provision, being diverted to these new managerialist activities. These issues are addressed in more detail in the chapters that follow.

One point is worth stressing at this juncture, however; despite the attempts to make the managers in the public sector more businesslike and to behave in ways akin to their private sector counterparts, there remain many differences between the public and private sectors. It is a failure to appreciate this that has led to some difficulties for private sector managers recruited into the public sector, especially some of the Next Steps Agencies' Chief Executives. For example:

As compared with the private sector, government:
1. faces more complex and ambiguous tasks;
2. has more difficulty implementing decisions;
3. employs more people with different motivations;
4. is more concerned with securing opportunities and capacities;
5. is more concerned with compensating for market failures;
6. engages in activities with greater symbolic significance;
7. is held to stricter standards of previous commitment and legality;
8. has a greater opportunity to respond to issues of fairness;
9. must operate or appear to operate in the public interest;
10. must maintain minimal levels of public support above that required in private industry. (Baber, 1987: 159–60)

In other words, public sector managers are 'driven not by the profit motive, although that may be a subsidiary goal, but by the principles of accountability' (Massey, 1993: 15). In the private sector company chief executive officers may possess a well-developed sense of community values and responsibilities, but if they do not make a profit acceptable to their shareholders they are sacked, or the company is bankrupted. It is a simpler environment for business managers to work in than their public sector counterparts who are accountable in many more (and more sophisticated) ways.

Why is public management important?

Public administration and public sector management matter because governments use the public sector to deliver goods and services to the public, either directly, as in the case of policing, defence, education and welfare payments, or indirectly, as in the case of family doctor services and the provision of roads and refuse collection. If the public sector fails then governments fail to deliver their manifesto pledges. If the public sector is corrupt or inefficient, or simply incompetent then society at large suffers and those who suffer most are the most vulnerable, the citizens who are least able to protect themselves and depend upon the government, via the public sector, to protect and nurture them. The study of public sector management is the study of how successful and democratic a society is at governing itself and advancing the interests of its citizens. Real democracy lies in making government accountable and responsive. In recent decades the impact of managerialism and consumerism, as explored in the succeeding chapters of this book, has been designed to deliver this modern version of democracy. In this book we discuss the way in which this has been done and how successful it has been.

In the rest of this chapter we will trace some of the main theories to have influenced public management and governmental attempts at implementing its modernisation in recent decades. We will begin with a discussion of some of the classical perspectives on public administration, including the work of theorists such as Weber, Woodrow Wilson and Haldane. We will then explore the influence of more recent reformers from what has been referred to as the Chicago, Virginia and the Austrian schools of neo-liberal public choice theory, as well as the impact of new public management, modernisation and Europeanisation on British public sector management.

Some classical perspectives

Unlike the natural sciences, where empirical research, in the form of observation and experimentation, are employed to discover previously unknown aspects of the physical world, social science practitioners often find themselves on a mission of rediscovery. The periodic announcements within the disciplines of the development of 'new' theories or 'novel sub-disciplines' are sometimes akin to Columbus informing the resident Native Americans that he had discovered them, both sets of peoples equally unaware of previous incursions by Vikings. While advances in the study of human genetic structures have demonstrated the essential unity of humanity and its slow evolution, advances in technology have allowed societies to develop sophisticated social and political structures, which in turn have facilitated further technological innovation.

New technologies and sociopolitical developments have encouraged and enabled governments to apply new managerial techniques to their administrative structures. Adherents of the more recent innovations have labelled them variously, 'New Public Management', or 'Re-engineering' or 'Re-inventing Government'. Just as the human genome has been passed down through the generations in an essentially unchanged form, with different physical environments favouring different aspects of the adaptable human species, so this administrative inheritance also possesses a long history. The changing technological and political environment has allowed long dormant approaches to social organisation to reappear in new guises. Re-labelled and re-packaged for a modern audience, many of those who implement the new public administration are unaware that they are merely inheritors of previously tried and trusted, but then discarded approaches to governance.

Administrative traditions

Whereas Price (1983) acerbically argues public administration is the 'seamy side of politics', or how governments actually get things done, Hood (1983: 3) defines public management (or public administration) more elegantly as 'the art of the state'. Arguing it is 'the problem of how to design and operate public services and the detailed work of executive government'. He applies an approach known as grid/group cultural theory to chart and explain the way in which different perspectives on managing the public sector vary across time and geographical space. Grid/group theory originated in the field of anthropology as an attempt to 'capture the diversity of human preferences about different "ways of life" and relate those preferences to different possible styles of organisation, each of which has its advantages and disadvantages' (Hood, 1998: 7). The 'grid' element refers to the way in which our lives are structured and circumscribed by rules and regulations, limiting individual freedom, while the 'group' element 'denotes the extent to which individual choice is constrained by group choice, by binding the individual into a collective body. For example, if we live in a community which involves common pooling of resources and is differentiated from the outside world' (Hood, 1998: 8).

A further illustration of this point is provided by the work of Shils, especially in the eponymous, *The Virtue of Civility* (1997). Grosby notes that:

Time and again over a period of fifty-five years, Shils observed that the coherence and stability of any society depend at least in part on the

existence of the image of that society; on the attachment of the society's members to that image; and, concomitantly, on the attachments
that the members of that society form with one another. (See Shils,
1997: viii)

He continues:

There are, if you will, two bearers of life: the individual who makes
choices and decisions, and the achievements – the language, traditions,
laws – of the lives of many individuals of the larger collectivity.
Determining the proper relation between these two bearers of life
presents a great problem. (See Shils, 1997: ix)

And:

The violence against human nature perpetrated by ideology in all its
various manifestations is in denial of the plurality of ends that man
pursues ... In opposition to the totalitarian temptation of ideology
stands liberalism's acknowledgement of a plurality of ends. Because
this acknowledgement contains the potential for conflict, it is important that the virtue of a citizen – of civility – be cultivated in a manner
that confines this potential. (See Shils, 1997: xi)

In other words, the perpetual conflict between the role of the individual
and the responsibilities they have to themselves and their families is set
against their duties as citizens to society at large.

It is the role of government, or the state, to regulate this conflict, but in
so doing the state must also engage in the conflict over the proper limits
to its power over civil society. Shils himself argued that:

The institutional arrangements required for the freedom of expression
of beliefs and the representation of interests and ideals – both of which
can be divisive – can function effectively in society if those who use
them for their own particularistic ends are at the same time restrained
by an admixture of civility. . . . The institutions in which beliefs and
desires or interests are proposed and confronted in argument and the
institutions in which beliefs and interests are taken into account and
digested discriminatingly into law cannot work acceptably without
some constituent civility and consensus of the contending parties.
(Shils, 1997: 3)

Such a view is recognised and extended by Hood (following Olson (1971) and Hirschman (1970)), who points out that egalitarian forms of organisation involving:

> relatively weak formal leadership and [which] rely heavily on community 'participative' decision-making involving most or all of the members, are chronically vulnerable to collapse if opportunistic members either exit or seek to 'free ride' on the contributions of the few naïve public-spirited members, who will eventually themselves be discouraged. (Hood, 1998: 10)

That these perspectives remain at the heart of much of the debate surrounding the role of the state and its proper relationship to civil society is testimony to their durability. It is a debate that would be recognisable to the ancients. For example, the Roman writer Cicero debated the notion of the role of the state and its administrative functions (Dunsire, 1973: 1–5). Even earlier than this, Chinese writers from 330 BC, such as Shen Pu-Hai and the legalists, argued for a government conducted according to a legally binding constitution, rather than the Confucian principles of public service (Hood, 1998: 15–16).

There is a multiplicity of ways in which a society may structure its public sector, but these may be generalised into three broad types of public administration, or public sector management:

1. as a hierarchy;
2. in an individualist way;
3. in an egalitarian way.

We will introduce each of these in turn.

Hierarchical approaches

There are three hierarchical traditions and Hood's typology labels them Confucianism, Cameralism and Progressivist/Fabianism (Hood, 1998: 73–114). It may be argued that there are other labels that could be applied, but Hood's have the benefit that they at least clearly demonstrate the classical lineage of the debate. It will be seen that much of what Hood labels *Confucianism* may be found in Weber's work (although Weber (1986) himself was at pains to distance himself from any such claim) and echoes of the ancient debate exist in much of our modern systems of government. Hierarchical systems are structured according to clear sets of rules and regulations, with a hierarchy of offices stressing orderly behaviour and proper 'codes of conduct':

1. The Chinese Empire developed a system of public administration based on Confucian principles of competitive examinations leading to merit-based appointment, fixed contracts and a hierarchy of offices that lasted from the Han dynasty for nearly two thousand years until the early years of the twentieth century. It placed an emphasis on study and the acquisition of knowledge and experience leading to wisdom, with a special emphasis on ethical sensitivity, rather than technical skills (Hood, 1998: 73–80). The hierarchy of office meant that those at the top, the mandarins, although enjoying great privilege, were also expected to take the blame when things went awry. It was a clear example of appointment to office, limited span of control and merit-based promotion that would be the basis for many of the systems that were to take root in the West from the late nineteenth century onwards (Hood, 1998: 75–82).

2. The cameralists were mostly associated with German states (but also Sweden and Russia) during a period of absolutism from the early sixteenth century until the Napoleonic era (Hood, 1998: 82–90). The cameralists concentrated on developing public sector management according to economics (largely mercantilist and superseded by liberalism), public finance (the notion of fiduciary responsibility and oversight), and policy science (what we would now call policy analysis and social policy). The cameralists evolved the notion of teams collectively responsible for decision making, rather than hierarchies headed by a single office-holder. These teams were set above the rest of society to establish a clear set of rules and policies and operated rather like the Catholic Church's College of Cardinals, from which its inspiration was drawn (Hood, 1998: 85). The underlying assumptions for this were:

    *   the absolute power of the state and its ruler;
    *   the pursuit of economic wealth and development structured by the state and its concomitant imposition of social order (Hood, 1998: 86);
    *   the government actively managing the economy and civil society, overcoming sectional interests inimical to modernisation (Dunsire, 1973: 54–64);

- the establishment of a professional public service independent of interest groups and loyal to the ruler (Dunsire, 1973: 54–64);
- economic development was a process from which all members of society were deemed to benefit, an assumption challenged by liberals and egalitarians (Hood, 1998: 86–9).

3. Fabianism and Progressivism grew out of modern party-political struggles rather than absolutist doctrines and the ruling houses of Europe (Hood, 1998: 90). 'What these movements have in common is a belief in what Beatrice Webb ... conceived as a "Jesuitical corps" of dedicated and selfless professionals to establish an orderly, well-planned world free of corruption and muddle' (Hood, 1998: 90). These movements are characterised by the pursuit of good public management through independent regulation by technocrats; public administration structured as a profession; a belief in the need to have accountable government overseeing and structuring economic and social advances. Like cameralism, therefore, progressivism and Fabianism, were top-down in their approach and therefore hierarchical. Progressivism was a powerful movement in the United States during the 1880s through to the 1930s and many of its ideas remain attractive, especially its opposition to powerful corporations, organised crime and corrupt politicians. Fabianism was popular in the United Kingdom and some of its (now former) colonies, especially India at about the same time. Although identified with the political 'left' nonetheless Fabianism had a distinctly non-egalitarian approach to organising the apparatus of the state (Parsons, 1995: 161–2; Hood, 1998: 87–97). Its approach may still be seen in some of the policies and perspectives of New Labour, first elected to office in 1997 (Savage and Atkinson, 2001).

The hierarchical, or top-down approach to organising public administration remains a powerful perspective for politicians seeking to deliver on their electoral mandate. It is leavened, however, by two other organising perspectives.

Individualist approaches

The first of these is individualism and it is this perspective that has had a great deal of influence in restructuring public administrations for over twenty years. These approaches begin 'from the assumption that the world is populated by rational egoists who are bent on outsmarting one another to get something for nothing' (Hood, 1998: 98). It is an organising perspective rooted in classical economic theories of human behaviour, a topic returned to later in this chapter. There are various schools associated with it, the so-called *Austrian, Chicago* and *Virginia* schools, each of which adopts a different propensity within the perspective (Denham, 1996). All of them, but in particular the Virginia School of James Buchanan, have heavily influenced the debate on public sector management in recent years and are themselves the product of American individualism and populism. They are therefore equipped with a theoretical heritage that may be traced back to John Locke, Adam Smith and Algernon Sidney (Buchanan, 1997).

The Virginia School developed the theory of Public Choice, which challenged the notion that government can act in a disinterested way for the public good or indeed that government is able to deliver on its promises at all (Denham, 1996: 14). It is interesting to note that in *The Calculus of Consent*, Buchanan argued if an individual cannot know how different rules will affect them, then they will need to choose between rules in terms of some criterion of generality. This is a process, Buchanan notes, that is remarkably close to the *veil of ignorance* central to John Rawls' *Theory of Justice* (Buchanan, 1999: 23–4). Rawls is often claimed as one of their own by proponents of egalitarianism because of the impact his work has had in the fields of human rights and civil liberties. It is in the concern for individual rights that the egalitarians and individualists meet, in theoretical terms. It is no accident that two of the leading exponents of these perspectives are drawn from the ranks of US social scientists, developing a priori beliefs in the rights of individuals and limits to government power that draw heavily for inspiration on the traditions of Locke and Sidney.

Individualistic perspectives reject the top-down approach to government and challenge the notion of government as a 'good thing'. They argue it is simply one among many players in the policy process and public officials, as rational individuals, will act in their own interest, not some abstract notion of the common good, however that may be defined. The organising principles for public sector management, according to this perspective, should construct rules that ensure the individual self-interest of public officials coincide with the public interest, that is they do right by pursuing their own ends (Hood, 1998: 94–119; Dunleavy, 1991). Introducing targets for them to achieve and then rewarding them through incentives may do this, as may performance-related pay. Another way is to introduce greater competition and marketisation into the public sector through the competitive provision of public services (Hood, 1998: 94–119; Massey, 1997). Many of the reforms in British and American public administration have been driven by this perspective.

Egalitarian approaches

As a general guide to their perspective, egalitarians are opposed to both markets and bureaucracies as the primary organising principle for public sector management (Hood, 1998: 120). But, it should be noted, there are many varieties of egalitarianism; a perspective often (but not always) associated with the political Left, such as social democracy and Marxism (Dunleavy and O'Leary, 1987). The most recent impact upon public sector management, however, has come from communitarianism, rather than Marxism, which in any case has often taken a top-down hierarchical approach in practice, some elements of the Chinese Cultural Revolution notwithstanding (Chang, 1991: 362–73, 405–8).

Parsons notes the rise of 'communitarianism' through the 1980s and 1990s as a non-Marxist, but egalitarian community-based rebuttal of the individualist perspective (1995: 51–2). The work of exponents such as Walzer and also Taylor sought 'the renewal of the idea of community … as a source for an alternative to the individualism of the 1980s' (Parsons, 1995: 51–2). In quoting the journalist Seamus Milne, Parsons captures the communitarian approach:

> Communitarianism can be summed up in two essential ideas. Modern atomised societies, its supporters argue, have lost a sense of community and social solidarity. The vital social fabric between the state and the individual – everything from voluntary associations and geographical communities to schools, families, churches and trade unions – has withered under the impact of rampant market individualism. It must be protected or rebuilt. In a related ethical thrust, the communitarians believe that selfish liberalism has created an alienated social wasteland, shifting the balance between rights and duties too far in the direction of rights. A new emphasis on individual and mutual responsibility is needed to right the balance. (Parsons, 1995: 52, quote from *The Guardian*, 7 October 1994)

In other words, communitarian perspectives resurrect the old notion of a *social contract* between the state and civil society and between different parts of society, with rights and duties balancing each other.

Etzioni was to the forefront of this and his work influenced both the Clinton administration in the United States and New Labour's approach to policy making in the United Kingdom (Etzioni, 1993). Etzioni argued:

> As communitarians see it, a strong but scaled-back core of the welfare state therefore should be maintained. Other tasks, currently undertaken by the state, should be turned over to individuals, families and communities. The philosophical underpinning for this change requires the development of a new sense of both personal and mutual responsibility. But how do we work out which activities should be dealt with at which level of society? By applying the principle of subsidiarity. This says that responsibility for any situation belongs first to those who are nearest to the problem. Only if a solution cannot be found by the individual does responsibility devolve to the family. Only if the family cannot cope should the local community become involved. Only if the problem is too big for it should the state become involved. (Etzioni, 1994, quoted in Parsons, 1995: 53)

This approach harks back to an atavistic sense of community, a pioneering frontier spirit of self-confident individualism tempered by ethical commitments to the other members of society. As an approach to structuring public sector organisations, it favours 'group self-management, control by mutuality, and maximum face-to-face accountability' (Hood, 1998: 122). It is, of course, only one version of egalitarianism, there are other more radical elements to this perspective. These include radical (or 'dark') green movements; radical feminist movements, and the more 'traditional' Marxist and neo-Marxist organisations, but with the caveat noted above (Hood, 1998: 122–43; Parsons, 1995: 145–53, 130–1; Page, 1985: 107–62; Stivers, 1993).

The concomitant to the different approaches to structuring public administrations, approaches that reflect disparate a priori views about what constitutes the 'proper' role of the state and the relationship between individuals and the state, is a varying set of perspectives on how to control public sector managers. Much of the rest of this book addresses these issues in more detail, but it is clear that a perspective based upon the need for a hierarchical view of society adopts a different stance on the need for oversight and review as contrasted to an individualistic perspective. The former opts for a command and control method of oversight and accountability, while the latter has a preference for market or competition solutions (Hood, 1998: 52–70; Horton and Farnham, 1999). For egalitarian approaches, the preference is for control by mutuality, or 'groupism' (Hood, 1998: 60–5). This is as much the case for community-based groups as for some of the higher professions, such as medicine and law, or collegiate institutions such as churches and universities.

It should be clear from the above that despite academic attempts to devise neat typologies, the plethora of approaches within each of the aforementioned major perspectives ensures there is an untidy overlap in the 'real-world' experience of practitioners. Those who advocate egalitarian structures in society are often content to implement their policies using top-down hierarchical and centralised methods of control and oversight (Savage and Atkinson, 2002). Conversely, there is within many hierarchical organisations an element of collegiality and mutuality, especially in those organisations employing large numbers of professionals (Massey, 1988). Likewise, both approaches in modern British and US public sector management have inserted into their organisational workings large elements of competition and marketisation (Aberbach and Rockman, 2000; Minogue, Polidano and Hume, 1998; Greenwood *et al.*, 2002).

Theory and practice: early modernisation and 'objective' public sector management

There has often been an overlap between management theories developed in business schools and the application of novel organising principles to the public sector. There is a long chronology testifying to the influence of business theory upon public administration. This takes us from the work of the scientific management school of writers (Taylor, Gulick, Urwick, Simon), through the human relations school, and mid-to-late-twentieth-century developments such as zero-based budgeting, planning-programme-budgeting systems, public choice theory, and total quality management (Parsons, 1995; Massey, 1993; Self, 1977: 19–31; Hughes, 1998). Alongside and often within these business or economics-based schools of thought, were writers who specifically sought to influence public sector management. These included Weber, Haldane, Woodrow Wilson and later, Niskanen, Olson, and Osborne and Gaebler (1992) (Hughes, 1998; Horton and Farnham, 1999; Parsons, 1995).

The scientific management tradition is hierarchical and highly structured, with top-down oversight of those hierarchies by bosses, or chief executives. The work of Taylor, based upon his observations of Fordist industrial settings, insisted that:

1. Work ought to be standardised to find the 'one best way of working'; and
2. Work ought to be closely controlled in order to maintain high standards and compliance to instructions (Hughes, 1998: 33).
3. This involved the development of practices such as 'time-and-motion' studies; a wage-incentive system such as piece-work or performance-related pay;
4. Administrative systems should be restructured to more closely resemble the 'scientific' breakdown of specific work functions found in Fordist production lines (Hughes, 1998: 33–4).

At the same time as the scientific management school were setting out their theories, Max Weber in Germany and Lord Haldane in Britain were proposing the restructuring of the administrative systems of their respective countries: in Weber's case through his theory of bureaucracy, in Haldane's from his position as a senior civil servant (Hennessy, 1990).

The two schools together – scientific management and Weber's theory of bureaucracy – heavily influenced the structure and behaviour of western public administration systems for most of the twentieth century and they retain a vestigial grip on much of their workings. Weber set out six principles for organising bureaucracy, distilling them from his belief in structuring public administration along rational/legal lines, rather than according to traditional models or those based upon a charismatic leader or chief (Weber, 1946; Hughes, 1998: 27–8). Weber's principles are:

1. Administration is divided into fixed and official jurisdictions, or offices, each of which is structured or ordered by rules, laws and/ or regulations.
2. There is a hierarchy of offices and different grades of authority leading to an ordered system of oversight and subordination. Lower-graded officials and their offices are supervised by those with a higher rank.
3. Management is based on and operated through written files and documents. The group of officials who constitute an office, their work and their documents make up a 'bureau' and this is kept distinct from their private life. That is, officials must maintain the distinction between their public office and their private interests.
4. Officials must be well-trained to carry out their jobs.

5. Officials must have no other fiduciary interests or occupations. That is, their official work must be a full-time occupation.
6. The bureau is operated along a constant and stable set of rules which may be learned and the knowledge of these rules involves jurisprudence and administrative law as well as business management. The learning of these rules is itself a legal/rational and technical training (Hughes, 1998: 27; Weber (in Rourke 1986): 62–73).

Hughes (1998: 27) makes the point that:

> The principles of bureaucracy have become so ingrained in society that these points seem obvious, but they did represent a substantial advance on early administration.

Indeed, they were an attempt to rationalise and systematise public administration in a way that may be seen as the first comprehensive attempt at modernisation. It was also a concerted effort to root out the nepotism and corruption of previous generations in Britain, Germany and the United States and advance a system based on technical skill, personal ability and merit (Massey, 1993) (see Tomalin (2002) for an example of eighteenth-century civil service practice). This early process of modernisation placed public sector management within the context of a body of administrative law and/or practice, ensuring officials' authority to act was located within this legal framework.

In addition to the issue of control within a bureaucracy, there is the primary concern of the control over the administrative system. This issue, one much discussed by Confucians and cameralists, remains at the heart of the issue of modernisation in Britain. In liberal democracies, as well as other types of system, this must mean political control or, rather, the ability of politicians to control their appointed officials. From the time of its foundation the US political system had sought a separation of powers between the legislature, judiciary and executive (Ellis, 2000). Woodrow Wilson, in examining the spoils system, whereby a newly elected president was able to appoint large numbers of allies and friends to powerful (and often lucrative) positions within the executive, sought to institute a similar separation between politicians and administrators. This was in order to facilitate political control, but also to insulate officials from overt party political interference in the administrative process.

The issue of political control over the administration, then, may be seen to be complex in that as the democratically elected policy makers – politicians – can expect, as a constitutional right, to set the policies for public sector managers. Yet, at the same time, these officials are expected to serve a broader spectrum than political self-interest, they are expected to behave in the national interest, however that may be defined. As such, Wilson argued that they needed to be protected from the short-term and selfish interests of party politicians and enabled to carry out their administrative duties in an impartial manner according to law and to the best of their ability. In developing a similar approach to that of Weber, but within the US context, he proposed a strict separation of politics from administration. As a process it has never been fully implemented, but it has nonetheless, been very influential and it has had enough of an impact in the US to allow a separate administrative realm to emerge (Aberbach and Rockman, 2000; Hughes, 1998: 30–4; Massey, 1993).

Within the traditional or Weberian model of administration, Hughes outlines three main factors we need to be concerned with. These are:

1. There needs to be a clear line of accountability. Officials both advise ministers and deliver services to the public. In both roles they are accountable to ministers and through them to Parliament and the electorate.
2. Following on from this, there is a strict separation between matters of policy (which are the preserve of ministers) and administration (which is the responsibility of officials). In reality this separation is a porous thing and its boundaries have never been so clear that mistakes and misunderstandings have been avoided. Again, much modernisation in recent years has sought to address this issue. But events such as the removal of Derek Lewis as Head of the Prison Service, and Martin Sixsmith as Head of Communications from the then Department of Transport, illustrate the problems encountered on a daily basis by individuals in the machinery of government (Wicks, 2002).
3. The third aspect of political control is that the administration (or rather its officials) is presumed to be anonymous and neutral. This allows officials to 'speak truth unto power' without being personally associated with any of the decisions. Officials are non-party-political and are able to serve any leader with the same degree of loyalty and without favour. That this aspect of the relationship between politicians and officials is under strain has become obvious with events such as those mentioned in (2) above, some observers even referring to its existence as a myth (Hughes, 1998: 33–4).

Although the reality of this model of political control is different to the theory, that any deviation from it in practice leads to adverse comment is a testament to its abiding attraction. In reality this model is now a description of times past, the flaws in its character being subject to considerable adverse comment.

We will return to these in a later part of this chapter and again in Chapters 3 and 4. Suffice to conclude this section by noting that traditional bureaucratic structures of the kind advocated by Weber and Taylor and implemented by Haldane, Wilson and others in the US, UK and Germany, although a great advance on the nepotism and corruption of previous regimes, were also constraining. Critics pointed to the stifling of entrepreneurial ability, the excessive caution engendered by strict hierarchies and limited span of control and the unreality of the separation between politics and administration. The merging of politicians and officials into a seamless web was an essential prerequisite for informed policy making, they were two elements of the one whole, with politicians always at the apex of the hierarchy (Massey, 1993). Indeed, the politics/administration dichotomy not only did not exist, but the perpetuation of its myth contributed to attempts by successive governments in the United Kingdom to assert control over an administrative system already subservient to a considerable degree. In this politicians mistook the inability of officials to deliver on government promises as wilful refusal or obstinacy rather than what it really is, a symptom of a hollowed out state within a differentiated polity (Rhodes *et al.*, 2003). The belief that they should be in charge and that officials were not doing as they were told, thereby frustrating the democratic mandate, has led ministers to chase the chimera of modernisation in an attempt to reassert control. Yet for public sector management in the United Kingdom, under the redefining impact of Europeanisation and globalisation the power structures have shifted, the levers have moved or been disconnected; politicians, however, have yet to publicly acknowledge this fact.

Economic 'overload' and the public choice solution

Under the watchful eye of Haldane's successors, the post-war reconstruction of Britain took place. It was a top-down implementation of an overwhelmingly popular policy of constructing the Welfare State (Smith, 1979; Marquand, 1991). In the period from 1945 to 1975 the growth in the size of the peace-time public sector and the proportion of the economy taken in taxes to fund it grew to nearly half the nation's GDP (Middlemas, 1979). The size of the home civil service grew in proportion to this, as the number of officials required to deliver (and to oversee the delivery of) services rose. The number of non-industrial civil servants peaked at nearly 570,000 in 1978 (Rhodes *et al.*, 2003: 10). But this was a fraction of the number of public servants overall, which included those employed in local government, various quangos, the nationalised industries, the armed services and the criminal justice system.

The tax burden combined with a period of high inflation and rising unemployment from 1974 to bring about what some analysts referred to as the fiscal crisis of the state. This is where a perception grew among some US and British observers that the commitments of the welfare state were outstripping the ability of taxpayers to fund it (O'Connor, 1973). This critique chimed with the analysis of the public choice theorists, namely that the nature of bureaucracy is inherently wasteful and markets are a more efficient way of allocating scarce national resources. In other words, they advocated an individualist approach to the allocation of national resources, rather than a hierarchical approach. Their perspective seeks to push the boundary between the state and civil society back from a welfarist perspective of state domination of the policy process in the direction of a more privatised, civil-dominated society. Their critique emanates from three (theoretically linked) general perspectives, or schools of thought.

The Chicago School

From the early 1950s onwards, the group of influential neo-liberal economists based at the University of Chicago, began a steady critique of 'big' government, reaching the peak of their influence with the governments of Ronald Reagan in the United States and Margaret Thatcher in the United Kingdom. Their analysis remains a powerful force in modern political discourse. Included in their number was Milton Friedman, whose books, *Capitalism and Freedom* (1962) and *Free to Choose* (1980), encapsulate much of the New Right's argument. This may be summarised as the belief that there is a causal connection between capitalism and freedom and that whereas liberty ultimately depends on capitalist economics, political activity is destructive of economic liberty and by logical extension, therefore, of liberty itself (Denham, 1996: 4).

The Chicago School of economists argue that the links between liberty (and here they see liberty as a positivist manifestation, that is as a simple concept devoid of intrinsic moral value) and capitalist economics are empirically observable and predictable. The members of this approach argue:

> On empirical grounds, that only free markets can co-ordinate effectively the disparate elements in a complex society and that attempts on the part of the state to improve on the market will destroy both freedom and prosperity. (Denham, 1996: 5)

With the slide of western economies into inflation, high unemployment and expensive tax-funded welfare provision, this empirically based theory, arguing that government intervention was not only unsuccessful, but actually made matters worse and threatened individual liberty, became attractive to politicians.

The Austrian School

Named after a group of neo-liberal economists, originally from Austria, such as F.A. Hayek, the Austrian School differs from the Chicago economists in that it is not so relentlessly empirical and does not alienate the role of the individual from the decision-making process. Chicago economists have tended to: 'construct a metaphysical conception of the person whereby he or she is merely a passive respondent to mechanical processes, an agent that only reacts to external stimuli, a creature and not a creator of the world' (Denham, 1996: 6). For Austrians, however, the economy and those involved in it, are engaged in a continuous process of discovery and for them, the main problem with welfarist economics is that it is based on imperfect knowledge and ignores this central importance overshadowing all decisions taken by policy makers (Denham, 1996: 7).

For the Austrian School, the individual is released from the metaphysical chains of the Chicago economists, and the boundaries imposed upon human action by the collectivising advocates of mass state-provided welfare. Instead he or she is the central element in economic reasoning, individuals use their imperfect knowledge intelligently to make a series of highly complex economic decisions on a daily basis, this must necessarily be a subjective process. Advocates of the Austrian perspective, therefore: 'Are subjectivists, emphasising the purposefulness of human action; they are unhappy with theoretical constructions which emphasise equilibrium to the exclusion of market processes' (Denham, 1996: 9). The role of the market to both allocate and regulate resources and entrepreneurial activity in a manner that is more efficient than any state agency is the key to the Austrian perspective. They argue that different people know different things and the market 'gathers and transmits these discrete (and often contradictory) pieces of information, thereby co-ordinating that actions and plans of market actors' (Denham, 1996: 11).

Such an individualistic perspective is bound to conflict with the egalitarian notions of social justice inherent to welfare economists and those hierarchical bureaucracies of the Fabian and social democratic left. The Austrian economists doubt whether government attempts to overcome 'market failure' through welfare provision can succeed, given the knowledge deficit inherent to the bureaucratic institutions used. Such institutions would need to be pragmatic and entrepreneurial in operation, something that statist welfare hierarchies singularly appear to lack. Furthermore, the Austrian School refer to the whole notion of social justice as a 'mirage', contending that it lacks any meaning and is simply a rhetorical term used by politicians and advocates of welfare expenditure and redistributive taxation schemes (Denham, 1996: 12–13). Such a notion poses a threat to individual liberty.

The Virginia School

As already noted in the forgoing sections, the Virginia School of economists developed public choice theory from their interpretation of liberal economics, as applied to political science and policy making. The work of writers such as Buchanan, Tullock, Niskanen and Olsen led to several reinterpretations of the neo-liberal perspective on the role of the state in general and democratically elected governments in particular (Parsons, 1995: 306–23). These may be distilled into the following points:

1. Public choice writers emphasise the importance of political institutions in the policy process. Furthermore, within those institutions, officials act as rational utility-maximisers, that is they use the position and power of their office to further their personal aims.
2. The role and impact of interest groups, especially their impact on policy making through lobbying bureaucrats, mean these groups seek to privilege themselves over others. Many of the more powerful groups attempt to achieve monopoly rights granted by government over certain areas of activity, that is, control over scarce resources. This is termed 'rent-seeking'.

3. Public choice writers also claim to have discovered a 'political business cycle'. They argue that politicians are vote-maximisers and will use their political power to manipulate the business cycle in their own self-interest, cutting taxes to create an economic boom before elections, and raising them again afterwards.

4. Public choice theory argues that government has an inherent tendency to expand and needs to be kept in check.

5. While public choice theorists approve of democracy as a way of removing governments without recourse to violence, they question, given the aforementioned points, whether government is truly democratic and able to reflect voters' preferences.

6. Public choice writers have led the way for a series of constitutional reforms designed to make government properly responsive to voters' wishes, including sunset laws, item or line vetoes on budgets, fuller citizen participation in policy making through consultation and balanced budget rules. These institutional changes being implemented to make the costs and benefits of government activity more in line with each other and more transparent. (Denham, 1996: 14–17; Parsons, 1995: 306–25)

Taken together, the three schools of thought led British governments (and many others around the world) from 1975 onwards to implement what has variously been described as new public management (NPM), re-engineering or re-inventing of government. It is a modernising process that continues in various forms and draws upon several of the perspectives discussed so far. It does so in often bewilderingly complex ways, attempting to reflect the demands made upon modern public administrations. It is further complicated in Europe by the impact of European integration and the Europeanisation of public administration. For the British, this has also meant a sometimes painful clash as the Anglo-American tradition has collided with the statist traditions of continental Europe.

New public management and modernisation

The following chapters discuss the various techniques, mechanisms and institutions adopted within British public sector management as a result of the impact of NPM and the quest for modernisation. The purpose of this section is to provide a guide to the impact of the neo-liberal (individualist) critique of classical public administration and the way in which it has structured the debate and the subsequent and continuing slew of reforms. There have been several linking threads drawn from the Chicago, Austrian and Virginia schools. These have been as influential in the United Kingdom, Australia and New Zealand as in the United States (Hughes, 1998; Considine and Painter, 1997). These threads or goals have been:

1. To reduce the role and extent of the 'state' in order to enhance that of the private sector;
2. To facilitate the acquisition of entrepreneurial skills and activities within society generally;
3. To prevent future expansion of the public sector, often through the creation of a powerful coalition of interests to counter the perceived welfare-demanding coalitions which have linked their interests to those of the bureaucrats;
4. To de-politicise many (mainly economic) policy decisions through their being entrusted to professional experts, rather than the whim of politicians and bureaucrats perceived to be in the thrall of self-serving interest groups;
5. To inculcate public sector organisations with the best techniques of private sector practice in order to bring the discipline and inherent efficiencies of the marketplace to the activities of the state;
6. To entrench the divisions between the private and public in such a way that individual civil liberties are protected by inalienable property rights, which act as a flexible bulwark against the power of the state and the temptations of state employees and elected politicians to behave in an arbitrary and capricious manner, abusing their power, power loaned to them in trust by the citizenry. (Massey, 1993: 7–8)

As Hughes remarks, these points explore the dynamics of the 'larger picture' while Hood also concentrated on the mechanics of the internal changes within public administration. Hood had seven main observations. He noted:

1. A move to 'let managers manage' with the development of hands on professional management that elevated the role of managers above that of professionals in some parts of the public sector.
2. The implementation of explicit standards and measures of performance.

3. Greater emphasis on output controls, with resources being directed to areas according to measured performance indicators.
4. A move to disaggregate units in the public sector, through privatisation and agencification.
5. A shift to greater competition through the use of contracts and public tendering procedures.
6. A stress on private sector styles of management and flexibility in hiring and rewarding staff.
7. A stress on greater parsimony and discipline in resource use, cutting costs and resisting interest group and public sector union demands for favourable treatment. (Hood, 1991: 4–5, quoted in Hughes, 1998: 61–2; also Massey, 1993: 19–40)

Much of the rest of this book explores these issues and their implementation into British public sector management in more detail.

The implementation of the public choice agenda in various manifestations of new public management has continued apace despite criticism from academics and practitioners, indeed it has continued as a process of continuing modernisation, akin to a rather perverse variation on Trotsky's theory of Permanent Revolution. It has been criticised for lacking the empirical evidence to substantiate the changes implemented in British public administration (Jordan, 1997) and for having at its heart 'the seldom-tested assumption that better management will prove an effective solvent for a wide range of economic and social ills' (Pollitt, 1990: 1). Parsons (2000: 5) has criticised it on its own ground, arguing that whereas the Virginia School has emphasised the need for NPM due to the existence of uncertainty in the decision-making process, the work of Schon could lead to different conclusions regarding the way to deal with that uncertainty. Schon believed in the value of learning organisations, structured from the bottom up as communities of interest. This is in contrast to market-led approaches, and while Schon's perspective celebrates liberty and individualism, it also makes room for community and ethical considerations apart from those of economist empiricism (Parsons, 2000: 6–7).

Parsons follows Pollitt in his condemnation of NPM as neo-Taylorist, as a new-variant scientific management rather than modernisation in a meaningful sense. It has the measurement of performance at its core, rather than anything truly novel and innovative. He argues:

NPM is the nearest we have come in this country, for a few hundred years at least, to a kind of state religion. To question or to deny its essential doctrines is to place oneself beyond the pale. To shout as it parades past that it is stark naked – that the emperor has no clothes – is to risk being bundled away or being injected with a tranquilliser or sent to a gulag. (2000: 12)

Such a culture does not lead to the development of learning organisations, able to respond to the needs of customers and citizens, but the establishment of a monitoring and audit culture. It is a stunted, withered thing in which officials are afraid to make innovative decisions and managers enforce obeisance to the latest centrally directed performance targets.

The Labour government elected to office in Britain in 1997 is committed to modernisation and it is clear, as we shall see in later chapters, that this includes a large dose of NPM, but NPM set within a context of the steady Europeanisation of British public administration. This constitutes one of the strongest dynamics within the current debate on modernising the UK's public sector, with some observers arguing that the whole process has led to a hollowing-out of the state and the development of a more differentiated polity (Rhodes *et al.*, 2003).

The 1999 White Paper, *Modernising Government* (Cm 4310), however, confirmed a hierarchical approach to the process of modernisation. This is a paradox in that although NPM is located within the individualistic theoretical terrain of public choice and Virginia school of economists, Labour have sought its implementation by employing the kind of centralised, mechanistic and statist bureaucracy emphatically opposed by the neo-liberals. The White Paper affirms a belief in the efficacy of government to deliver services to the nation in a coherent and efficient way, policies however, that have at their heart the steady Europeanisation of the British policy process. The *Europeanisation* of British public administration is the context in which policy-making must now be located. It is a process that amounts to a form of international socialisation (Fennig, 2000). Lodge identifies four possible triggers for this process:

1. *Coercive triggers*: (a) requirements to comply with European legislation; (b) rulings by the European Court of Justice; (c) and European Commission executive acts.
2. *Mimetic triggers*: (a) increased interaction among civil servants leading to the adoption of 'best-practice'; (b) national co-ordination networks through things like peer-group review for the implementation of EU employment policy and monetary policy, among other fields.

3. *Professionalisation as a trigger*: (a) policy networks as part of the transnationalisation of societal actors leading to the 'logic of exchange' in areas such as regulatory agencies for telecommunications; (b) the emergence of policy communities.

4. *Domestic politics as a trigger*: (a) strategic competitive adjustment, whereby domestic institutions and regulations are adjusted to comply with European standards to ensure protection of domestic markets. (b) Secondly there is the way Europeanisation shapes domestic policy opportunities through legitimising particular policy beliefs and options. (c) Finally, domestic triggers are found in the lobbying of elite groups to force the adjustment of domestic laws, regulations and institutions to the European model in order to ensure access to resources and the global 'playing field'. (2002: 48–9)

Modernisation, then, is a complex process that involves the continuing impact of the neo-liberal reform agenda, but in Britain, at least, the integration of European policy making and the Europeanisation of governance also heavily influence this process. It is fraught with contradictory dynamics: the hierarchical centralised approach of British government contrasted with the decentralised individualistic approach of neo-liberals; and the homogenising effect of Europeanisation, contrasted with the need to develop entrepreneurial learning organisations able to respond to the individual and complex needs of different groups of citizens.

Conclusion

In this chapter we have traced the major traditions of administrative thought and their development and application in recent years. What is often portrayed as modernisation may be seen to have roots in more classical – indeed ancient – traditions, but it is the economic, social and political context of a society that decides which administrative characteristics will thrive.

The work of Hood has identified the major traits to be found. He located these using grid/group cultural theory. These traits are based upon a priori perspectives on how best to organise society and where to draw the boundaries between the role of the state and civil society. We then explored the hierarchical, individualist and communitarian approaches, with a special emphasis on the impact of the neo-liberals on restructuring and modernising public sector management in recent years. Finally, we began the location of many aspects of British public sector modernisation within the context of European integration and Europeanisation, a topic to which we return from time to time in the following chapters. In Chapter 3 we explore the response of the political parties to these dynamics before looking in more detail at economic and financial management reforms.

3

The Response of the Parties

The theme of this chapter is the adoption of the key tenets of new public management by the major UK political parties.

Approaches to the management and administration of government services have not traditionally been subject to overt party-political factors in Britain. Before the 1980s, the history of modern British government reveals relatively few instances of party conflicts arising over matters of public administration. The major exception to this was what might be described as the macro-change to the overall management of public services signalled by the policies of the 1945–51 Labour governments, which ushered in an era of relatively widespread public ownership and government interventionism. To some extent, the managerial practices and approaches deployed at that time were not particularly new. Their roots could be discerned in the two periods of wartime government (1939–45 and 1914–18), and also to some degree in the last extended period of Liberal government (1905–15). Nonetheless, because the immediate post-1945 Labour governments embraced an extensive policy of nationalisation and peacetime economic planning, the Conservatives, in opposition, launched repeated attacks on the 'socialistic' administrative culture which was apparently being engendered. However, in spite of such attempts by the major parties to differentiate between their governing styles, in practice, in the following years there seemed little to distinguish the managerial approaches adopted by the parties once in power. This was the era of 'Butskellism' (a term coined from an amalgam of the names of successive Labour and Conservative Chancellors of the Exchequer in the early 1950s, Hugh Gaitskell and Rab Butler) and the 'post-war consensus'. During this period, while the electoral rhetoric of the major parties might suggest that there were fundamental ideological differences separating them, once they were in power, the Labour and Conservative parties subscribed to broadly similar policies in key strategic areas. Thus, both were committed to the concept of the 'mixed economy', full employment, and a range of social welfare policies arranged around the idea of the welfare state. There were some indications that this broad consensus was breaking down during the 1970s, and it was to come apart quite dramatically following the 1979 General Election.

The similar approach taken by the major parties towards issues of management and administration in the public sector was perhaps an understated element of this consensus. Although there was an adherence to fairly traditional methods of administration, it is important to stress that neither of the major parties of government was averse to managerial modernisation in some forms. Perhaps the best illustration of this could be seen at the level of central government. Both the Plowden Report of 1961 and the Fulton Report of 1968 (published during periods of Conservative and Labour government, respectively) signalled the increasing importance of management in government. In particular, Plowden gave new emphasis to important elements of financial management, including budgetary control systems, resource allocation and 'efficiency drives'. It was argued that the management functions of senior civil servants were at least as important as their policy advice roles. Its overall impact was to be mixed, but Fulton gave further emphasis to the importance of management, and its recommendations led directly to the establishment of new management education arrangements for senior civil servants (via the Civil Service College).

Although many of the main tenets and features of what became known as the new public management had their roots in the period before 1979, it was during the extended period of Conservative government which started in that year that fundamental changes in the management of public services in Britain were introduced. In this chapter, we examine the way in which the Conservative Party in government established the public sector reform agenda which paved the way for the introduction of the new public management in Britain. As we shall see, in this period of heightened partisanship, the opposition parties initially responded with a mixture of scepticism and outright antagonism to most aspects of the new approach. However, as time passed the rhetoric and policies of the Labour Party and the Liberal Democrats gradually changed, and their positions shifted in relation to such key new public management themes as privatisation, performance management, consumerism, and the introduction of markets in the public sector. A new political consensus emerged around the Conservative agenda, in much the same way as the post-war consensus largely developed around the Labour Party agenda at that time. The new public management thus occupied a pivotal position in the move away from 'big', interventionist government. Final proof of the adoption of this new consensus came in the form of the overt embrace of the new public management by the Blair government, within the framework of its modernisation programme.

Conservative managerialism

As the traditional party of 'business' the Conservatives tended to favour the development of close links between the personnel and practices of the private sector on the one hand, and those of government on the other. To some extent, this was a feature of the pragmatism with which the party liked to be associated: matters of governance were generally deemed to be susceptible to 'common-sense' solutions based on managerial efficiency. Although this might be illustrated with reference to virtually any period of Conservative government, it could be seen particularly vividly in the early phase of the Heath administration.

Even as Leader of the Opposition during the 1960s, Edward Heath planned a 'quiet revolution' which would have the objective of revamping the government machine through the introduction of a series of managerial reforms. By 1969 Heath's Conservative Party was being advised by a team of businessmen put together under Richard Meyjes of Shell (Campbell, 1993: 316). Following the election victory of 1970, Meyjes, together with Derek Rayner from Marks & Spencer and a small cadre of similar business types seconded to Whitehall, started to work on the details of the managerial 'revolution'. Their key recommendations were encapsulated in the White Paper entitled *The Reorganisation of Central Government*, which was published in October 1970. The managerialist approach of the Conservative businessmen was combined with elements of the prescription for change proffered by the Fulton Report (on the civil service) of 1968. Reform of the administrative structure (the creation of 'giant' departments coupled with some experiments in 'hiving-off' functions to executive agencies) were coupled with the introduction of techniques and practices gleaned from the world of corporate business, including devolved budgets, 'management by objectives' and rational policy planning (encapsulated in the Programme Analysis and Review scheme). At the level of local government, structural reorganisations took place and the concept of 'corporate management' spread, with its emphasis on reducing 'departmentalism', creating a co-ordinated approach to the management of local authorities, carving out spheres of autonomy for officials and minimising political interference in the details of service delivery. This pattern of 'macro' structural and organisation change coupled with 'micro' reforms of managerial systems and methods was to become familiar.

Ultimately, however, the managerialism of the Heath government received a mixed verdict, at best. Managerial theory is awash with whims, fads and fashions, and almost as soon as the British government had embraced the concept of 'giantism' for administrative structures, this approach was swept away by a new orthodoxy which necessitated further reordering of the administrative map. The predicted rewards which were to be generated by the adoption of the new managerial methods and techniques did not appear to be forthcoming – at least in the short term – and as economic and political crises mounted, it became increasingly difficult for many ministers and civil servants to focus on the requirements of internal managerial change. At a more fundamental level, there were elements of official and political resistance to the wave of managerialism. Some senior civil servants undoubtedly viewed the new prescriptions with a degree of antipathy, perceiving managerialism as an attack on civil service values and culture. One official wrote about 'The Great Management Hoax' (Sisson, 1976). Politically, the managerialist tide seemed to turn after 1974 as some of the ministers in the Labour governments of the mid- to late 1970s openly doubted the applicability of business-orientated schemes and methods to the world of government and public administration. Some of the new approaches which had been introduced in the early 1970s were now allowed effectively to wither on the vine (Programme Analysis and Review, for example). It should be noted that even within the Conservative Party there were those who believed that Heath's close interest in the technicalities of management was more of a weakness than a strength, and perhaps even indicative of a fundamental political failing. Alan Clark's scathing view, as a leading backbencher of the time, was that Heath saw politics 'as a correspondence course in management studies' (Clark, 1998: 342).

By the time of the election of the next Conservative administration, in 1979, certain key conditions were in place which ensured that the new wave of managerialists would have more success. The important lessons of the past had been learned, and, in particular, this meant that the incoming Conservative ministers and their special advisers would be much more selective about the extent to which civil servants would be trusted with the keys of reform. More importantly, perhaps, there was to be a sustained and demonstrable commitment to widespread managerial change from a number of senior figures, led by the prime minister. While it was undoubtedly true that Edward Heath had placed his weight behind the managerial changes introduced in the early 1970s, he later became distracted and even engulfed by the political and economic crises facing his government. Margaret Thatcher was to keep her eye 'on the ball', partly because the cause of managerial reform became inextricably linked with the political purposes of her government. Managerialism was equated with the attacks on the 'nanny state' and big government, on inefficiency and financial waste. Organisational culture was to change, as well as techniques and processes. One of the novel aspects of the emerging new public management would be its proximity to politics. It was not to be the preserve of technocrats – it touched upon big political questions including the proper role and function of the state in a modern society. Finally, as we note below, the Thatcherites, unlike the Heathites before them, were possessed with a kind of missionary zeal, deriving from their adherence to the philosophical certainties of the New Right.

None of this should be taken to imply that the Thatcher government started work in the summer of 1979 with a new public management blueprint to hand. Quite apart from anything else, as we have seen, the very concept of NPM did not develop for some time after the election of this government. It would be more accurate to say that the government moved quickly to establish a series of managerial reforms in some areas, while others took time to develop and were influenced in part by ideas and policies emerging from private sector business practice, management theory and the experience of governments in other countries.

New Right ideology also influenced the attitude of the Thatcher governments towards public sector management, although the relationship between this broad set of ideas and theories and the practical implementation of managerial reform is complex and somewhat confused (Hickie, 1995). While it would be a mistake to suggest that ministers in the Thatcher governments were driven solely or even mainly by ideology, there can be little doubt that the perception of public administration and management held by the prime minister and her closest colleagues owed a great deal to the 'radical simplifying assumptions' (Hickie, 1995: 115) of a particular strand of New Right ideology, public choice theory. At the core of public choice theory was the concept of self-interested public bureaucracies, with a built-in incentive towards the growth and over-provision of public services (because these lead to bigger departmental budgets, higher salaries, more promotion opportunities) and an inherent tendency to become incompetent and inefficient. The answer to such problems, according to the proponents of public choice ideas, was the advent of competition, markets and consumerism. For the Conservatives of the 1980s, this perspective, allied to the traditional Tory inclination towards business and newly emerging business and management theories, concepts and practices, was to help create a reformist imperative and influence the shape of the new public management.

The influence of New Right public choice theories, traditional Tory business values and emerging business and management practices could be seen in the privatisation drive. The policy of privatisation was a relatively slow starter in the sense that it did not even feature in the 1979 Conservative Party manifesto and only began to have a serious impact as a policy in the second term of the Thatcher government (Jackson and Price, 1994; Marsh, 1991). As we shall see in Chapter 5, privatisation takes many different shapes and forms, including the total or partial conversion of a public corporation or nationalised industry into a limited company, government disposal of all or some of the shares it holds in specific bodies, breaking the monopoly held by a state concern, or the advent of competitive tendering or market testing in public bodies (the latter does not necessarily amount to 'privatisation', although it can lead to the introduction of private sector managerial methods and practices or to the provision of a service by a private company for a fixed term). The rationale behind privatisation had three key dimensions, as summarised in Box 3.1. The Thatcherite Conservatives equated state control and public ownership with fat, flabby and inefficient organisations, over-dependent on subsidy, unaware of their true cost and unable to meet the demands of their customers. Allied to this perception was the attraction of easing the strain on the Public Sector Borrowing Requirement by transferring large

---

***Box 3.1* The rationale for privatisation**

- Efficiency
  - state control/public ownership equated with inefficiency and lack of competitiveness
- Control of public expenditure
  - ease problem of public sector pay
  - reduce Public Sector Borrowing Requirement
  - generate income (and facilitate tax cuts)
- Ideology
  - encourage economic freedom and market forces
  - break 'dependency culture' and create 'property- and share-owning democracy'
  - reduce scale and power of state bureaucracy

numbers of workers from the public to the private sector, reducing Treasury lending and providing a flow of funds into the Exchequer through the sale of assets. Finally, there was an ideological imperative, which became increasingly significant as time passed. Privatisation fitted neatly into the Thatcherite crusade to encourage economic 'freedom', create a 'property and share owning democracy' and cut the state machine down to size. As Marsh (1991: 406–61) notes, while the initial emphasis 'was upon controlling the money supply, reducing public borrowing and cutting income tax', as the policy developed 'the government embraced privatisation for political rather than economic reasons'.

While privatisation took some time to develop as a keystone of the Conservative government's approach to public administration and management (as we shall see in Chapter 6), the drive for modernisation and efficiency in the public sector, beginning with the civil service, was much more prominent from an early stage. The single most important development in this sphere was to be the appointment of Derek Rayner, a veteran of the Heath government's team of businessmen, to head the Efficiency Unit within the Private Office at Number 10 Downing Street. Physical proximity to Thatcher was significant and symbolic: the managerial revolution was seen to have the consistent and full-hearted support of the prime minister. During the 18 years of Conservative government the Efficiency Unit, under successive heads (Rayner returned to Marks & Spencer in 1983) and under two prime ministers (the Unit retained its prominence in the Major years), was to spearhead a series of managerial initiatives which would be applied not only in Whitehall (although the civil service was the main focus of attention for the Unit) but throughout the public sector. The programme of 'scrutinies' designed to achieve cost savings and improve value for money was to be a continuous feature of the Efficiency unit's work (see Pyper, 1995: 57–62) and, although debates raged about the precise savings achieved, the managerial approaches engendered by the scrutinies (including ongoing fundamental examination of activities, programmes and methods) spread rapidly within Whitehall and beyond ('Raynerism' became a feature of NHS management too).

The scrutinies and the general work of the Efficiency Unit spawned a number of extremely important managerial offshoots, including the Financial Management Initiative which encapsulated a range of new approaches to the micro-management of resources (see Chapter 4) and the Next Steps programme which brought about a fundamental restructuring of the government machine through the process which came to be known as agencification (see Chapter 5).

As noted at several junctures in this book, the transition from the Thatcher years to the period of the Major government saw a marked shift in tone and emphasis. The privatisation drive and the search for economy and efficiency continued apace, but new managerial approaches to public services were emerging. Influenced in part by developments in the United States (as was Thatcher during the Reagan years, when the transatlantic trade in New Right ideology had been at its peak), and in part by an avowedly more sympathetic attitude towards public services, the Conservatives began to focus on the types of issues raised by the *Reinventing Government* agenda (Aberbach and Rockman, 2001; Osborne and Gaebler, 1992). Questions were now being asked about how to develop more varied forms of public sector accountability, treat the consumers of services as customers, encourage competition between service providers, develop meaningful comparisons between similar services with the aim of identifying the best managerial practices, focus on outcomes and decentralise decisions (Riddell, 1994: 37). The practical implications of all of this are discussed throughout the remaining chapters of this book.

The extent to which the new public management grew to become a significant force during the years of Conservative government after 1979 should not be underestimated. Martin Smith (1996: 163) noted that 'the language of managerialism has come to dominate the Conservative attitude to the state'. To some extent, this can be attributed to the influence of the New Right critique of bureaucracy, although, as Smith points out (1996: 165), the form of the state even under Thatcher fell far short of the minimalist ideal of this camp. Other influences were also at play. The re-emergence of some traditional Tory values under the party's leaders in the 1980s and 1990s is easily overlooked when analysts emphasise the extent to which Thatcherism in particular marked a departure from the party's roots. However, as Adonis (1994: 149) pointed out, the party was traditionally committed to business values, low taxes and a small state, and to some extent the Thatcherite managerialism 'marked a *reaction*, a return to values deeply rooted in the party's history, values the party had never wholly foreworn even when most compromised by accommodation'. Finally, the party's 'business' orientation meant that it was open to influence by the prevailing and emerging theories and concepts in the private sector, as well as to attempts to transplant and adapt corporate business practices to public sector requirements. Box 3.2 summarises the key components of Conservative Manageralism. Whatever the contributory factors, the result was clear: 'One of the legacies of 18 years of reforming Conservative governments from 1979 to 1997 was a

---

Box 3.2 **Conservative managerialism: key components**

- New Right Public Choice critique of bureaucracy
- Traditional Tory values
- Emerging business and management theories and concepts

---

well-entrenched system of "new public management"' (Horton and Farnham, 1999: 247). Nonetheless, although it was 'well-entrenched', this system of public management was distinctly problematic. 'The claims made on behalf of the new managerialism are not ... immune from challenge ...' (Painter, 1999: 99). The extent to which the quality of public services actually improved and greater value for money was achieved were open to question. The NPM reforms were introduced in varying degrees in different parts of the public sector, and there were increasing problems (including those involving ethics) associated with the crude transplantation of private sector practices and values to the system of government (Painter, 1999: 87–98).

The conversion of the opposition

It is impossible to understand the response of the opposition parties to the emerging new public management as an isolated phenomenon without reference to the fundamental internal changes taking place within and around these parties. During the period when NPM was emerging in Britain, the opposition parties were subjecting themselves to processes which have been variously described as reform, renewal and modernisation. These processes were influenced by many factors, some of which were intrinsic to the historical development of the parties themselves, some of which arose due to global political developments (the fall of Communism and end of the Cold War produced a crisis in socialism and led to a fundamental reorientation within many centre-left parties) and some of which simply stemmed from the extended period of Conservative government. The changes which took place within the opposition parties ultimately led them to accommodate the main features of the new public management.

While our focus in this chapter is mainly on the major parties of government, Conservative and Labour, the general stance of the Liberal Democrats can be briefly summarised.

Formed by a merger between the Liberal Party and the Social Democratic Party in 1988, the Liberal Democrats draw upon at least two political traditions (it might be argued that even within the old Liberal Party there were numerous distinct philosophical strands). The economic liberalism and *laissez-faire* approach of the nineteenth-century Liberal Party was transformed in the early part of the twentieth century by an avowedly interventionist 'New Liberalism' which was in the vanguard of the social and welfare reform movement (Cook, 1998: 42–51). Although the party was not to hold power in its own right at national level after 1915, it remained committed to broad ranging reform programmes and exercised some control at local government level in certain areas. The SDP was formed in 1980, by a leading group of social democrats in flight from the internal struggles of the Labour Party:

> The philosophies and policies of the Liberal Party and the SDP, though alike, were in important respects not the same. Liberals had held to a firm belief in liberty … underpinning their central commitment to a redistribution of power within society in the interests of individuals and communities … The SDP was notably more managerialist and less decentralist than the Liberal Party. (Brack, 1996: 86–7)

In the wake of the merger, the new party sought to differentiate itself both from the Conservatives' 'radicalism' on issues such as privatisation and what was still at that time seen as the outdated, traditionalist approach of the Labour Party. It is difficult to be precise about the specific policy orientation of the Liberal Democrats on all aspects of the new public management, due in part to the party's tendency during its early phases of development to focus on clarifying its general principles and keystone policies. However, in broad terms, by the early 1990s the Liberal Democrats had adopted a 'less interventionist, more free market' approach, and countenanced 'the possibility of private investment in public services' while also stressing the importance of market mechanisms (Brack, 1996: 88). Although this type of stance alienated some party members, the Liberal Democrats, like the emerging New Labourites, felt the strong pull of a new, Conservative-created orthodoxy on public management issues. The 1997 Liberal Democrat election manifesto was replete with the phraseology of consumerism and 'public–private partnerships'. While widening ownership of the public utilities was a stated objective, the principle of privatisation was not questioned (Liberal Democrats, 1997: 13, 19, 23, 29). The tone of the 2001 election manifesto (Liberal Democrats, 2001) was broadly similar, with great emphasis being given to performance targets in the public sector.

As we have noted, the philosophical and political changes brought about within the opposition parties during the 1980s and 1990s were about much more than the new public management. Nonetheless, these parties were obliged to respond to key features of what would come to be known as NPM, including the adoption of private sector methods and techniques within government, the spread of competition and markets, new budgetary systems, privatisation and consumerism. The changing responses to challenges of this type mirrored broader changes in their political outlook.

The attitude of the Labour Party to issues of public administration and management has always been bound up with its wider political and philosophical stance. Traditionally, the Labour Party was a 'broad church' within which trade unionists, moderate piecemeal social reformers and socialists competed for power and influence. During the period following the Second World War, the dominant feature of this amalgam had come to be characterised as 'revisionist social democracy' (Shaw, 1994: 2), although this faced frequent challenges from those on the left of the party who were styled democratic socialists. The defining statement of the social democratic approach was set out by the leading Labour intellectual and parliamentarian, Anthony Crosland (1956). In practice, and in government, revisionist social democracy implied a 'rapprochement between private corporate interests and the common good' (to be accomplished by means of Keynesian economics). While there was some direct public ownership of some key industries, the bulk of the economy was left in private hands, and limited state intervention was favoured as a means of regulating the excesses of the market. Social welfare programmes (especially social security, education, health and housing) were seen as the means by which the lives of the majority of the population could be improved.

In line with the spirit of the times, all of this was managed by large public sector bureaucracies at central and local levels. While it would be wrong to suggest that no thought was ever given to issues of 'management', these were generally deemed to be matters of detail, which could be safely left to those working in the middle to low ranks of the system.

However, the importance attached to management in government increased slowly but steadily as the challenges of governance became more acute. Certainly, by the mid-1960s there were clear indications that the Labour Party in government was beginning to take managerial issues seriously. One sign of this was the establishment in 1966 of the Fulton Committee to inquire into the running of the civil service. The Fulton

Report, published in 1968, recommended, inter alia, the creation of the Civil Service College as a facilitator of management education for senior officials, new ways of managing the work of government departments (including devolved budgets and the creation of some executive agencies), and, in a general sense, raising the profile of management in government. The Wilson government accepted the report's findings and recommendations, although the implementation of Fulton by the Conservative and Labour governments of the 1970s was to be partial, at best, for a whole range of reasons.

The next phase of what would become Labour's evolution into a (perhaps *the*?) party of new public management came as the consequences of the 1974–79 governments' failures worked themselves out. It is no exaggeration to say that the policy compromises forced on Labour by inflation and rising unemployment brought about the final crisis for revisionist social democracy and initiated a battle for the soul of the party and for control over its future direction. By the time the Labour government fell from power in 1979, Keynesianism had been ditched, monetarism embraced (albeit with some reluctance) and internal battles were already starting to break out over the party's future.

In opposition, the party's major factions fought for control over organisation and policy. Both left and right (broadly defined as a coalition of elements around Tony Benn on the democratic socialist wing and the regrouped revisionist social democrats around James Callaghan, Denis Healey and Michael Foot on the centre-right) claimed victories in the numerous skirmishes of this time. Some of the leading social democrats, dismayed at the apparent resurgence of the far left within the party, resigned and went off to form their own party, the Social Democratic Party (which, as we have already noted, ultimately merged with the Liberal Party, to form the Liberal Democrats). Labour went into the 1983 General Election with a programme which, although representing a victory for the left on many key policies, was, when viewed overall, effectively 'a compromise between two positions' (Shaw, 1994: 13). The party's subsequent crushing defeat (it emerged with only 28 per cent of the vote and 209 MPs) was the catalyst for fundamental change. Although it was by no means an entirely smooth and steady process, between 1983 and 1997 Labour in opposition was transformed. The 'modernisation' of Labour saw both the democratic socialists and the revisionist social democrats eclipsed, as the party shed many of its traditional ideas, policies and procedures and rebranded itself as New Labour. In this process, the new public management, pursued heretofore by the Conservatives in government, was embraced by the major opposition party with some vigour and enthusiasm, and it became clear that a 'modernisation' agenda would be pursued by New Labour in government.

Labour's managerialists, although thin on the ground, were never quite as rare as the party's image as a collection of trade unionists and socialist intellectuals suggested. The ranks of Labour's parliamentarians had come to contain a number of people who were capable of thinking analytically about managerial issues. Perhaps the most prominent of these was John Garrett, who brought the approach of management consultancy to his writings on the civil service and government (Garrett, 1980). However, the period after 1983 was remarkable in the sense that many of the party's policies were gradually (in some cases abruptly!) moulded around the managerial agenda. This was partly a simple reaction to electoral defeat, partly a product of longer-term changes within the party itself, and partly the consequence of broad social and economic factors:

> the British economy had become interlocked with a global economy ... At the same time, service industries were replacing manufacturing, leading to a consumer culture rather than the producer culture with which Labour had been traditionally associated ... An information economy was emerging in which skill and talent had become critical as knowledge and education played a greater role ... In these circumstances, a new socialism ... was needed. (Foote, 1997: 345)

During these long years in opposition, the Labour Party's position on many aspects of public management shifted. The Rayner scrutiny programme was viewed initially by the Labour opposition as a stalking horse for staff cuts and privatisation. Similar scepticism characterised Labour's approach to Next Steps, although the official party line on this came to be broadly supportive of the reform. Initial opposition to the principle and detail of market testing and the Private Finance Initiative waned as time passed, although questions were posed about the true value of the 'efficiency savings' generated, the sums spent on private management consultants and the extent to which private companies were complying with their government contracts (Labour Research, 1993; Mandelson and Liddle, 1996: 252–3). In the end Labour was committed only to a moratorium on market testing, but, when the time came, even this was speedily dropped after the 1997 election. The Major government's failure to back the Citizen's Charter (see Chapter 5) with additional financial resources and the Charter's relative weaknesses in securing redress of grievances were mocked, but the concept of 'Charterism' was ultimately embraced by Labour on the grounds that it had originated within a Labour-controlled local authority.

The most vehement opposition was reserved for the policy of privatisation, which was attacked by Labour throughout the 1980s. The party's critique of this policy focused on the extent to which state monopolies had simply been replaced by private monopolies in some spheres (such as the gas and water utilities), social costs (including redundancies), dismantling of the public service principle, loss of public accountability, enrichment of institutional shareholders, and the apparent failure of the Conservative government to secure the full value of the state's assets (due to the 'sale of the century' approach to the share flotations). The principle of privatisation continued to arouse Labour's ire during the early 1990s, although by this point the party was admitting that not all of the Conservative privatisations would be reversible by a Labour government. Labour's 1997 General Election manifesto virtually ignored the subject. Only rail privatisation, which was reluctantly accepted as a *fait accompli*, was given a mention (Labour Party, 1997: 29). By this stage, it was becoming clear that Labour's ministers might actually favour the introduction of limited privatisation measures in certain spheres.

Slowly, therefore, a broad consensus seemed to have developed between the government and the official opposition with regard to at least some of the key elements of public management. One clear example of this came in 1994, with the publication of the Conservative government's *Continuity and Change* White Paper (Prime Minister, 1994). Token criticism of this document could not disguise the basic similarity in approach between the two major parties on important issues related to NPM. To some extent this was due to Labour's gradual embrace of the central tenets of the new public management – itself indicative of the common ground occupied by Labour's 'modernisers', the Labor administrations in Australia and New Zealand, and the Clinton presidency's proponents of 'reinventing government' (see Aberbach and Rockman, 2001; Borins, 2002; Carroll and Steane, 2002; Halligan, 2001).

One measure of the changing attitude towards managerialism within Labour's ranks was the adoption of management principles to the continuing process of internal reform within the party itself, and the alacrity with which the modernisers embraced business values:

In preparation for office, members of the shadow Cabinet were even sent on a business school mangement course! Indeed, Peter Mandelson used a commercial analogy in describing 'Old Labour' as the equivalent of a company that had lost touch with its customer base, making it essential for the party to rebrand the product it had to offer in the electoral market place. (Painter, 1999: 99)

By the time of the 1997 General Election, Labour was seeking to distinguish its public service policy from that of the Conservatives, mainly on the issues of ethics and openness. The Scott inquiry and the subsequent report into the 'arms for Iraq' affair had raised serious questions about the extent to which senior officials had colluded with Conservative ministers to mislead Parliament and withhold embarrassing information. Labour's commitment to change included plans for a Freedom of Information Act. Beyond this, however, the party's 1997 election manifesto (Labour Party, 1997) had nothing specific to say about the civil service (the part of the government machine which would be key to the development of new public management), and there seemed to be no clear agenda to guide the developing relationship between the new government and the administrative system it had last encountered 18 years before.

New Labour, new public management

Once in office, the Blair government wasted no time in demonstrating its commitment to the new public management. Even at a very early stage in the life of the new administration, the symbolism of NPM could be seen. In one bastion of Whitehall traditionalism, the Foreign Office, Robin Cook began a process of organisational 'rebranding' by publishing a 'mission statement'. Other ministers followed this lead, introducing motivational techniques in order to encourage civil servants to take 'ownership' of departmental and agency objectives (Painter, 1999: 99–100). The prime minister announced that progress in achieving the government's election pledges would be set out in the form of a corporate business-style annual report.

Beyond the symbolism, other developments were indicative of a firm commitment to the new public management. As we shall see in more detail in Chapter 6, the government quickly dropped its proposed moratorium on market testing in favour of a more selective use of the policy within the framework of *Best Value* in local government, and *Better Quality Services*, its civil service equivalent. These initiatives sought to replace the 'dogmatism' of compulsory competitive tendering and

market testing with a more 'pragmatic' approach. The aim was to identify the best supplier of a particular service through consideration of
competitive tendering, although unlike the previous system, there would
be no compulsion to do this, provided robust internal reviews of service
provision were sufficient to have satisfied the external auditors (and in
the case of the civil service, the Cabinet Office, the Treasury and a key
Cabinet Committee).

The procedures surrounding the most controversial form of contractualisation, the Private Finance Initiative, were overhauled (see Chapter 6
for full details), but the basic principles remained intact, despite growing
criticism from within the Labour Party. Privatisation was not to be
eschewed. The government's plans for the future of the London Underground and the air traffic control system, to cite two examples, were
cloaked in the jargon of 'public–private partnerships', but effectively
involved significant elements of privatisation.

A fundamental aspect of the NPM agenda is the emphasis given to
consumerism. In Chapter 6 we shall see in detail how the development of
'charterism' fitted into this. The Labour Government's approach was initially set out in 1997 by David Clark, the Chancellor of the Duchy of
Lancaster and Public Service Minister, when he announced that the
Citizen's Charter would continue, albeit subject to 'relaunching' and
'refocusing'. In the event, this took place within a developing 'quality'
and 'performance' agenda encompassing *Service First*, the title given to
the relaunched Charter programme, and a range of associated initiatives.
These included the People's Panel, a 5,000-strong nationally representative
group charged with telling the government 'what people really think'
about public services and the efforts being taken to improve them. A typical New Labour product, this adopted the focus group approach to give
the government feedback on public service issues and operated between
1998 and January 2002, at which point the Cabinet Office announced its
end, on the grounds that there was now less need for a centrally based
body of this kind, since departments and agencies had developed their
own customer consultation initiatives.

Beyond this, the government showed a clear determination to expand
the previous administration's deployment of managerial devices such as
benchmarking (the practice of comparing the management processes and
procedures used in different organisations, with a view to transferring the
best practices from one to others), performance indicators and public
service agreements (designed to set out in detail what people can expect
in return for public expenditure on specific services).

The whole strategy for the application of new public management
principles and practices within the future framework for governance was

to be set out in a White Paper. After much delay, this was published in March 1999, under the title *Modernising Government* (Prime Minister, 1999). This document drew together many of the managerial themes and processes which had been developing piecemeal during the life of the Blair administration, and indeed before. The *Modernising Government* White Paper (for a summary, see Box 3.3) was in many respects, a typical Blair product, with its short phraseology gleaned from the world

---

Box 3.3   **Labour embraces NPM:** *Modernising Government* **White Paper**

Central objective:

'Better government to make life better for people'

Aims:

- Ensure that policy making is more 'joined up' and strategic
- Focus on public service users, not providers
- Deliver high quality and efficient public services

New reforms:

- 'Government Direct': Public services available 24 hours a day, seven days a week, where there is a demand.
- 'Joined-up government': Co-ordination of public services and more strategic policy making.
- Removal of unnecessary regulation: Requirements that departments avoid imposing new regulatory burdens and submit those deemed necessary to Regulatory Impact Assessments.
- 'Information Age' government: Target for all dealings with government to be deliverable electronically by 2008.
- 'Learning Labs': To encourage new ways of front-line working and suspend rules that stifle innovation.
- Incentives: For public service staff – including financial rewards for those who identify savings or service improvements.
- New focus on delivery within Whitehall: Permanent Secretaries to pursue delivery of key government targets, recruit more 'outsiders', promote able young staff.

Key commitments:

- Forward-looking policy making:
  - Identify and spread best practice via new Centre for Management and Policy Studies (which will incorporate the Civil Service College)
  - Joint training of ministers and civil servants
  - Peer review of departments

$\longrightarrow$

$\rightarrow$

- Responsive public services:
  - Remove obstacles to joined-up working through local partnerships, one-stop shops and other means
  - Involve and meet the needs of different groups in society

- Quality public services:
  - Review all government department services and activities over 5 years to identify best suppliers
  - Set new targets for all public bodies with focus on real improvements in quality and effectiveness
  - Monitor performance closely to strike balance between intervention when things go wrong and allowing successful organisations freedom to manage

- 'Information Age' government:
  - An IT strategy for government to coordinate development of digital signatures, smart cards, websites and call centres
  - benchmark progress against targets for electronic services

- Public service:
  - To be valued, not denigrated
  - Modernise the civil service (including revision of performance management arrangements; tackle under representation of women, ethnic minorities and people with disabilities; build capacity for innovation)
  - Establish a public sector employment forum to bring together and develop key players across the public sector

of image-makers and PR consultants. Not all of the snappy concepts seemed full of meaning (even the 'central objective' was slightly opaque). Nonetheless, the White Paper's contents epitomised the government's approach and emphasised the significance and centrality of the new public management in the New Labour project. The pace of reform was incessant, however, and only two years after its launch the Modernising Government initiative effectively evolved into a component of the new 'focus on delivery' and 'reforming public services' agenda.

Of course, while it was feasible and possibly politically necessary for the new party of government to adopt the phraseology and techniques of the new public management, it was not necessarily the case that this approach to governance, even when clad in the garb of the 'Third Way' (the 'way' between rampant free market capitalism and state socialism) would facilitate the sweeping transformation of public services claimed by its proponents. Members of the public dealing with the Child Support Agency at almost any point during its perennial crises, or the Passport Agency during the virtual collapse of its services in 1999 (to take but two examples) could be excused for their failure to take seriously the jargon about 'customers', 'stakeholders', 'service standards', 'quality', 'managerial improvements' and the efficacy of 'public–private partnerships'. The publication of a 'mission statement' did not prevent the Foreign Office becoming embroiled in a series of major policy failings early in the life of the new administration (one of which, the 'arms to Sierra Leone' affair, bore more than a passing similarity to the type of scandal which had dogged the former Conservative government!). In truth, the more astute analysts (see, for example, Painter, 1999; and Horton and Farnham, 1999) have recognised that the political claims for the wonders of the new public management and modernisation are often inflated. To a considerable extent, political leaders have made exaggerated claims for the benefits of NPM, often without any real evaluation of its impact and outcomes. Party members and the general public beyond, have been expected to take a great deal 'on faith' (Horton and Farnham, 1999: 250).

The new public management undoubtedly has some negative consequences. Among these are its tendency to spawn its own bureaucracies, the destruction of professionalism in certain parts of the public sector, the toleration of non-consultative and domineering managerial styles, lower morale in workforces, the devaluation of certain types of accountability and denigration of the traditional public service ethic. Political parties which have invested their credibility in the methods and techniques of NPM are reluctant to admit to this downside. In government, the Labour Party has attempted to differentiate its approach from that of the previous Conservative governments, and effectively give its managerialism a softer, friendlier and more accommodating image. Hence the emphasis on constitutional and political reforms rather than mere market reforms as the route to enhance citizenship. The concepts of communitarianism and stakeholderism were initially stressed as means by which the harshness and rigidity of market solutions and naked competitiveness might be alleviated (Painter, 1999: 100), but the currency of these concepts was fairly limited, and they were superceded, in time, by the 'Third Way', a much broader-based set of ideas. The debates about the content and meaning of the 'Third Way' (see Giddens, 1998, 2000, 2002) raised a number of serious issues. However, at one level it seemed to offer a broad conceptual bridge linking the early manifestations of managerialism, the new public management, and the Blairite modernisation programme (for more on these linkages, see Newman, 2001, 2002). 'Third Way' initiatives, including 'partnerships' in service delivery, 'inclusion' in policy formation, and coordinated (or 'joined-up') modes of governance were proffered as the routes to modernised governance and enhanced public management. However, as Horton and Farnham (1999: 255–8) note, and Giddens (2000) acknowledges (without necessarily accepting!), there was some dispute about the real distinctiveness of the 'Third Way' of governance. In time, Prime Minister Blair and his ministers came to make fewer explicit references to the 'Third Way', opting instead to deploy the even broader concept of 'modernisation' as the *leitmotiv* of their managerial reforms.

Ultimately, the differences between the New Labour and Conservative approaches to public management in some respects at least do not appear to be fundamental or striking. 'More significant, perhaps, are the areas of similarity' (Horton and Farnham, 1999: 255).

Conclusion

In this chapter we have outlined the way in which the major parties in Britain have responded and reacted to the challenges posed by changing approaches to public management. As the party most closely associated with 'business', and as the dominant force in British government and politics for almost two decades before 1997, the Conservatives embraced the new public management and successfully entrenched its doctrines and ethos throughout the system of government. In opposition, the Liberal Democrats and the Labour Party slowly adjusted to this new reality, eventually accepted that a fundamental break had been made with key aspects of the post-war consensus on *dirigisme*, and adopted the new public management and modernisation as an appropriate set of means through which a new consensus on governance could be activated.

Some of these themes can now be pursued in more detail, as we turn our attention to matters of economic and financial management.

4

Economic and Financial Management

There is a fairly clear relationship between the broad economic and financial management approaches adopted by governments and the managerial culture which develops within governing institutions. The relationship could perhaps best be characterised as one of complex, mutual interdependence, in the sense that new approaches to public management, administration and governance tend to develop partly as a consequence of changes in the financial and economic environment, while these new approaches themselves simultaneously have an influence on some of the specific features of that environment. In simple terms, the financial and economic strategies of governments affect the style and ethos of public administration and management, and vice versa.

In this chapter, we set out the centrality of finance and economics to the new public management, while offering an account of the changing framework of macroeconomic policy occasioned by the flight from Keynesianism, and the general impact this had on UK public administration and management. Thereafter, we examine some of the key features and aspects of the developing new public management in this sphere, including some reflections upon the impact of the Blair government on the nature and character of public finance and economics.

A changing framework: the flight from Keynesianism

During the period between the Second World War and the mid-1970s, successive British governments pursued economic policies which drew to a significant extent upon the ideas of John Maynard Keynes. This is not to say that these ideas were ever implemented in full, or in the manner Keynes had envisaged. Indeed, some commentators argue that there was a failure to give the Keynesian approach its proper chance because basic features of the British system militated against it. According to Hutton (1996: 32), 'The shortcomings of Britain's constitutional arrangements derailed the attempt at establishing a Keynesian social democracy and divided the Labour Party'. As we shall see, it is certainly true to say that Keynesian techniques were subject to manipulation and compromise. Whether this was due to inherent constitutional failings in Britain or to political expediency is a moot point. Regardless of whether or not we agree with Hutton, it is the case (and one which he recognises) that the economic approach taken by governments in this period could broadly be characterised as Keynesian.

The central characteristic of the Keynesian approach was an assumption that government intervention was necessary in order to regulate economic activity and levels of employment. Budgetary policy could be utilised in order to sustain high levels of activity, while in times of falling economic activity and rising unemployment, deficit spending (that is, an excess of government expenditure over revenue) would be used in order to stimulate recovery.

William Keegan (1985: 18) succinctly summarises the basic features of the Keynesian prescription:

> government could and should intervene to stabilise economic activity and employment. It must increase its own spending – new roads and buildings gave work to construction companies, this in turn brought jobs to suppliers of materials, and plumbers; the need to furnish houses brought extra orders to the furniture and refrigerator firms; and so forth. The government could also precipitate economic recovery by cutting taxes, or raising unemployment and welfare payments.

Although Keynes had originally envisaged only periodic economic and financial interventions by government, in the interest of general economic regulation and management, post-war governments of both parties came to utilise the Keynesian techniques with great frequency, for a variety of political and economic reasons. As a result, governments became hooked upon the habit of continuous intervention and economic fine-tuning.

The practice of government in the United Kingdom came to be associated with detailed financial and economic planning at the macro level. Governance became characterised by interventionism, *dirigisme*, and welfare statism. This had certain consequences for the culture, ethos and practice of public administration and management. As Metcalf and Richards (1990: 185) note, despite the Keynesian proclivity for macro planning, financial management practices at the micro level within the machinery of government were deemed to have little intrinsic importance, and were largely left to develop in an unstructured, unco-ordinated fashion:

> the predominantly Keynesian economic philosophy encouraged a belief in the beneficial effects of growing public spending on economic performance. Since public spending *per se* was beneficial in macro economic terms, there was little interest in the efficiency or effectiveness of spending in achieving policy objectives at the micro-level. Improvements in management and efficiency were regarded as insignificant factors in macro economic policy-making.

The inherent inflationary pressures generated by the use or misuse of Keynesianism by successive governments, coupled with frequent foreign exchange crises, gradually undermined confidence in this economic approach. By 1970 the Bank of England was unofficially experimenting with monetary targets as the route to medium-term control of inflation, but it was only in the wake of a major international crisis in the mid-1970s that the final flight from Keynesianism began:

> during the oil crisis of 1974–75, the lamps went out on the accepted pattern of economic policy-making. For the simple rule 'reflate if unemployment is excessive and deflate if the balance of payments is in crisis' was unworkable in an environment where both unemployment and the foreign payments deficit, and, for good measure, inflation as well, stood at post-war record levels and still rising. (Mosley, 1988: 190)

The policy vacuum was to be filled by a revived and retuned version of the economic orthodoxy of the earlier part of the century. Monetarism, at its simplest, was based on the assumption that inflation was caused by variations in the money supply: if the latter could be reduced, inflation would fall. This implied the need for reduced government deficits (since these were met by borrowing and borrowing created a growth in the money supply) and, in consequence, an end to the policy of deficit spending for purposes such as achieving target levels of employment. The new approach also precluded the use of interest rates as an instrument of policy, since the growth of the money supply was the prime target and that would be adversely affected by tinkering with the price at which money could be borrowed.

Denis Healey, the Labour Chancellor of the Exchequer, formally refused to resort to Keynesian demand techniques even in the face of rising unemployment in 1975, and he reacted to the sterling crisis of 1976 by signalling the government's intention to cut the budget deficit in order to achieve a reduction in the money supply. Mosley (1988: 191–2) observes that the flight from Keynesianism and the move to a new approach to economic policy 'was three-quarters complete' before the election of the Thatcher government in 1979 brought an explicit rejection of high employment as a prime policy target, and the embrace of the monetarist prescriptions. This was to have significant implications for the practice of public management and administration.

From monetarism to pragmatism

In its purest form, the monetarist experiment in Britain was fairly short-lived, failed to achieve many of the key objectives of the Conservative government, and was ultimately subject to compromise and dilution. Nonetheless, there was to be no return to Keynesianism.

Margaret Thatcher's first administration adopted the concept of a Medium Term Financial Strategy, incorporating four-yearly targets for reduced monetary growth and budget deficits, supposedly as an alternative to the 'stop–go' short-termism inherent in Keynesianism. However, in practice, control over both the money supply and public expenditure, as originally defined, continued to elude the government. Like its predecessors, it could not resist the temptation of manipulating the economy (now primarily via interest rates) in order to enhance its electoral chances, and, as its failure to meet its own monetary targets became increasingly obvious, it began to seek new, more amenable definitions of the money supply (Mullard, 1993: 197). This move away from the dogmatism of the economic theorists and towards a more pragmatic approach in the sphere of the money supply was mirrored in the realm of public expenditure, where the target shifted from a real-term reduction to a reduction of public expenditure as a ratio of Gross Domestic Product. By the late 1980s, the Chancellor of the Exchequer, Nigel Lawson, was actually citing rises in public expenditure as a government achievement (Mullard, 1993: 198–200). The demise of Margaret Thatcher in 1990 and the subsequent Major government resulted in more open debates within the Conservative Party regarding the merits of different types of public spending, an acceptance that the Conservative governments' attempts to control fewer elements of the economy better had, in practice, produced mixed results, and an awareness that many of the economic successes of the 1980s had been built on a system of public finance which was bolstered by North Sea oil receipts coupled with the proceeds of successive major privatisations. The scale of privatisation was significant. By the early 1990s, 46 major companies and dozens of smaller ones had been transferred from the public to the private sector. Nearly one million jobs had been transferred, and the share of Gross Domestic Product accounted for by the nationalised industries and the public corporations fell had fallen from to only 3 per cent (from around 9 per cent in 1979) (HM Treasury, 1992: 104).

If the flight from Keynesianism was a rather messy and unco-ordinated affair, comprising, in varying measures, *realpolitik* (evinced in the actions of the Labour government in the mid- to late 1970s), economic and political dogma (epitomised by the approach of the early Thatcher administrations), consolidation and compromise (the later Thatcher period and the Major era), its impact on the nature and style of public administration and management was more clear-cut. The overwhelming domestic concern of British governments in the period from the mid-1970s onwards was the scale and nature of public expenditure. In this context, financial discipline became the *idée fixe* of the emergent style of public administration, which was described, successively, as a 'new managerialism' and then as the 'new public management'.

In fact, the claimed originality was somewhat bogus. Antecedents of the managerial changes could be discerned in earlier phases of British public administration (Pyper, 1995: 55–6), and many of the UK changes were heavily influenced by public sector reforms in the United States and the Antipodes. Nonetheless, it was clear by the 1980s that the scale of the managerial changes was more significant than anything which had gone before: there was a more consistent and overt attempt to change organisational culture as well as processes and techniques, and there was a genuine and sustained political force behind the changes. As we have shown in Chapters 1 and 2, the concept of new public management is multifaceted, and it contains some quite disparate elements. What can often appear as a jumble of managerial fads and fashions, current themes and transient ideas, is bound together by the prominence of financial discipline. This pre-eminent concern stemmed directly from the flight from Keynesianism and the move into a new era of public finance and economics, in which there was an overwhelming concern with the scale and shape of public expenditure and a corresponding imperative: to achieve value for money. There was a certain irony in the fact that interference in the details of public sector financial management was being spearheaded by a government which lost no opportunity to proclaim its adherence to the tenets of economic liberalism and *laissez faire*.

Most of the new public management's core elements placed an overt emphasis upon finance. Obvious examples of this were: the development of financial information systems; the application of new budgetary techniques; identification of accountable cost centres; contractualisation and marketisation in service provision; and, in a general sense, the elevation of financial management and managers within public sector organisations. Some of these themes are explored elsewhere in this book. Here, we can note that the transition from public administration in the Keynesian era to new public management in the post-Keynesian period brought with it a narrowing of the governing focus. The prevailing concern with closer financial control spawned a variety of methods and techniques which were geared towards achieving better control of tighter budgets at all levels of the system of government. Let us now examine some of the manifestations of this.

Budgetary systems and techniques

The flight from Keynesianism and the concomitant tightening of public finances helped to spawn new approaches to the management of budgets throughout the public sector. Experiments with new budgetary systems and techniques became enmeshed, in time, with the development of the new public management.

Traditionally, public sector budgetary systems had been characterised by 'incrementalism'. From the 1970s onwards, newer approaches, which had their theoretical origins in some of the decision-making debates taking place in the United States during the 1950s, injected elements of 'rationality' into public sector budgeting in Britain. It should not be thought that these elements of 'rationality' entirely superseded the traditional, 'incrementalist' features of budgeting: in fact, public sector budgeting remained fundamentally 'incremental' in character. Nonetheless, the experiments with 'rationality', coinciding as they did with the early rise of the new public management, epitomised a new approach to the management of financial resources in hard times.

What are the key features and characteristics of traditional, 'incremental' budgets? The basic analytical concepts were developed by the American political scientist Aaron Wildavsky, drawing on earlier work in the sphere of decision making by Charles Lindblom and Robert Dahl (Dahl, 1956; Lindblom, 1965; Wildavsky, 1964, 1975), although numerous other academics were to contribute to the understanding of traditional budgeting. In fact, traditional budgets were said to exhibit a range of features, including their adherence to an annual cycle, their relatively simplified structures and their highly politicised frameworks (Jordan, 1987). However, the single most significant feature of the traditional budget, and arguably its defining characteristic, is its 'incrementalism'. In simple terms, this involves establishing a starting point for the budgetary process, a 'base', which is the settlement of the previous financial year. In effect, therefore, this means that the greatest part of the budget is the product of previous decisions. Wildavsky (1964: 13) illustrates this with reference to a maritime analogy:

> The budget may be conceived of as an iceberg with by far the largest part below the surface outside the control of anyone. Many items in the budget are standard and simply re-enacted every year unless there is a special reason to challenge them.

In this light, the focus of budgetary choice and decision making is at the margins – changes to the overall size and shape of the budget will be incremental. The implications of this are quite significant. Within the budgetary process, those bidding for financial resources tend to see their role as advocates of additional spending based fundamentally upon the existing broad pattern of resource allocation. In other words, those with the largest budgets in previous years expect to continue to have the largest budgets, with appropriate incremental additions, in the coming years. Analysis of the general shape and size of the whole budget, and of the relative importance of its component parts, tends to be limited, and there is little attempt to correlate budgetary choices with strategic policy objectives.

While this summary of the incremental budget is inevitably rather broad and generalised, and open to the criticism that it omits the more complex features of even the most traditional budgetary systems, it should convey an understanding of the appropriate facets of this budgetary type.

In British central government, the budgetary system came to be structured around the annual PESC cycle, so called because of the central co-ordinating role allocated to the Public Expenditure Survey Committee (Likierman, 1988; Pyper, 1991; Thain and Wright, 1992). In key respects, this has been a fundamentally incrementalist process, within which the budget settlement of the past year becomes the base for future spending bids from departmental ministers. Metcalf and Richards (1990: 185) capture the flavour of the PESC process:

> Giving statutory force to the conclusions emerging from the Public Expenditure Survey system moved the budgetary process into the

annual parliamentary ritual of estimates and votes. The process rolled forward each year. Like many planning and budgetary systems ... the Public Expenditure Survey was a creature of its time, with characteristic weaknesses and blind spots. It was built on growth assumptions – next year will be like this year only more so. Programmes could be rolled forward with only marginal adjustments of priorities and resources from year to year.

Thain and Wright (1992: 8) also emphasise the fundamentally incrementalist nature of the PESC cycle when examining the budgetary base: 'The decision on "what can be afforded" in any future year, is derived from immediate past decisions.'

The tighter economic and financial circumstances of the 1970s and 1980s saw the advent of a number of adjuncts to the PESC cycle, which can be viewed as attempts to introduce slightly more sophisticated, less incremental, elements to the central government budgetary system. By the 1990s, further moves were taking place, apparently in the direction of introducing overt 'rationality' to the system. There is a sense in which all of these changes can be linked with the advent of the new public management. We shall move on to examine some of these developments in subsequent sections of this chapter. However, it was at the level of local government that some of the earliest British experiments with 'rational' (or at least, less traditional, less incremental) budgets began.

If the academic theories of Lindblom and Dahl provided much of the basis for Wildavsky's ideas on budgets characterised by incrementalism, the theories and concepts of another American social scientist, Herbert Simon (1957), provided the critics of incrementalism with an alternative approach. In fact, Lindblom had developed the concept of incrementalism, or 'the science of muddling through', as a critique of what he saw as Simon's unrealistic concept of rational decision making. Rational decision making came to be closely associated with the rise of new managerial practices in American corporate business during the 1960s, and there was an increasing attempt to transfer this concept, together with many of the other new business approaches, to public administration and management. In particular, there were attempts to apply rationality to public sector budgets in, for example, the Defense Department in the mid-1960s, and by Jimmy Carter as, successively, Governor of Georgia and President of the United States.

The basic concept of rational budgeting was deceptively simple. The process of rational decision making was applied to the specific sphere of budgeting, to facilitate greater analysis and bring about more strategic budgetary decisions. Thus, the annual budgetary process is linked to medium- and long-term strategic plans, more detailed data are generated and analysed before decisions are reached about the future allocation of resources, and information is presented in a fashion designed to clarify choices. Numerous variants of rational budgetary systems emerged, under the general umbrella of Planning, Programming, Budgetary Systems (PPBS). A particular form of PPBS, Zero-Base Budgeting, epitomised the rational approach (Wholey, 1978). Zero-Base Budgeting (ZBB), in its purest form, totally dispensed with the idea that the previous year's budget could serve as the base for future calculations. Instead, the practitioners of ZBB would divide all proposed spending programmes into units of manageable size, subject them to detailed scrutiny, and establish an order of priority across these units. This is the key element of ZBB, and, indeed, of rational budgeting theory as a whole: there are no built-in assumptions about the status of existing spending programmes – all must be subjected to fresh examination in order to justify their place in the budget each year. Given adequate financial resources, the entire spending order could be financed. However, if the total funds available are not sufficient to cover the entire rank order, the lower priority items are simply left unfunded.

In Britain, a number of local authorities began to experiment with rationality in their budgetary processes. In part, these experiments seem to have been prompted by the commitment of senior officers and councillors to the new managerialism sweeping through the public sector ('rationality' seemed better suited to the emerging norms of corporate and strategic management than old-style 'incrementalism'), and in part by the need to find innovative means of managing limited financial resources. In the era of rate-capping, tight revenue grant settlements, central government oversight (and, via external auditors, enforcement) of local government spending limits, the new approaches to budgeting spread (Elcock and Jordan, 1987; Elcock, Jordan *et al.*, 1989; Midwinter and Monaghan, 1993).

However, the experiments with rationality in British local government tended to produce, at best, hybrid budgetary systems, in which some elements of rationality were combined with a fundamentally incrementalist approach. As Grant Jordan (1987: 22) pointed out:

> in few local authorities have the moves to rationality been substantial and where such attempts have been made they have had to live uneasily with the tradition ... of incrementalism.

Such conclusions reflected the perspective of Wildavsky, who believed that in the real world of public sector budgeting, beneath the descriptive terminology of rationality, one could usually uncover the incrementalist tradition, which is driven by the realities of poltics! Notwithstanding this, it would be wrong to ignore the significance of the experiments with rationality. In almost every case, these left their imprint upon the budgetary processes of the local authorities concerned, and they clearly added a new dimension to the management of financial resources within the world of local government. In a very real way, these new approaches represented an important feature of the new public management, as traditional political power-broking within the budgetary process was now allied to the presentation and analysis of data generated by local authority managers. Full-blooded budgetary rationality is probably unworkable and perhaps undesirable, but the addition of elements of rationality to the world of local authority budgeting brought a new approach to the management of scarce financial resources, and, incidentally, helped to elevate the role of managers within local councils.

The Financial Management Initiative and its consequences

We have already noted that the PESC budgetary cycle within central government was fundamentally incrementalist in character. However, new approaches to the management of public finances brought in their wake a series of schemes and programmes designed, in part, to add elements of sophistication to the crude traditionalism of central government budgeting.

A relatively early example of this was the PAR (Programme Analysis and Review) system, introduced during the twilight period of Keynesianism, in the early 1970s. In some senses, PAR epitomised applied rationality. Peter Hennessy (1989: 222) described it as an attempt to 'ruthlessly question existing commitments and put brain behind the crude brawn of PESC'. PARs proliferated throughout Whitehall, with the aim of examining the fundamental principles underpinning departmental spending programmes, and comparing these with other possible priorities, perhaps emanating from elsewhere in the government machine. Detailed comparative data were produced, with the aim of allowing ministers and senior civil servants scope to make rational decisions about the composition of their departmental spending programmes. Although many of PAR's key features were to recur in subsequent variants of this scheme, this particular wave of financial managerialism subsided within a relatively short period. Following its brief heyday, PAR 'became slow, top heavy and the victim of the relentless, interdepartmental grind'

(Hennessy, 1989: 236). Civil service antipathy towards PAR and other features of the managerialist approach (see, for example, Sisson, 1976) was coupled with a degree of ministerial scepticism regarding the applicability of business-oriented schemes in the world of government (Pyper, 1995: 55). PAR was officially abolished in 1979, as the new public management started to take root.

As we have already noted in other contexts, the main differences between early managerial initiatives, such as PAR, and the later products of the new public management, lay only partly in their substantive content. Of significant, and perhaps equal, importance were the circumstances and environment within which they were introduced. PAR's successors emerged in the post-Keynesian climate, in which the financial imperatives were much stronger. More than this, the political and official culture had started to alter to the extent that a new breed of civil servants and ministers were keen to draw upon the lessons of the earlier experiments and the growing body of literature which argued for the transferability of business practices to the world of government. Under the Thatcher governments and their successors, ministers and officials began to demonstrate a sustained commitment to the introduction of managerial techniques, with a particular emphasis on the management of financial resources.

> The climate within Whitehall has changed since the mid-1970s. Not only have the policy processes been affected by the introduction and operation of tight cash limits, and the development of cash planning, the 'mood' has been affected by manpower cuts, a continuing squeeze on civil service pay, by value-for-money exercises like the Rayner scrutinies and the investigations of the revitalised National Audit Office, and the emphasis on the need to improve the capacity and performance of line managers. (Thain and Wright, 1996: 47)

The Financial Management Initiative epitomised the new approach. The Initiative had its origins in an efficiency scrutiny carried out within the Department of the Environment, but it was formally launched for application throughout Whitehall in spring 1982. Co-ordinated by a joint Treasury/Cabinet Office unit, the objectives of the FMI were set out in a White Paper (White Paper, 1982) and updated at intervals thereafter. The basic objectives of the FMI were to develop departmental systems and organisations within which managers at every level had clear objectives, the means to measure outputs and performance in relation to objectives, well-defined responsibility for securing the best use of resources, and access to all the information required (especially about costs) in order to effectively exercise their responsibilities. In fact the Financial Management Initiative was something of a misnomer: the FMI's implications extended beyond purely financial matters and it 'achieved public prominence as a symbol of governmental commitment to lasting reforms of public management' (Metcalf and Richards, 1990: 183).

Within this broad framework, government departments were encouraged to develop their own versions of FMI. The most significant common characteristics which emerged were management information systems, financial information systems, devolved budgets, value for money testing, performance indicators and rational budgeting techniques (see Box 4.1).

The impact of the FMI was undoubtedly more significant and lasting than that of PAR. In particular, although there was a degree of variation across Whitehall departments, the FMI apparently played a significant part in engendering new approaches to certain aspects of the management of financial resources (Metcalf and Richards, 1990: 177–210; Richards, 1987). However, there is more of a mixed verdict on the outcome of the initiative's broader aims, to transform the practice of management in government, or, in the words of one of its creators, to create 'a fundamentally new approach to the management of central government operations' (Oates, 1988: 1). We have already noted the need for observers to be sceptical about extravagant claims of novelty in the

---

Box 4.1   FMI common characteristics

- **management information systems** for senior civil servants and ministers, modelled on the original 'MINIS' developed in the Department of the Environment.
- **financial information systems**, designed to allow ministers, senior civil servants and line managers to distinguish between administrative costs on the one hand, and programme expenditure (on services, implementation of policies and so on) on the other.
- **devolved budgets**, brought about through the establishment of cost centres and the identification of accountable line managers who were to be given considerable delegated authority over the more detailed elements of their budgets.
- **value for money testing** on a systematic and regular basis.
- **performance indicators** and measures of output, designed to measure the extent to which specific objectives were being achieved.
- **rational budgeting techniques**, to allow basic questions to be posed about the principles and priorities in departmental expenditure programmes.

sphere of public management, and the FMI should be no exception to this rule. It was not 'fundamentally new' – in fact, it extended and consolidated a number of past and present trends and initiatives, while also giving added impetus to some newer concepts (see Jackson, 1988: vi). Furthermore, the FMI's limited successes in developing certain financial management practices within central government were not replicated in the realm of civil service management broadly defined, where 'the initiative ... failed to create more than small incremental improvements. There has been no quantum leap' (Richards, 1987: 40). The specific reasons for the broader failure of the FMI need not concern us here, but we can note that this was to be a contributory factor behind the wide-ranging, combined structural and managerial reform of the civil service brought about by the Next Steps initiative (see Chapter 5). This should not be taken to imply that the FMI was formally ditched: on the contrary, its specifically financial dimensions were rolled on into the restructured and reformed civil service of the 1990s.

Towards a new rationality at the centre?

While the Financial Management Initiative was focused primarily upon the 'micro' level of central government finances, successive governments began to introduce a number of important changes at the 'macro' level, in the realm of economic and financial strategic decision making. In some respects, at least, these changes seemed to represent a move towards the introduction of more 'rational' approaches to decision making in this sphere, and they certainly reflected a willingness to embrace newer methods of managing economic and financial policy. Four interrelated developments are worthy of note:

- combining the annual budget and public expenditure statements
- strategic public expenditure reviews
- introducing resource accounting and budgeting techniques
- reforming the Treasury–Bank of England relationship.

Let us comment upon each of these in turn.

Traditionally, the PESC cycle operated on the basis that central government departments would formulate their final expenditure 'bids' for the forthcoming financial year during the previous spring and summer. These would be subjected to Treasury scrutiny, and agreement reached (often involving a compromise between a spending department's 'bid' and the Treasury's target) in the autumn during a process of bilateral meetings between the Chief Secretary to the Treasury and the spending ministers, or, in extremely difficult cases, within a Cabinet committee known as the 'Star Chamber' (see Pyper, 1991). The outcome of this process would be announced during the Chancellor of the Exchequer's Autumn Financial Statement in November, while the Budget Statement in the following spring would specify the means through which the government would be raising the money to finance its spending commitments.

While there were quite sound reasons for this procedure, there was also a certain artificiality in managing the two key elements of the process separately. Following its re-election in 1992, the Major government moved to introduce a new system, within which the management of expenditure and fiscal policy would be combined. Accordingly, in 1993 the last of the traditional budgets took place in March, and the first of the new, annual 'unified' budgets was presented in November. Under this scheme, the former Autumn Financial Statement was effectively merged with the Budget Statement, so that the government's expenditure plans for the next three years could be presented at the same time as its decisions about taxation for the same period. An additional feature of the new system was the requirement that, following the setting of the overall agreed total figure for forthcoming public expenditure, new spending proposals emanating from departmental ministers would only be accepted on the understanding that cuts would be made in other parts of the budget (Parry, Hood and James, 1997).

Although it chose to switch the date of the main budget back to the spring (while introducing a new 'pre-budget' report in November), the Blair government completely accepted the rationale for this method of managing the creation and presentation of public expenditure and fiscal policy and continued with the holistic approach. Nonetheless, the apparent rationality of the new process offered no guarantee of success. In the pre-budget report of November 2002, Gordon Brown, the Chancellor of the Exchequer, was obliged to react to a substantial decrease in tax revenues (caused at least in part by global economic factors) by planning an increase in government borrowing by £29 billion over the figure he had predicted in the April Budget (Denny, 2002).

Alongside these developments new applications were being found for rational budgetary techniques, at the level of strategic, programme expenditure. In February 1993, John Major's government initiated a series of 'fundamental expenditure reviews' within key areas of public spending. Co-ordinated by the Chief Secretary to the Treasury, these were to supplement the normal PESC scrutiny of expenditure proposals and were designed to facilitate long-term, strategic analysis of the main spending programmes. A rolling programme of reviews was developed, covering, inter alia, health, social security, education, home affairs, urban expenditure, employment, transport, and then the expenditure programmes of the Department of Trade and Industry, the Inland Revenue, Customs and Excise, the Treasury and the government's legal departments (Gillie, 1994: 37). The social security review, conducted by Peter Lilley, was perhaps the most high-profile and controversial of these exercises. Its direct consequences included a range of changes in the benefits system, including the replacement of invalidity benefit with a new incapacity benefit which was subject to tax, replacing unemployment benefit with a job seekers' allowance which was available for six rather than nine months, and phasing in a raising of women's pensionable age to 65 (Gillie, 1994: 37–8; Hulme, 1994: 181–5).

While it seems sensible to view the fundamental expenditure reviews as a feature of, or an adjunct to, the new public management, it is perhaps wise not to push the association too far in every case. Observers of the Treasury's review, which led to a restructuring of this key strategic department of state and a rearrangement of the central managerial components of the PESC within the Treasury, noted the pivotal role of a Harvard Business School-educated Treasury official (Jeremy Heywood) and the involvement of 'a godfather from industry' (Sir Colin Southgate of Thorn EMI). Nonetheless, doubts remained about the ultimate impact of business and management ideas in this review:

> although FER [fundamental expenditure review] used the obligatory business-school vocabulary of delayering, empowerment, mission ownership and team working, it is doubtful how far its ideas drew directly on any specific ... business model ... some of FER's key themes seem to have derived more from internal and relatively long-standing Treasury debates and particular Treasury-specific issues. Moreover, the FER doctrine that Ministry of Economics/Finance Ministry tensions within the Treasury should be ... explicitly institutionalised into a 'creative tension', is not obviously derived from business management practice ... [and] could be seen as ideologically suspect from the conventional New Public Management view that better management in the public sector can only be achieved by prior agreement on goals. (Parry, Hood and James, 1997: 411–12)

With specific reference to the latter point, it might be argued that the Blair government's reordering of the relationship between the Treasury and the Bank of England, to which we turn below, was more in line with new public management orthodoxy and the modernisation agenda.

Following the General Election of 1997, the new Labour government accepted the outgoing administration's overall public expenditure commitments for the forthcoming two years, while reserving the right to shift cash around within the agreed total, in order to prioritise certain programmes, including health and education. However, the new government also made it clear that its longer-term expenditure plans would be moulded by the outcome of a Comprehensive Spending Review (CSR) which would cover every department and expenditure programme and result in fixed total expenditure plans, over three-year cycles. This involved a lengthy, item-by-item analysis of spending programmes. A zero-based mode of analysis was adopted. The results of this CSR were announced in July 1998 (HM Government, 1998). Box 4.2 sets out its main features.

The second Spending Review was conducted in 2000 (see www. hm-treasury.gov.uk/Spending_Review for details). Although this did not repeat the item-by-item approach of the 1998 CSR, it subjected some issues to detailed examination, by means of 15 cross-cutting reviews of

---

Box 4.2   **The Comprehensive Spending Review, July 1998**

Increased spending in key policy areas, including:

Health	+£21 billion over three years
Education	+£19 billion over three years
Transport	+£1.7 billion over three years
Science	+£4.4 billion over three years
Cities and Housing	+£4.4 billion over three years
Museums, Arts, Sport	+£290 million over three years
Overseas Aid	increase from 0.25% to 0.3% of national income

Plus: Interest payments on government debt to be cut by £5 billion a year by end of parliament

All to be achieved by imposing spending cuts in Defence, Agriculture, Legal Aid, Foreign Office, Trade and Industry

And by imposing efficiency targets of 3% to 10% on government departments

And by forcing public sector pay reviews to take account of departmental spending limits, inflation and efficiency targets

policy initiatives which straddled traditional departmental boundaries. The 2000 Spending Review established new spending plans through to 2003–04 by taking 2002–03 (the last year of the planning cycle set up by the 1998 CSR) as the first year of the new plan.

The third Spending Review was concluded in July 2002 (Chancellor of the Exchequer, 2002). This set out the government's expenditure plans through to 2006 while making specific links between the spending programmes of government departments and the performance targets they would be expected to meet (the latter were couched in the form of Public Service Agreements).

Even in advance of the initial CSR's outcome, it was clear that one consequence would be the adoption of a different form of accounting and budgeting throughout the system of government and public administration. Resource accounting and budgeting, widely used within the private sector, began to feature, in some forms at least, within central government executive agencies and NHS trusts in the early 1990s (Mellett, 1998: 4). Wider applications were signalled in a series of exchanges between the Treasury, the National Audit Office and the House of Commons Treasury and Civil Service Select Committee between 1994 and 1997. Green and White Papers and a manual of guidance were published (HM Government, 1994, 1995; HM Treasury, 1997) and an implementation programme emerged (Likierman, 1998: 17–19). The formal introduction of resource accounting and budgeting throughout central government, and beyond, was a core principle underpinning the CSR and the successive Spending Reviews. What is resource accounting and budgeting, and why is it potentially significant?

In simple terms, it involves combining the conventional accounting for financial resources with accounting for what might be termed extra-financial resources (including assets such as property), value for money testing (already becoming common in the public sector during the 1980s) and output measurement. Andrew Likierman (1998: 18) summarises the main features:

> Resource accounting is a set of accruals accounting techniques for reporting on the expenditure ... and a framework for analysing expenditure by departmental aims and objectives, relating those to outputs wherever possible. Resource budgeting is planning and controlling public expenditure on a resource accounting basis.

The entire system involves establishing much closer connections between a range of 'inputs' (these go beyond the normal cash inputs to include the cost of departmental assets of various kinds), stated aims and objectives, and measurable 'outputs'. In practice, this means taking a holistic approach to the process of budgeting and accounting, ultimately reaching judgements on a department's use of its resources in pursuit of targets such as increasing literacy levels, reducing the numbers of deaths from cancer and heart disease, and so on. As part of the move towards resource accounting and budgeting a National Asset Register has been compiled, within which £120 billion of government land and properties were initially logged. Some government departments (for example, the Ministry of Defence, with its lucrative assets) were obliged to consider selling off some assets (with the prospect of keeping up to £100 million of the proceeds each year) rather than having these weigh in the balance against them under the resource accounting and budgeting system (White, 1998).

Finally, it is appropriate for us to note the significance of a major structural change at the heart of the central government economic and financial management process: the reordering of the relationship between the Treasury and the Bank of England in the immediate aftermath of Labour's 1997 election victory. Only five days into the new administration, the Chancellor of the Exchequer, Gordon Brown, announced that the first stage of a Treasury reorganisation would involve reversing the arrangements for managing interest rate policy which had existed since 1946. The Bank of England was to be given operational control over interest rates, with immediate effect. The origins of this policy lay in a Fabian pamphlet, written by Ed Balls in 1992. On becoming Brown's policy adviser, Balls further developed the idea, which was then agreed with Tony Blair (Draper, 1997: 25–8; Thomas, 1997). The Labour Party's election manifesto had made only oblique mention of the future management of monetary policy, and the precise timing of the announcement was decided upon only after the election.

In practice, the decision gave the Bank of England a significant degree of independence from the Treasury. Under the new system, the Chancellor of the Exchequer would establish a target for inflation, and the Bank would then have operational control over the setting of interest rates to achieve this. The management of this key decision would be handled by a new monetary policy committee within the Bank (comprised of the governor, two deputy governors, the Bank officials responsible for monetary policy and market operations, and four outsiders appointed by the Chancellor), which would meet monthly to set interest rates.

In some senses, this epitomised key features of the new public management and modernisation. It combined structural reorganisation with apparent de-politicisation. The creation of at least one facet of monetary policy was to be removed from the realm of politics, and handed over to the 'experts'. However, as with many other aspects of the new public management, this raised serious – and as yet unanswered – questions, particularly in relation to accountability. Even if one assumes that it is appropriate for a policy which has a widespread and fundamental impact upon the lives of ordinary people to be 'removed from politics' (a rather sweeping assumption!), is it also appropriate for a group of unelected technocrats, with whom the electorate has no direct relationship, to be given control of this policy? The government attempted to fill the perceived accountability gap by strengthening the powers of the Bank of England's governing body, the Court, and enhancing the role of the House of Commons Treasury Select Committee, but the implications of all this for accountability can only be assessed in the longer term.

In conclusion, we can say that if one of the symptoms of the new public management's presence is a change in the culture and environment within which government operates, it is difficult to cast serious doubt on the proposition that the move to a combined management of the budget and public expenditure processes, coupled with the successive strategic public expenditure reviews, the advent of resource accounting and budgeting and the creation of a new Treasury–Bank of England axis signify just such a presence at the heart of British central government.

Conclusion

In this chapter we have attempted to illustrate some of the connections between, and the relationship of, the prevailing economic and financial environment within which government operates, and the style of public administration and management which characterise the polity. During the past three decades in Britain, we have witnessed a shift away from the established Keynesian orthodoxy and an associated move into a new governing culture in the realm of finance and economics. Even as we write, the changes continue, and while it is not always possible to differentiate clearly and definitively between those which would occur in any case, and those which stem primarily from the tenets of the new public management and the imperatives of modernisation, the general impact of these developments upon financial and economic strategies at all levels of the system of government and public administration is undoubtedly significant.

5

Restructuring the State Machine

A concern with organisational and institutional structures has ever been prevalent within public administration and management. As one informed observer notes:

> there has been a view that many problems of management could be solved if only the structures were right. The search for the best size of organisation, the correct hierarchy between levels of government or levels of management, or the most effective size of management teams has preoccupied governments and managers. (Flynn, 1997: 198)

Often drawing upon the current vogue in management 'science' or organisational theory, politicians and bureaucrats have a penchant for moulding and re-moulding the shapes and structures of the polities within which they function. For a decade or so from the mid-1960s organisational fashion dictated the creation of 'giant' structures, designed to harvest the rewards of 'economies of scale' and strategic planning. In Britain, this was epitomised by the Heath government's plans for the reorganisation of central government (White Paper, 1970), which built upon some emerging trends and enshrined the doctrine of 'giantism' by proposing a series of organisational amalgamations leading to the creation of 'super-departments' including the Department of the Environment and the Department of Trade and Industry.

To some extent, this organisational trend was also apparent in the National Health Service restructuring of 1974 and the local government reforms implemented in 1974–75. The latter included the creation of the monstrous Strathclyde Regional Council and a plethora of other authorities north and south of the border, the establishment of which showed little concern for established patterns of local community and identity but maximum respect for modish management principles.

Such structures were the offspring of a union between managerialism and big government, or *dirigisme*. Three decades on, the prevailing ideas about the shape and structure of the system of public administration are, similarly, the outcome of a meeting between a new public management and a leaner state machine. The purpose of this chapter is to set out the main features of this meeting. Decisions about the overall shape and size of the public sector were taken forward through the twin mechanisms of privatisation and restructuring. The elements of the system which were to remain in the public sector were restructured and reorganised with the aim of inculcating new managerial approaches and facilitating improved local and sub-central management. The latter involved incorporating the new managerial orthodoxies of decentralisation, delegation and localism. However, as we shall see, there was an inherent and growing tension between the principle of decentralisation and the continuing desire of the centre to retain control over fundamentals. This tension emerged in the form of conflict between, for example, some parts of Whitehall and certain executive agencies, central and local government, and the central management of the NHS and the periphery. It might be argued that this was exacerbated by the tendency to believe that matters of 'policy' and matters of 'management' are fundamentally distinctive with little or no areas of overlap between the two.

As a first step towards understanding these themes and issues, let us turn our attention to the process which led to a fundamental reordering of the system of public administration and management.

Moulding the overall shape and structure of the public sector: the privatisation catalyst

How does privatisation impinge upon a discussion of governmental modernisation and the new public management? Surely the whole point of this policy, in its most familiar form, the state sell-off, is that it dispenses with the need for *public* management by transferring former public holdings into the private sector? This is undoubtedly true. However, our concern here is with the role of privatisation as a catalyst: in a very real sense, it was a device which brought about the restructuring of the public sector.

In the previous chapter, we showed that the financial imperative formed a central element of the new public management. The desire of successive governments to control public expenditure led to the search for new managerial approaches which might facilitate the achievement of that goal. In this context, the policy of privatisation became doubly attractive: it offered the opportunity for government to shed responsibility for the costs of significant parts of the former public sector, while at the same time generating income through the sales. The policy also encapsulated one of the central strategic components of the emerging new public management: deciding where the main boundaries would be drawn between the public and private sectors and where the key areas of interchange between the two sectors would be. In Chapter 6, a detailed analysis of privatisation is offered. Here, we view privatisation in the context of its role as a policy which helped facilitate the fundamental reshaping and reordering of the public sector.

Running parallel to the privatisation policy was a complementary attempt to introduce the imperatives of the market and competition to virtually every area of the public sector, via mechanisms such as competitive tendering, market testing and the attraction of private finance to public sector projects. It is appropriate for these themes to be explored in the context of Chapter 6.

A third strand of policy, and one which will be examined later in this chapter, is the continuing, almost continuous, attempt to restructure those institutions which remained within the public sector, with a view to making them more efficient and inculcating within them new managerial practices and procedures.

Let us begin, however, by discussing the catalytic effect of privatisation upon the shape and structure of the British public sector. When we asserted, above, that privatisation was one of the keystones of the new public management, our intention was to emphasise the importance of this policy as a facilitator of major decisions regarding the core and peripheral activities of the state rather than to imply that it was uncritically accepted by observers and analysts. Like many of their colleagues, those oracles of US public managerialism, Osborne and Gaebler, were distinctly sceptical about the value of privatisation. In *Reinventing Government*, which became a key point of reference for politicians and officials at all levels of the American system of government, Osborne and Gaebler (1992: 45) argued that privatisation was '*one* answer, not *the* answer' to some of the challenges of public management, and they pointed to the dangers of uncritical acceptance of the arguments of the ideological proponents of this policy, likening the latter to 'snake oil salesmen'. However, it should be noted that privatisation had already become a distinguishing feature of state policy in Britain some time before the thoughts of Osborne and Gaebler were published. In some respects, at least, the sellers of snake oil (perhaps defined, in the British context as the creation of a 'property- and share-owning democracy', or the advent of a new era of high efficiency and effectiveness) had long since departed from the scene! The ideological dimension of privatisation can be pored over indefinitely, but its practical impact upon the size and shape of the public administration system can be summarised in a straightforward fashion.

The policy of privatisation came to affect public services at all levels of the system of government. In local government, the National Health Service, central government and the burgeoning 'quangocracy', assets and services were shifted from the public to the private sector during the 1980s and 1990s.

Privatisation emerged from three imperatives. The Thatcherite Conservatives, in power from 1979 until 1990, equated state control and public ownership with fat, flabby and inefficient organisations, over-dependent on subsidy, unaware of their true cost and unable to meet the demands of their customers. Privatisation would directly address this problem. Allied to this view was the attraction of easing the strain on the Public Sector Borrowing Requirement by transferring large numbers of workers from the public to the private sector, reducing Treasury lending and providing a flow of funds into the Treasury through the sale of assets accompanying privatisation. Finally, there was an ideological imperative, which became increasingly significant as time passed. Privatisation became a key element of the Thatcherite crusade to encourage economic 'freedom', create a 'property- and share-owning democracy' and cut the state machine down to size. In the course of a relatively short period, British government disengaged from a whole series of enterprises, services and utilities. In some cases, privatisation took the form of total conversion from public corporation to limited company, in others the conversion was partial, while a further category involved the disposal of the government's minority shareholdings. During the Thatcher and Major governments the state shifted significant holdings into the private sector, including: British Petroleum, British Aerospace, Jaguar Cars, British Telecom, British Gas, British Airways, Rolls-Royce, the Rover Group, British Steel, the water utilities in England and Wales, the electricity generators and suppliers, British Coal and British Rail.

From 1997 onwards, the Labour government was willing to retain privatisation as an option, but largely for pragmatic rather than ideological reasons. Major share flotations and the introduction of private ownership were not totally discarded. In the early phase of its life, the new Labour government announced its intention to sell off 60 per cent of the Commonwealth Development Corporation, and, more dramatically, in June 1998 the Chancellor of the Exchequer set out a planned sale of public assets worth £4 billion a year for the next three years. As it was rolled out, this privatisation programme would include moving the Stationery Office into the private sector, and selling 51 per cent of the National Air Traffic Control system and the Royal Mint (Elliot and MacAskill, 1998). However, New Labour's preference was for the creation of public–private 'partnerships' through devices such as Best Value, Better Quality Services and the Private Finance Initiative, which are discussed in Chapter 6. The Blair administration adopted a more partial and selective use of the privatisation option. Although this government disavowed the ideological imperative towards privatisation, it appeared to be as willing as its predecessors to deploy the policy as a means towards governmental restructuring and generating income from sales. The distinctly new public management process of deciding what was 'core business', and shedding the rest, continued.

The steady disengagement of government from the ownership of former public utilities – including gas supply, electricity generation and supply, the telecommunications service, and water services (in England and Wales) – was accompanied by the assumption of a new role: that of regulator. In these cases, therefore, the divestment of a service function, and the concomitant restructuring of the public sector, was coupled with the establishment of new organs of public administration/management. The new regulatory agencies, normally created as non-departmental public bodies, included the Offices of Gas Supply (OFGAS), Telecommunications (OFTEL), Electricity Regulation (OFFER), Water Services (OFWAT) and Rail Regulation (OFRAIL). The gas and electricity regulatory agencies were subsequently merged, becoming the Office of Gas and Electricity Markets (OFGEM). In Chapter 8, we discuss the role played by these bodies in securing public accountability.

Restructuring within the centre: agencification

Running parallel to, and in tandem with, the policy of privatisation was a revived interest in certain aspects of the concept of decentralisation. In particular, during the 1980s, governments became increasingly attracted to the principle of decentralising executive, managerial and service delivery functions within a framework of continuing policy control from the centre. Within a relatively short period, the Next Steps initiative transformed the structure and shape of UK central government.

Commentators and analysts disagree about the overall impact of this process of change. Some argue that the widespread creation of agencies altered the fundamental cohesiveness of the civil service, effectively resulting in a process of Balkanisation which broke the service up into increasingly independent components (see, for example, Chapman, 1992, 1997). Others (see, for example, Hennessy, 1993; Butler, 1993) have adopted a more relaxed perspective, and see these changes in the context of the evolutionary tradition of the civil service. What is beyond doubt is the fact that this process of agencification came to symbolise the concept of new public management in central government. The decentralisation of executive functions within a broad programme of structural reform became the necessary precondition for the advent of a range of localised management initiatives.

The modern roots of this approach to restructuring could be traced to the 1968 Fulton Report, which recommended the 'hiving-off' of certain functions into executive agencies. In the years after Fulton, some significant agencies were created, including the Defence Procurement Executive (part of the Ministry of Defence), the Property Service Agency (part of the Department of the Environment) and the Manpower Services Commission (part of the Department of Employment). These agencies were charged with responsibility for delivering specified services to the armed forces (in the case of the DPE), government departments generally (in the case of the PSA) and the unemployed (in the case of the MSC). The new bodies were led by politically appointed chairmen, and had significant financial and operational freedoms, while remaining constitutionally accountable to ministers.

In the late 1980s, this form of decentralisation was revived and expanded to become the *leitmotiv* of central government reform. The Next Steps programme, launched in 1988, took the concept of decentralisation much further than the Fulton-inspired experiments of the 1970s, and initiated the wide-ranging reform process which led to the agencification of the civil service (for an analysis of this process, see James, 2003). Next Steps stemmed from the relative failure of the early Thatcherite reforms in central government. These had been focused on the programme of efficiency scrutinies co-ordinated by the Prime Minister's special adviser Derek Rayner and the resulting Financial Management Initiative (for more on these, see Brereton, 1992; Holland, 1988; Jackson, 1988; Metcalf and Richards, 1990: 117–210; Oates, 1988; Pyper, 1995: 57–64; Richards, 1987), although bringing significant managerial changes in their wake, had, in the view of the Prime Minister, failed to radically change the civil service's management culture.

Under Rayner's successor, Robin Ibbs, the Downing Street Efficiency Unit reviewed the managerial reforms which had been introduced in the civil service, and examined the nature of the factors preventing further change. Its findings were set out in the Ibbs – or Next Steps – report, which made some key recommendations about future policy (Efficiency Unit, 1988). Structural reform leading to the creation of executive agencies was identified as a prerequisite for the modernisation of the civil service. It was estimated that 95 per cent of the civil service was concerned with executive work involving policy implementation and service delivery, and this work would be most appropriately devolved to agencies. The agencies would be accountable to their core, parent departments, but would function with significant day-to-day freedom, under the leadership of chief executives.

In February 1988 the Conservative government of Margaret Thatcher committed itself to implementing the Next Steps initiative. As the reform process rolled on, it came to be seen as the late-twentieth-century version of the Victorian era's Northcote–Trevelyan Report (for details, see Drewry, 1988; Greer, 1992, 1994; James, 2003; Massey, 1995; Pyper, 1995: 70–8). By the early part of the twenty-first century, UK central government had been fundamentally restructured to the point where 78 per cent of all civil servants worked in executive agencies, of which 127 were Next Steps agencies (see Box 5.1 for a full list of executive agencies).

The Next Steps model of recruitment and pay was important because it gradually spread to other parts of the civil service. Agency chief executives were, in the main, recruited via open competition, with a significant element of the appointments (34 per cent by the late 1990s) going to external candidates (Next Steps Team, 1998: 68–9). Renewable, fixed-term contracts and performance-linked salaries were key to the contracts of the new breed of civil service managers.

The individual executive agencies were reviewed periodically. During this process, consideration would be given to possible alternative futures for the agency (including re-absorption into the parent department, privatisation and merger). Consequently, some agencies (see the examples in Box 5.2) (including HMSO and the Recruitment and Assessment Services Agency) were abolished.

From the outset, issues and questions arose regarding the pace and nature of the evolution of Next Steps as a modernising process. At a relatively early stage, the Fraser Report (Efficiency Unit, 1991) argued the case for greater 'empowering' of chief executives, on the grounds that many core, parent, departments seemed to be unwilling to delegate to the fullest possible extent, and the volume of contact between departments and agencies appeared to be unnecessarily high. As a consequence of this, the Framework Documents which established the basic working relationship between departments and agencies were to be periodically revised and the exclusion of any executive function from the remit of the chief executives would have to be fully justified. Around the same time, regular surveys by Price Waterhouse, the management consultants, revealed a continuing concern on the part of chief executives about the demands of parent departments and the Cabinet Office (Price Waterhouse, 1991: 9; 1992: 6–8). These tensions resurfaced in the aftermath of the 1992 General Election, when Sir Peter Kemp, the Permanent Secretary charged with managing the Next Steps project, was effectively dismissed by his new minister, William Waldegrave, on the grounds that a new approach was needed in the new department being set up to handle the strategic management of the civil service (the Office of Public Service and Science, later the Office of Public Service). Unusually, an alternative post was not found for Kemp, and he was obliged to resign. His strong belief in the need for cultural diversity within the executive agencies clashed with the Major government's plans to impose new efficiency targets on the chief executives, and his *enfant terrible* image left him without support within the group of senior mandarins led by Sir Robin Butler. There is some evidence to suggest that the departure of Kemp marked a turning point in the development of Next Steps: while the pace of agency creation was not affected, there was a certain loss of momentum in the drive to give chief executives increased operational freedoms (Theakston, 1995: 136).

This issue epitomises a crucial dilemma which lies at the heart of the new public management schemes for decentralisation and delegation. Ultimately, politicians and managers at the centre will only be prepared to go so far down the path of decentralisation. At a given point, their instinctive desire to control and micro-manage will overcome any adherence to the concepts of full-blooded decentralisation and delegation. In part, this might be attributed to a dawning realisation that aspects of the management theories underpinning Next Steps were seriously flawed. The emphasis on the existence of a policy–management dichotomy, coupled with an unwillingness to recognise the close interplay between policy and management in key spheres of government work subjected to the Next Steps treatment (for example, employment services, social security benefits, child support, prisons), produced serious problems of accountability (of which, more in Chapter 8; see also Hogwood, Judge and McVicar, 2001).

In this light, it might be argued that Major's instinct for consolidation was timely, as the aforementioned fears about the 'Balkanisation' of the

Box 5.1 **Executive agencies**

Parent department	Agencies
Attorney General	Treasury Solicitor's Department
Cabinet Office	Government Car and Dispatch Agency; Central Office of Information
Department for Culture, Media and Sport	Royal Parks Agency
Department for Environment, Food and Rural Affairs	Central Science Laboratory; Centre for Environment, Fisheries and Aquaculture Science; Pesticides Safety Directorate; Rural Payments Agency; Veterinary Laboratories Agency; Veterinary Medicines Directorate
Department of Health	Medical Devices Agency; Medicines Control Agency; NHS Estates; NHS Pensions Agency; NHS Purchasing and Supply Agency
Department of Trade and Industry	Companies House; Employment Tribunals Service; Insolvency Service; National Weights and Measures Laboratory; Patent Office; Radiocommunications Agency; Small Business Service
Department for Transport, Local Government and the Regions	Driver and Vehicle Licensing Agency; Driving Standards Agency; Fire Service College; Highways Agency; Maritime and Coastguard Agency; Planning Inspectorate; Ordnance Survey; Queen Elizabeth II Conference Centre,; The Rent Service; Vehicle Certification Agency; Vehicle Inspectorate
Department for Work and Pensions	Appeals Service Agency; Benefits Agency (closed March 2002); Child Support Agency; Employment Service (closed March 2002). New from April 2002: Jobcentre Plus; The Pension Service
Food Standards Agency	Meat Hygiene Service
Forestry Commission	Forest Enterprise; Forest Research
Foreign Office	Wilton Park
Treasury	Debt Management Office; Royal Mint; National Savings; Office for National Statistics
Home Office	Forensic Science Service; HM Prison Service; United Kingdom Passport Agency
Inland Revenue	Valuation Office

Lord Chancellor's Dept	Court Service; Public Guardianship Office; HM Land Registry; Public Record Office
Ministry of Defence	Armed Forces Personnel Administration; Army Base Repair Organisation; Army Personnel Centre; Army Training and Recruiting Agency; British Forces Post Office; Defence Analytical Services Agency; Defence Aviation Repair Agency; Defence Bills Agency; Defence Communications Services Agency; Defence Dental Agency; Defence Estates; Defence Geographic and Imagery Intelligence Agency; Defence Housing Executive; Defence Intelligence and Security Centre; Defence Medical Training Organisation; Defence Procurement Agency; defence Science and Technology Agency; Defence Secondary Care Agency; Defence Storage and Distribution Agency; Defence Transport and Movements; Defence Vetting Agency; Disposal Sales Agency; Duke of York's Royal Military School; Medical Supplies Agency; Meteorological Office; MoD Police; Naval Manning Agency; Naval Recruiting and Training Agency; Pay and Personnel Agency; Queen Victoria School; RAF Personnel Management Agency; RAF Training Group Defence Agency;Service Children's Education; UK Hydrographic Office; War Pensions Agency; Warship Support Agency
Northern Ireland Office	Compensation Agency; Forensic Science Agency; Northern Ireland Prison Service
Northern Ireland Executive	Business Development Agency; Construction Service; Driver and Vehicle Licensing; Driver and Vehicle Testing Agency; Environment and Heritage Service; Forest Service; Government Purchasing Agency; Health Estates; Industrial Research and Technology Unit; Land Registers of Northern Ireland; Northern Ireland Child Support Agency; Northern Ireland Statistics and Research; Ordnance Survey of Northern Ireland; Planning Service; Public Record Office of Northern Ireland; Rate Collection Agency; Rivers Agency; Roads Service; Social Security Agency (Northern Ireland); Valuation and Lands Agency; Water Service
Scottish Executive	Communities Scotland; Fisheries Research Services; HM Inspectorate of Education; Historic Scotland; National Archives of Scotland; Scottish Agricultural Science Agency; Scottish Court Service; Scottish Fisheries Protection Agency; Scottish Public Pensions Agency; Scottish Prison Service; Student Awards Agency for Scotland; Registers of Scotland
Welsh Assembly	Cadw: Welsh Historic Monuments; Welsh European Funding Office

Source: Reproduced from Office of Public Services Reform (2002).

Box 5.2   Some former Next Steps agencies

Reason for abolition	Agency
Privatisation	DVOIT, National Engineering Laboratory, HMSO, Paymaster, Building Research Establishment, Laboratory of the Government Chemist, Transport Research Laboratory, National Resources Institute, Chessington Computer Centre, Occupational and Health Service Agency, Recruitment and Assessment Services Agency
Contracted out	Accounts Services Agency, National Physical Laboratory, Teachers' Pensions Agency
Subject to mergers	Warren Spring Laboratory, Central Science Laboratory, Chemical and Biological Defence Establishment, Defence Operational Analysis Centre, Defence Research Agency, Coastguard, Marine Safety Agency
Subject to demerger	Defence Accounts Agency
Functions abolished	Resettlement Agency
Change of status	Historic Royal Palaces (became a non-departmental public body)
Returned to a department	Security Facilities Executive Agency

Source: Data from Next Steps Team (1998: 64–5).

---

civil service and the concomitant erosion of its fundamental principles had been growing (Chapman, 1992). Nonetheless, his government's continued adherence to the principles of delegated management was signalled by the passage of the 1993 Civil Service Management of Functions Act, which allowed the component parts of the increasingly federal civil service to determine a wider range of terms and conditions of service without reference to the centre.

One vitally important feature of Next Steps, apparent from the outset, was its attraction of broad, cross-party approval. This effectively guaranteed the programme's long-term significance. In particular, the Labour Party's attitude towards Next Steps was originally, and remained, broadly supportive. Criticisms, when they came, tended to focus on the *causes célèbres* associated with the breakdown in accountability arrangements within the Prison Service Agency and the Child Support Agency. At these times, opposition attacks would be based upon the issues of ministerial conduct or lack of accountability, while the general principles and impact of Next Steps would be lauded. Before the 1997 General Election, Tony Blair's senior policy advisers on the civil service admitted that executive agencies 'have improved the delivery of government services through better management and delegation' (Mandelson and Liddle, 1996: 251). Following its election in 1997, the Labour government recognised the accountability problems posed by the child support and prisons cases. The Child Support Agency was subjected to much closer ministerial oversight through a review process which also saw the establishment in 1999 of the CSA Standards Committee to provide the Chief Executive with an independent commentary on the quality of decision making and service delivery within the agency. However, repeated attempts to modernize the computer system on which the day-to-day work of the CSA depended met with failure, and its flaws were still apparent in 2003 when yet another new formula was announced for the calculation of the awards managed by the agency. Meanwhile, the accountability arrangements for the Prison Service were changed, with ministers assuming full responsibility for accounting to Parliament for this sensitive area of public policy and management.

Next Steps moved into its concluding phase under the Blair government. A natural conclusion had been reached in the process of agency creation, and by this stage the effect of agencification was apparent in virtually every part of the civil service. In summer 2002 a major official review of the history, development and future of the executive agency scheme was published (Office of Public Services Reform, 2002), and this reached the conclusion that the agency model had been an overall success. In true modernising style, however, the report emphasised the need for agencies to continually evolve in order to deliver consistently improving public services.

Restructuring the centre itself: devolution

Agencification involved a fundamental reordering of the traditional departmental structures at the level of central government. The process of devolution implied restructuring of a different type, with the aim of creating (in varying degrees) administrative, policy making and legislative bodies within the sub-national and regional entities of the United Kingdom, which would inherit duties and responsibilities which had formerly been the province of central government departments of state. This process was complex, and its implementation was varied according to local demands and circumstances:

> The UK's is an instance of asymmetric devolution, similar to Spain's region-building process of the late 1970s and early 1980s, in the sense that distinct regions are being given different sets of powers at variable times and speeds. (Holliday, 2000: 100)

The weakest and most diluted strain of devolution could be seen in the English regions. Compared with Scotland, Wales and Northern Ireland, the English regions lacked a strong sense of a identity, 'national' sentiment, political weight and even geographical coherence.

The Blair government came to office committed to legislate 'to allow the people, region by region, to decide in a referendum whether they want directly elected regional government' (Labour Party, 1997: 35). However, there was little sense of urgency in this area of policy. In the special case of London, direct elections took place in the spring of 2000, resulting in Ken Livingstone's election to a four-year term. Livingstone was re-elected in 2004. The mayor's powers over budgetary and policy matters (he is required to create policies to address London-wide issues) are shared with the Greater London Authority (which has operational responsibilities for transport, development, policing, and fire and emergency planning). The London Assembly (25 members), also elected on a four-year term, scrutinises the work of the mayor, and shares some of the mayor's powers of appointment to the Greater London Authority. Although some commentators (see, for example, Pimlott and Rao, 2002) were prepared to be generous in their assessments of the initial period of the new 'London government', others pointed to the relative lack of powers and internal politics as factors which limited the impact of the Mayor and the Assembly. Travers (2003: 191, 193) noted that 'Few Londoners could point to any aspect of their lives affected by the new Mayor ... The assembly itself has not found anything like an effective role.'

Devolution in other parts of England was to be managed by the Department of the Environment, Transport and the Regions, and its local government successor, located within the Office of the Deputy Prime Minister. The first stage of the process involved an attempt to supplement the role of the regional government offices of Whitehall by coordinating the formation of a group of Regional Development Agencies, which were to aid economic growth. The work of these quangos was supplemented by the establishment of regional chambers, which were designed to facilitate representation of the relevant local authorities and other interested groups. It was initially believed that these chambers might evolve into proper elected regional assemblies, but in the event it proved difficult to achieve a consensus on a timetable for this. In some regions, including the North-East, there was evidence of strong support for an elected assembly, but this was not the case in other parts of England.

Eventually, in November 2002, the Regional Assemblies (Preparations) Bill was introduced. This set out arrangements for consultation exercises to take place within the English regions, and allowed for subsequent referenda where there is clear evidence of interest in holding a vote. The referenda (which might be held in only a small number of the regions) could approve the establishment of new regional assemblies, which would take the form of large unitary authorities dealing with all matters of local governance. By autumn 2003, the deputy prime minister was taking this process into its next phase, with plans taking shape for consultative referenda. In summer 2004 these were agreed for two regions, although the proposed referendum for a third region (the North-West) was postponed, apparently due to a combination of political and technical problems. Against all the predictions, the referendum in the North-East in autumn 2004 produced a massive 'no' vote.

At the other end of the spectrum from the English regions, the Scottish devolution package was relatively strong. In the wake of its election in 1997 the Blair government moved quickly to deliver its manifesto commitment, and complete the 'unfinished business' of the last Labour administration in the 1970s. A White Paper was published in the summer of 1997, a pre-legislative referendum in September confirmed in principle the support of the Scottish people for a Parliament with tax-varying powers (although the basic funding of the devolved administration would come via the extant block grant system determined by the Barnett Formula), and the Scotland Act received Royal Assent in November 1998. The Scottish Parliament was elected on fixed, four-year terms, with the first elections taking place in May 1999.

The major impact of the Scottish devolution settlement was the augmentation of the extant arrangements for significant administrative and limited policy devolution via the Scottish Office, with much more widespread policy devolution and, crucially, legislative devolution (for some analysis of the theory and practice of devolved governance, see, for example, Hassan, 1999; Hassan and Warhurst, 2000, 2002; McConnell, 2000).

To a considerable extent, the Scottish Parliament modelled its procedures on those of Westminster. However, there were some important differences. The working hours were more conventional, and the debating mode simpler. The most significant innovation was in the nature of the committee system. The 16 committees combined the functions of the Westminster select and standing committees, and added some more. This gave them powers to conduct inquiries, scrutinise the legislation proposed by the Executive, and even initiate their own legislation (see Lynch, 2001).

With the Scottish Office transformed into a rump (and renamed the Scotland Office), the vast majority of its officials transferred to work in the new Scottish Executive, which was headed by a Cabinet led by a First Minister. Civil servants working for the Scottish Executive (and its Welsh counterpart) remained part of the unified Home Civil Service, with no changes to their status or conditions of service (for detailed analysis of devolution's implications for the civil service, see Pyper, 1999; Parry and Jones, 2000; Parry, 2001; Pyper and Kirkpatrick, 2001). A series of 'concordats' was produced, with the aim of establishing the ground rules for the relationships between the Cabinet Office, Whitehall departments and the new departments of the Scottish and Welsh administrations, and again, the focus here was on the need for official coordination and unity.

Within the Scottish Executive, organisational reconfiguration reflected the changed policy imperatives and the need to develop working relationships with the new ministerial team, and with the Parliament. Detailed analysis of this organisational and structural aspect of devolution can be found in Parry (2001) and Parry and Jones (2000). Officials and ministers in the Executive faced an increased volume of work, caused by the effect of full legislative programmes and demands for policy initiatives from organised interests, the public more broadly, and the MSPs. For civil servants, there were also changes in the nature of their work, stemming from the change from working for a Secretary of State and a small ministerial team, to serving the First Minister and a full array of Cabinet and sub-Cabinet ministers. The need to carry out 'Cabinet Office' types of function led to the creation of a new Executive Secretariat. Finally, increased accountability demands accompanied devolution. These were brought about by the creation of the Scottish Parliament (with its committee system and arrangements for ministerial questions and scrutiny debates), coupled with increased volumes of correspondence and refocused external audit (centred on Audit Scotland) and ombudsman systems (the move to a combined Scottish Public Services Ombudsman in 2002).

The arrangements for Welsh devolution were a diluted version of those put in place for Scotland. The sequence of events in 1997 and 1998 was broadly similar for both countries. Shortly after the 1997 General Election the government's proposals for Wales were published in a White Paper, and a pre-legislative referendum was held in September. Wales had voted decisively against devolution in 1979, and nearly rejected the idea once again. The result was an extremely narrow 'yes' vote. The Government of Wales Bill was introduced in the House of Commons in November 1997 and passed quickly, receiving Royal Assent in July 1998. Elections to the Welsh National Assembly were held on the same day as those for the Scottish Parliament in May 1999.

Power was devolved to the National Assembly as a corporate body, but in order to facilitate a cabinet style of executive (rather than, for example, a local-government-style committee system) the Assembly delegated its decision-making functions to the First Secretary (elected by the whole Assembly) who was then in a position to make ministerial appointments. The National Assembly inherited the policy responsibilities of the former Welsh Office, which (like the former Scottish Office) was scaled down, given an essentially co-ordinating role, and restyled as the Wales Office. Unlike the Scottish Parliament, the Assembly was given secondary rather than primary legislative powers, which meant that it could pass only Assembly Orders to complete the details of Acts passed by the Westminster Parliament. A second significant difference with the Scottish model was that the Welsh Assembly had no tax-varying powers and would be entirely reliant upon the block grant from London (which continued to be shaped by the Welsh variant of the Barnett Formula).

Civil servants working in Wales, like their colleagues in Edinburgh, remained part of the unified Home Civil Service, but their formal position was different. The officials would work for the National Assembly as a corporate body, and not simply for the First Secretary and the Assembly Cabinet. It was argued (see Osmond 1998, 1999) that this arrangement contained the potential for tensions and conflicts of loyalty to develop as these officials attempt to follow three lines of responsibility (to the Assembly, the Cabinet and Whitehall). Civil servants in Wales had to adopt new methods of operation in order to cope with the demands placed upon them by individual AMs (Assembly Members), Assembly Committees, the First Minister and Assembly Secretaries. Additionally, the Assembly's committee system was a structural novelty, designed to facilitate policy making as well as oversight and scrutiny. The Assembly Secretaries (ministers) became members of the committees which covered their ministerial portfolios, although they were not permitted to chair the committees (Laffin and Thomas, 2000).

In the early years of Scottish and Welsh devolution, an obvious tension arose between the modernising tendencies of the Blair government – with its clear commitment to the doctrines and practices of the new public management – and the governing administrations in Edinburgh and Cardiff. The coalitions between Labour (predominantly a left-leaning, 'old' Labour variant) and the Liberal Democrats in Scotland and Wales were markedly less enthusiastic about certain aspects of the Blair agenda, and this led to some instances of policy divergence (over the funding of residential care for the elderly and student finances, for example) within the devolved United Kingdom.

Northern Ireland is, in every sense, a special case of devolution. It had experienced devolution within the United Kingdom between 1922 and 1972. However, the Unionist-dominated Stormont Parliament had a mixed record, and the breakdown in law and order in the province in the late 1960s was to lead, eventually, to the introduction of 'direct rule' via a department of central government, the Northern Ireland Office. The years since then have been characterised by continued violence of varying degrees of intensity, and repeated attempts to introduced a devolved settlement which carries cross-community support. The first attempt, the Sunningdale Agreement of 1973, led to the resumption of limited devolution in the form of a power-sharing arrangement which sought to guarantee representation on the executive to nationalist politicians. This was aborted in the face of opposition from hard-line Unionists in 1974. As the violence continued, the Northern Ireland Office re-emerged as basis for government. Fresh attempts to restore devolution, including the 'rolling devolution' project of 1982, ended in failure. Eventually, a chain of events set in motion by the 1985 Anglo–Irish Agreement, led to a new settlement, which was set out in the 'Good Friday', Belfast Agreement of 1998 (see McConnell, 2000; Meehan, 1999). This put in place a framework for the resumption of devolved government in Northern Ireland. However, this process has been incomplete, and subject to sporadic interruptions.

Under the terms of the Good Friday Agreement, members were elected to the Northern Ireland Assembly in June 1998. The Assembly was to assume full legislative and executive authority over matters previously within the remit of six Northern Ireland Office departments: agriculture, economic development, education, the environment, finance and personnel, and health and social services. Certain key policy spheres, including defence and foreign affairs, were reserved for Westminster in perpetuity, but other areas, such as law and order, might be devolved in future, provided there was clear evidence of cross-community support for this. An Executive Committee of 12 ministers, including the first minister and the deputy first minister, would lead the devolved administration. Assembly business would be carried out through debates and within 16 Standing and Departmental Committees, as well as an array of ad hoc committees. Both scrutiny and policy-making functions would be assigned to the Departmental Committees, and they would give approval to secondary legislation and deal with the committee stage of primary legislation. As was the case in the Executive, the committees would be required to give proper recognition to the representatives and views of all elements of the community.

When the Assembly first met in the summer of 1998, the Ulster Unionist leader David Trimble was elected as First Minister and the SDLP's Seamus Mallon as Deputy First Minister. Negotiations then broke down over the issue of the nomination of ministers to the Executive Committee. Under the terms of the Belfast Agreement all legitimate political perspectives were to have representation, but the Unionists refused to allow Sinn Fein to have ministers until progress was made with arms decommissioning by the Provisional IRA. As a result of this impasse, the Assembly was suspended by the Secretary of State for Northern Ireland. The Assembly was reconvened in November 1999, and a ministerial team nominated, following a review of the process conducted by the US Senator George Mitchell. However, devolution was suspended once more for some months in 2000, and again, 'indefinitely', from autumn 2002 due to continuing disputes between the Ulster Unionists and Sinn Fein over progress with arms decommissioning. Fresh Assembly elections were called in autumn 2003, although the prospects for the formation of a ministerial team looked uncertain in the face of further disagreements about the significance of new statements and actions from the Provisional IRA regarding weapons.

Restructuring beyond the centre: local government and the NHS

In other parts of the body politic, specifically in local government and the National Health Service, many of the modernisation and new public management structural concepts and themes were also in evidence. Although agencification along Next Steps lines was not replicated in these spheres, certain facets of the central government restructuring exercises could be discerned in local government and the health service. In particular, the coupling of external structural changes with internal management reforms was apparent. Additionally, there was an adherence to the concept of a policy–management dichotomy, the structural dimensions of which involved the creation of 'splits' between 'clients' and 'contractors' (in the context of local government competitive tendering) and 'purchasers' and 'providers' (in the context of the ultimately abortive NHS internal market). The creation of the NHS Executive (and its Scottish and Welsh equivalents) as an entity with operational freedom from the Department of Health is another illustration of the developing policy–management dichotomy. The local government and NHS restructuring exercises also provided a contrast between the prevailing rhetoric of delegation and localism, and the reality of increasing central control (from within the structures of local authorities and the health service, and also from central government). The 'command and control' approach of New Labour has been particularly marked in the spheres of local government and the NHS, with a proliferation of inspectorates bent on enforcing the centre's will. Furthermore, as structures changed, there was a distinct move away from the elective principle in certain areas of service provision, epitomised by the dilution of local authority rights of representation on Health Boards and the movement of water and sewerage services from local government (to the private sector in England and Wales, and to central government quangos in Scotland).

Reforming the structure of British local government has become something of a perennial occupation for central government ministers with time on their hands and more than a passing interest in the current vogue in management theory. As we have already noted, the penchant for 'giantism' and so-called economies of scale contributed to the climate in which the major structural overhauls of 1974–5 transformed the shape of local government in England, Wales and Scotland (although it should be noted that these reforms were substantially based upon reports emanating from Royal Commissions). The flaws in the new structures quickly became apparent, and these were exacerbated with the coming of a period of economic entrenchment, ever-increasing limits on the capacity of local authorities to raise revenue, and developing tensions between central and local government (see Young and Rao, 1997: chapters 7 and 8).

Political motivations, coupled with the first obvious signs of a commitment to 'simplify' the structure of local government, led the Thatcher government to abolish the Greater London Council and six English Metropolitan County Councils in 1986 (under the terms of the 1985 Local Government Act). Political factors, ranging from the perceived need to reduce the number of Labour-controlled local authorities, to the ambitions of the minister charged with responsibility for local government in England, would also be apparent during the next period of structural reform, in the final phase of the Major government (see Wilson and Game, 1998: 58–9; Leach, 1995: 50). Indeed, close observers of the system of local government, including Wilson and Game (1998) and Leach (1995), argue that the restructuring of local government in the 1990s was primarily driven by politics. However, there was also some evidence that the reforms were influenced, at least in part, by the new public management penchant for virtually constant programmes of rolling structural change, incorporating 'delayering' and 'downsizing'.

The overall impact of local government restructuring was significant. There was a marked reduction in the number of councils (see Box 5.3). In England, the initial radicalism of the process came to be diluted somewhat in the face of reduced ministerial enthusiasm following the departure of Michael Heseltine to another department and continuing antipathy from within the world of local government and the public at large (Wilson and Game, 1998: 59). In the end, a hybrid system emerged, with two tiers of local authority remaining in place in large parts of the

---

Box 5.3   The impact of local government structural reform in the 1990s

	England	*Wales*	*Scotland*
No. of Councils Pre-Reform	411	45	65
No. of Councils Post-Reform	387	22	32

Source: Adapted from Wilson and Game (1998: chapters 4 and 5).

Box 5.4   Creating unitary councils: some English examples

Former county council	*Former district councils*	*New unitary council*
Avon	Bristol City	Bristol
	Kingswood, Northavon	S. Gloucestershire
	Woodspring	North Somerset
	Bath City, Wansdyke	Bath & N.E. Somerset
Cleveland	Hartlepool	Hartlepool
	Middlesbrough	Middlesbrough
	Lanbaurgh-on-Tees	Redcar and Cleveland
	Stockton-on-Tees	Stockton-on-Tees
Leicestershire	Leicester City	Leicester
	Rutland	Rutland

Source: Extracted from Wilson and Game (1998: 60–1).

country, and a total of 46 new single-tier, or unitary, councils (see Box 5.4 for some illustrative examples).

This still represented a far-reaching reform of the local government structure in England. In Scotland and in Wales, the effects were even more sweeping, with unitary councils introduced across the board in each case, and the overall number of local authorities cut by more than half. However, as Wilson and Game point out (1998: 63), the move to single-tier, unitary councils did not necessarily bring about a simplification of the local government system, nor did it herald enhanced 'localism' and genuine decentralisation in every case. Paradoxically, the overall cut in the number of councils did not produce a situation in which fewer bodies were involved in the delivery of what had been local government services. In certain council areas, restructuring resulted in more bodies being responsible for fewer services. Meanwhile, some of the more important services (including water and sewerage in Scotland) were delivered by quangos appointed by ministers rather than by elected authorities and in other spheres (including responsibility for trunk roads) central government took over directly. In these cases, we see most clearly the tension between the new public management rhetoric of decentralisation, delegation and delayering and the reality of central government's desire to exert increased control over matters of finance, policy and service implementation.

In the National Health Service, although many of the details were different from those in local government, the broad themes associated with restructuring were familiar. Depending on definitions, it can be argued that at least four major restructuring processes have taken place in the NHS since it was introduced in 1948. If we detach ourselves from the details of these exercises, the prevailing general features would seem to be similar to those seen in the world of local government: a combination of political expediency and obeisance to current managerial fashion.

Tensions inherent to the organisation and management of health care in the UK led to a virtually continuous concern with structures. Klein (1995: 144) identified 'the cycle of experiments with delegation quickly followed by reversion to centralisation', while Ranade (1997: 2) criticised the 'policy see-saw, with governments alternating between periods of centralisation, the better to gain control, followed by a decentralising reaction against the rigidities which are caused as a consequence'.

Some of the most significant structural changes of all were presaged by the 1989 White Paper, *Working for Patients* (Department of Health, 1991) and given legislative force by the 1990 National Health Service and Community Care Act. It has been argued (Bruce, 1997: 184–5) that this initiative stemmed from the combined effect of a funding crisis, serious concerns about declining standards of patient care, and 'an ideological dimension'. The latter led directly to proposals for the advent of competitive markets (a typical feature of the new public management, discussed in detail in Chapter 6). As a result, the extant structure of health care, wherein District Health Authorities (Area Health Boards in Scotland) managed hospitals directly, was discarded in favour of a 'purchaser–provider split', within which the Health Authorities and Boards were given new roles as overseers of the health care needs of their resident populations (Bruce and Jonsson, 1996: 79).

The Health Authorities and Boards drew on their central government financing to became purchasers (later, 'commissioners') of health care, while the providers (in the form of the individual hospitals and community health services) took on new forms as Trusts. The revenue of the Trusts was to be produced through the negotiation of contracts with Health Authorities and Boards, the private sector of health care, and the new General Practitioner fundholders. The latter had budgets devolved to them from the District Health Authorities and Area Health Boards, and had increased flexibility to 'purchase' specialist hospital treatment for their patients. The government's strong encouragement to GP practices to apply for fundholding status, led to the emergence of an array of fundholding arrangements in England and Wales, although the new system was markedly unsuccessful in Scotland, where virtually all GP practices rejected the opportunity to have delegated funds.

These financial management reforms were accompanied by further structural changes in the wake of the 1989 White Paper. At the local level, the Family Practitioner Committees were initially reorganised into smaller management bodies, and then, in 1990, they re-emerged as Family Health Service Authorities (FHSAs). Following another review, in 1996 the FHSAs were merged with District Health Authorities to form unitary Health Authorities. The Regional Health Authorities in England were abolished, and replaced by regional offices of the Department of Health. At the same time, the new NHS Trusts were increasing in number, to the point where, in 1998 there were 450 Trusts in England and Wales (operating within a framework of 100 Health Authorities), and in Scotland there were 47 Trusts (within a framework of 15 Health Boards). The Trusts were quangos, in the sense that they were managed by boards containing executive and non-executive directors, whose appointment ultimately lay in the hands of central government ministers.

The overall effect of these restructuring exercises was to produce a quite bewildering array of bodies concerned, in one way or another, with the system of health care. New public management and modernisation had the effect of massively increasing the organisational complexity of the NHS. While the government's policy documents framing these changes were replete with the language of 'decentralisation', and 'delegated management', some observers (see, for example, Kendall, Moon, North and Horton, 1996: 211) could discern a familiar picture of increased centralisation and political direction.

Within the Blair government's modernisation agenda a partial rationalisation of the increasingly complex NHS structure was taken forward, but this also led to further waves of reorganisation. In the spirit of devolution, health White Papers were produced for each part of the UK between 1997 and 1999, but the published plans had a common theme: removal of the internal market (including the abolition of GP fundholding), retention of the distinction between those commissioning health services and those providing them, a primary care-led NHS (placing the commissioning of services in the hands of professionals closest to the patient, such as GPs and community nurses), more lay representation and greater openness (via more public meetings of NHS Boards and Trusts), and closer working relationships with local government (which retained responsibilities for social care, social services and environmental health throughout the earlier waves of change).

The outcome of these reforms for England was the creation of Primary Care Groups (PCGs) in 1999. These assumed health care planning and commissioning roles for their local populations. Gradually, these bodies became free-standing Primary Care Trusts (PCTs) which could combine commissioning with the provision of community health services. By 2003, there were 303 PCTs, receiving 75 per cent of the NHS budget, and it was anticipated that all PCGs would become PCTs by 2004 (see www.doh.gov.uk). Similar arrangements were put in place in Wales, with Local Health Groups based on local authority areas assuming the role of the English PCGs, although there were no plans to create Welsh PCTs. By contrast, in Scotland, there were to be no Primary Care Groups, but instead PCTs, funded by the Health Boards, were created, with GPs forming local health co-operatives under their auspices. The NHS in Scotland also committed itself to ending the separation of commissioning and provision, and emphasised the need for a new era of collaboration between Trusts and Health Boards.

Before these new arrangements could be fully implemented, a crisis during the winter of 1999–2000 led to yet another review, which produced a National Plan for investment and reform in the NHS (see Department of Health, 2000). This covered issues such as management processes, lay involvement, service quality and professional regulation, although further structural reform was also proposed. The new structural changes included the creation of a Modernisation Agency at national level (with boards at regional and local levels) charged with responsibility for managing the investment and reform agendas. The posts of Chief Executive of the NHS and Permanent Secretary of the Department were being combined, thus ending the division of responsibilities and roles put in place in the late 1980s. Organisational changes were also set in motion at lower levels of the system, when, during the launch event for the NHS Modernisation Agency in spring 2001, the Health Secretary announced new plans to cut the number of Health Authorities in England from 99 to 30, and abolish the ten regional offices. This signalled a further shift of financial power towards the Primary Care Trusts. Twenty eight new Strategic Health Authorities, covering populations of around 1.5 million people, were set up from the autumn of 2002, with the aim of 'ensuring coherence and developing strategies for the local health service' (see www.doh.gov.uk).

The image of the National Health Service as an arena of permanent revolution within which every variety of managerial fad and fashion (even in recycled forms) can be introduced in the name of modernisation was confirmed when the Blair government launched yet another structural reform in 2002–03, based on the concept of NHS Foundation Trusts. In a set of proposals which carried more than faint echoes of the previous Conservative government's ideas about GP fundholding, the 2003 Health and Social Care Bill planned to allow existing NHS Trusts to earn a degree of 'autonomy' which would allow them to become non-profit-making organisations freed from central control (while delivering national targets and standards), able to recruit and employ their own staff, raise money on the open market, and retain financial surpluses. The proposals were couched in the language of community involvement and local accountability. However, the devolved administrations in Scotland and Wales quickly made it clear that they did not intend to embrace this latest version of NHS modernisation, and the Bill became the subject of intense opposition in both the Commons and the Lords. In the wake of the legislation's rather stormy passage, the first ten Foundation Trusts were established in the spring of 2004, and the opportunity to assume the new status was being extended throughout the NHS in England (for more on these developments, see www.doh.gov.uk).

In this chapter our primary concern has been with what might be considered as one of the external manifestations of the new public management. Closely linked to these structural issues is another key facet of the managerial changes which have swept though the British public sector in recent years. The advent and spread of competition and markets, to which we have had occasional cause to refer in this chapter, now merits detailed consideration in its own right.

6

Competition, Markets and Consumerism

The notion of consumer sovereignty, of citizens as consumers of public services, was one of the core values of the Labour governments elected in 1997 and 2001. In 2000, the Cabinet Office noted that 'The Government is committed to making public services available 24 hours a day, seven days a week, where there is a demand', a policy partly informed by the extensive polling carried out by the MORI organisation via the *People's Panel* (March 2000, Issue 5, p. 1). It represented the continuation of a managerial approach to the provision of public services that sought to make the public sector more responsive to citizens, and to make it more like the private sector. The private sector, viewed as an exemplar, a notion imported to the public sector under Prime Ministers Thatcher and Major, was set to continue from the outset of the Blair administration. New Labour saw it as an important principle to be seen to be 'putting consumers at the heart of public services' (*People's Panel*, September 2000, Issue 7, p. 1). Competition, the use of markets and different forms of public participation in assessing service delivery and the formulation of policy are intrinsic to the managerialist approaches to government around the globe. The exact nature and procedures vary according to the local context, but the global fashion for these approaches is clear from the fact that they lay at the heart of many countries' public sector reforms.

The previous chapter explored the way in which the machinery of government and the apparatus and institutions of the state have been restructured. This followed on as a natural accompaniment to the discussion on the impact of managerialism and the economic and financial reforms delivered as part of a managerialist dynamic within government. In this chapter we return to the topic of neo-liberalism as a motivating force for change. But this time we concentrate upon the drivers for organisational changes established as they were, as an attempt at cultural change, by the application of greater competition into the public sector through the use of markets and consumerism. In doing so we first revisit privatisation and explore it within its managerialist context as one among a series of techniques employed by successive governments to deliver 'change'.

This is both *change*, used as a synonym for *modernisation*, and *change* as an attempt to establish *cultural change* within the institutional panoply of government and civil society. Indeed, it may be argued that the disparate authors of the managerialist project sought a Kuhnian paradigm shift within the governance of the UK. That it is a paradigm shift, with an increase in marketisation and of managerialism is accepted by many practitioners and observers of public administration (Ferlie and Fitzgerald, 2002: 342). The logic of the paradigm dictates that governing parties of different ideological backgrounds adopt both the values and norms as well as the tools of the New Public Management paradigm, and in the United Kingdom, some argue, this appears to have occurred (McLaughlin, Osbourne and Ferlie, 2002). We would argue the need to exercise some caution before wholly accepting the perspective of a paradigm shift.

It is worth remembering that Kuhn's is the generally accepted definition of a paradigm, one that borrows from his observations of the scientific community and the way in which there is a periodic epistemological advance within that community. It is therefore largely empiricist and positivistic in its application, although based upon a common perception of shared values, part of the paradox of positivism. Kuhn argues that a paradigm is: 'The entire constellation of beliefs, values, techniques and so on shared by members of a given community' (1970: 175). The nature of modern Western society is pluralistic. This implies it is not only multicultural and multidoctrinal, it is also highly atomised and individualistic, while being embedded within a globalising economy. As such there is more than one 'given community', there are several at any time; thus a paradigm shift in one community or constellation of kindred communities may, or may not be repeated in others. Indeed, so far as public sector management is concerned it may be more fruitful to adopt a sceptical view as to whether an old universal paradigm ever existed to be replaced, especially in the light of the discussions in previous chapters (Massey, 1997: 4–7). What existed before NPM (and continue to exist) are competing models. States have a propensity to adopt certain aspects of leading models over others, these change over time and do so according to a specific set of circumstance and within a context bounded by geography, history, economics and a range of sociopolitical factors. This is sometimes called a paradigm shift; usually it is more likely to be a propensity shift. It is a change of emphasis in order to adjust the public sector to cope with the prevailing exigencies and in the process utilise new technologies, where they are applicable (Margetts, 1997: 87–104). The adoption of various NPM techniques such as privatisation and marketisation are examples of this.

With privatisation providing an obvious link through from Chapters 4 and 5, the main focus of this chapter then turns to the different techniques employed by successive managerialist administrations in the United Kingdom to develop the evolving process of change. The marketisation of public services has involved the implementation of a series of techniques in British central and local government. These include compulsory competitive tendering (CCT), market testing, and Public Private Partnerships (PPP) through the Private Finance Initiative (PFI). Each of these has increased the use of contracts throughout the public sector, both for procurement and delivery purposes. There is also a discussion on the use of *consumerism* as a technique to implement managerialism through modernisation as a response to consumer demand. The different aspects of this have included the Citizen's Charter, with the apostrophe clearly denoting individual's rights rather than a plural interpretation. It has also involved the use of techniques such as Best Value reviews, quality audits and the short-lived 'People's Panel', as well as advances in 'e-government' (Bellamy and Taylor, 1998). Much of this is now mixed in with performance measurement and regulation through targets, the subject of Chapter 7.

Privatisation

In Chapter 2 we noted the different a priori approaches to the structuring of government, the relationship between the state and civil society and the way in which the two interrelate, especially through the nature of governance. Succeeding chapters have traced the impact of neo-liberal individualism, as defined through managerialism and NPM, upon the political parties and the structures of the machinery of government. There have been a variety of dynamics involved in this, some of them complementary, some contradictory. Ferlie and Fitzgerald have identified four of the more consistent drivers as (to paraphrase them):

1. A demand by a growing middle class for a more business-like approach to the delivery of public services, often linked to concomitant demands for lower taxes and a more efficient use of resources.

2. A decline of deference towards the traditional forms of authority. This must include the hierarchies of the civil service, as well as public sector professionals such as doctors and teachers. The new middle classes possess the ability (and a propensity) to exit from the public sector into private sector provision if dissatisfied, thereby weakening its coalition of support even further – for example, in the fields of education and health care.
3. There has been a rise in the power of professional managers, and the managerial perspective and 'way of doing things' similar to the rise of the professions in earlier generations (Wilding, 1982). Ironically, it is the rise of the professional manager that has itself been used as a technique to curb and redress the power of the professionals themselves. Ferlie and Fitzgerald believe this has contributed to a paradigm shift.
4. New kinds of management have been made possible through technological innovation (Ferlie and Fitzgerald, 2002: 343–4), especially in the fields of information technology, knowledge management and e-government.

To summarise this: 'change in the ideological sphere is crucial and reflects itself in more superficial spheres of structures and systems' and in Britain's public sector 'there has been a successful transition from a public administration archetype to a now embedded NPM archetype' (Ferlie and Fitzgerald, 2002: 342–3). Privatisation has been one of the tools used to achieve this change and is also a goal in itself.

The privatisation of swathes of the UK's public sector began tentatively, as noted in the foregoing chapters. The ideological and pragmatic foundation for it may be found in the taxpayers' revolts in the United States and subsequent attempts by US federal and state authorities to reduce the role of the state. From its gestation and nurturing in the fertile ground of the United States it crossed the Atlantic to find a welcoming home in the new Conservative administration of Mrs Thatcher. It has remained ensconced under two successive premiers. Various authors coined different phrases for the process, wherever it was located – these included 'Selling the State' (Veljanovski, 1987), the 'Retreat of the State' (Swann, 1988), or, more simply, 'Privatisation' (Savas, 1987; Ascher, 1987). The spate of books and articles in the 1980s and 1990s reflect both the novelty and the impact of the policy at that time. As the methodology of implementation has evolved the interest has not lessened, but the process of privatisation through (amongst other forms) the Private Finance Initiative (PFI) has matured.

Savas (1987: 4–11) identified four pressures for privatisation in the United States:

1. Pragmatic: the search for more cost-effective government.
2. Ideological: neo-liberal belief in the superiority of markets over government to allocate resources.
3. Commercial: private sector interests seeking increased business opportunities.
4. Populist: what in the UK would come to be known as consumerism, with the belief that people were entitled to choice and a better level of service associated with private providers.

For Savas, therefore, privatisation is both a means and an end in itself. In the United States and then in the United Kingdom, privatisation became firmly linked to the neo-liberal assault upon welfarist bureaucracies and was seen:

> As a method of controlling government, controlling the growth of government and also freeing resources in order to facilitate economic growth and efficiency. (Massey, 1993, 110)

But its advocates saw it as more than a tool; for them, it was part of their anti-state crusade, Bennett and Johnson declaring 'government is wasteful and inefficient; it always has been and always will be' (1981: 19, quoted in Massey, 1993: 110).

Hanke identified six major aims for privatisation. These neatly encapsulate the four dynamics (cited by Savas) for privatisation and include the dual role of the entity – as both a process and a product of managerialism. Hanke argued that privatisation pursues:

1. The improvement of economic performance of the assets or service functions concerned;
2. The de-politicisation of economic decisions;
3. The generation of public-budget revenues through sale receipts;
4. The reduction in public outlays, taxes and borrowing requirements;
5. The reduction in the power of public sector unions; and
6. The promotion of popular capitalism through the wider ownership of assets (1987: 2, quoted in Massey, 1993: 110).

For Veljanovski, the political and ideological attraction of privatisation supersedes any economic argument.

His analysis adds to Hanke's list the essentially British benefits of privatisation. These include the ability to raise revenues on the private market and reduce the public sector borrowing requirement and to promote an 'enterprise culture' (1987: 1). As such:

> The justification for privatisation does not derive from its economic attractiveness. It simply interprets the policy as a radical change in the institutional structure which shifts the locus of decision-making back to individuals and private organisations because that provides a more democratic basis for society and is necessary for a society based on individual autonomy ... The link between private property, markets and liberty is a strong one and is the primary defence of privatisation. (Veljanovski, 1987: 206)

This neatly encapsulates the a priori approach of many of the neo-liberals to privatisation and the programme of managerialism. It was not based upon empirically observed and tested experience, but on a basic instinct that was averse to the welfarist approach to governance (Barnekov, Boyle and Rich, 1989: 232; Ott and Hartley, 1991).

As we have discussed in the preceding chapters, privatisation has played a key role in the restructuring, reordering and modernisation of public administration into the new public management of the managerial state. The process has been as much about (successfully or unsuccessfully) attempting to secure a paradigm shift as it has about securing revenue for the Exchequer, breaking the monopoly power of public sector producers (and unions), or reducing the Public Sector Borrowing Requirement (the National Debt). The complexity of these motivations, both by those who have consistently been in favour and those who have consistently (and inconsistently) opposed it, means that the process has been far from straightforward. Indeed, the support and opposition of voters, trade unionists and public sector managers has taken a Byzantine series of twists and turns over the years as the different forms of privatisation have been introduced (Saunders and Harris, 1994). These range from outright sell-off, through share offers, contracting-out and partnerships with the private sector (Veljanovski, 1987; Saunders and Harris, 1994). There were lessons learned the hard way from the experience of privatisations. These included the experience of nuclear-fuelled electricity-generating power stations, or the railways that have proved deeply problematic. For these and other examples market solutions did not always provide the desired result, and the development of the PFI was intended to attempt to maintain a controlling interest for the public sector, while

---

Box 6.1   **Total proceeds from privatisation**

Year/company	Total proceeds (£bn)
81/82 – British Airways, Cable and Wireless, Britoil, Amersham	1,535
83 – Associated British Ports, British Petroleum	1,139
84 – British Telecommunications, Associated British Ports, BP, Enterprise Oil	2,050
85 – British Aerospace, Britoil, Cable and Wireless	2,706
86 – British Gas	4,458
87 – British Airways, Rolls Royce, British Airports Authority, BP	5,140
88 – British Steel	7,069
89 – the water companies	4,225
90 – Regional electricity companies	5,347
91 – Electricity-generating companies, BT (second tranche)	7,925
92 –	8,184
93 – Northern Ireland Electricity, BT (third tranche)	5,453
94 –	6,429
95 – Generating companies (second tranche)	2,493
96 – Rail Track, British Energy, Atomic Energy Authority	4,404

Data from www.hm-treasury.gov.uk

---

exploiting the financial and managerial resources of the private sector (Cory, 2003: 22–4).

To conclude this section it is worth noting the scale of privatisation in the UK. Since it began under the administration of Mrs Thatcher, 114 companies have been privatised with a total value (in 2001 values) of over £68 billion (Box 6.1).

Employment in the publicly owned industries has been greatly reduced through privatisation of the constituent companies (see Box 6.3. p. 114). This again reduces the demands made upon taxpayers not only in terms of wage and salary costs, but also for National Insurance and pensions contributions. The scale of the privatisation programme may be seen by the full list of central government privatisations given in Box 6.2. Local government privatisations are not given here, but were also substantial, especially through the process of compulsory competitive tendering, addressed in a later section of this chapter.

The next section takes this further, exploring how the process of privatisation kindled the marketisation of the state.

Box 6.2 **Publicly owned companies, subsequently privatised**

1. ADAS
2. AEA Facilities Management
3. AEA Technology
4. Agricultural Training Board
5. Amersham International
6. Appledore Shipbuilders Limited
7. Associated British Ports
8. Belfast International Airport
9. B. Aerospace
10. British Airports Authority
11. British Airways
12. British Airways Helicopters
13. BBC Transmission – Home
14. BBC Transmission – World
15. British Coal
16. British Energy
17. British Gas
18. British Petroleum
19. British Rail
20. BR. (Central Services)
21. BREL
22. BR. Freight
23. BR. Hotels
24. BR. Infrastructure Services
25. BR. Maintenance Limited
26. British Shipbuilders
27. British Steel
28. British Sugar Corporation
29. British Technology Group
30. British Telecom
31. Britoil
32. Brooke Marine Limited
33. Building Research Establishment
34. Busways
35. Cable & Wireless
36. Chessington Computer Services
37. Clark Kinkaid Limited
38. DAB
39. DERA (DSSD)
40. Doncaster Wagon Works
41. DTELS
42. DVOIT
43. Enterprise Oil
44. Fairey
45. Ferranti
46. FORWARD
47. General Practice Finance Corporation
48. Girobank
49. Govan Shipyard
50. Hall Russell Limited
51. Harland & Wolff
52. HMSO
53. Historic Property Restoration
54. Horwich Foundry
55. Hydraulics Research Station
56. ICL
57. Imnos
58. Insurance Services Group
59. International Aeradio
60. Istel
61. Jaguar
62. Laboratory of Government Chemist
63. Leyland Bus
64. Leyland Truck & Freight Rover
65. London Buses
66. National Bus Company
67. National Engineering Laboratory
68. National Freight Consortium
69. National Grid
70. National Health Service – Scotland CSA Building Div.
71. National Physical Laboratory
72. National Power
73. National Maritime Institute
74. National Seed Development Organisation
75. National Transcommunications Ltd.
76. Natural Resources Institute
77. Northern Ireland Electricity
78. Northern Ireland Generators
79. North Sea Oil Licences (Special Licensing Rounds)
80. Occupational Health/Safety Agency
81. Paymaster

→

$\rightarrow$

82. Powergen	100. Sealink
83. Professional/Executive Recruitment	101. Short Brothers
	102. Skills Training Agency
84. Property Services Agency (Building Management)	103. Swan Hunter Shipbuilders Limited
85. Property Services Agency (Projects)	104. Teachers Pensions Agency
	105. Technology Group Holdings
86. Rail Industry Privatisation	106. Train Operating Companies
87. Railtrack	107. Transport Research Laboratory
88. Recruitment & Assessment Services	108. Travellers Fare
89. Redpath Dorman Long	109. Trust Ports
90. Regional Electricity Co12	110. Unipart
	111. UK Accreditation Services
91. Rolling Stock Cos.	112. Vickers Shipbuilding & Engineering Limited
92. Rolls Royce	
93. Rover Group	113. Victaulic
94. Royal Ordnance	114. Vosper Thorneycroft Limited
95. Scott Lithgow	115. Water & Sewerage Cos: 10
96. Scottish Homes Building Div	116. WHCSA EstateCare Group
97. Scottish Hydro	117. Wytch Farm
98. Scottish Power	118. Yarrow Shipbuilders Limited
99. Scottish Transport Group	119. Yorkshire Rider

Reproduced from HM, Treasury, 2003, www.hm-treasury.gov.uk

Markets and marketisation

The process of marketisation and increasing competition in the public sector began with the Financial Management Initiative, discussed in Chapters 3 and 4 and progressed through the privatisation programme into the Private Finance Initiative and the Public Private Partnership programme of the Labour governments elected in 1997 and 2001. For New Labour the Public Private Partnerships (PPPs) are central to its modernisation programme, especially with regard to the effective delivery of public services (Massey, 2002: 34–5). The White Paper, *Public Private Partnerships: the Government's Approach* (HM Treasury, 2000), perceives PPPs as a powerful new approach to integrating the roles of the public and private sectors. This in turn builds upon the declarations made in the *Modernising Government* White Paper, which promised the delivery of public services 'to meet the needs of citizens, not the convenience

---

Box 6.3   **Employment in nationalised industries**

Year	No. employees in nationalised industries (000's)	Year	No. employees in nationalised industries (000's)
1971	1856	1987	864 Election of
1973	1731		Conservative
1974	1777 Election of		Government
	Labour Government	1988	791
1975	1816	1989	719
1976	1752	1990	675
1977	1866	1991	497
1978	1844	1992	457 Election of
1979	1849 Election of		Conservative
	Conservative		Government
	Government	1993	437
1981	1657	1995	344
1982	1554	1996	323
1983	1465 Election of	1997	295 Election of
	Conservative		Labour
	Government		Government
1984	1410	1998	302
1985	1131		

Data from www.hm-treasury.gov.uk

---

of public service providers' (1999: 25). There is a clear allusion here to the continuation of a more consumerist approach to the delivery of public services, something we return to later in this chapter.

Compulsory competitive tendering

The enforced marketisation of services in local authorities had been introduced under Mrs Thatcher's Conservative government at the same time as central government reforms and continued apace under Prime Minister Major. In many ways, at least initially, the marketisation of local government was more far-reaching than the reform of central government. Compulsory competitive tendering (CCT) was introduced under the Local Government, Planning and Land Act and the Local Government Acts of 1988 and 1992 as part of a stream of measures that steadily ratcheted up the requirement to marketise the activities of local authorities. Local authorities were forced to put out to tender or market test an increasing number of specified services, the terms and time-scales were determined by central government (Greenwood, Pyper and Wilson, 2002: 142–3).

CCT, in its various guises, was a largely successful attempt to transform the way in which local authorities operated. Local authorities could compete with the private sector to win contracts to continue to deliver services directly to their citizens, although some chose not to do so for some of their services, specifying they would favour 'out-of-house' bids. In many councils 'client/contractor splits were created, which allowed Direct Service Organisations (DSOs) to prepare bids and, if these were the most competitive, to perform contracts' (Greenwood, Pyper and Wilson, 2002: 143). Throughout the 1980s and 1990s, many contracts were awarded to the private companies that bid in these competitions and swathes of the public sector were transferred to the private sector under this comprehensive policy. The Labour Party originally intimated it would end compulsory CCT when it came to power, but although formally discontinued, the introduction of PPPs illustrated that the change was more one of emphasis than one of policy. The application of the PPP initiative to both the national and sub-national levels of government has much in common with CCT and is a full-blooded market-driven technique that leans heavily on New Right ideology and minimalist concepts of the state, as outlined in Chapter 1 above. In other words, due to the strong opposition expressed by public sector unions and Labour-controlled local authorities, the Labour government was obliged to signal a policy change. But in practice this was a change of emphasis, rather than substance. That is, the approach to public sector reform was varied, but the path pursued thereafter remained constant.

Public Private Partnerships

The Treasury's 2000 White Paper describes PPPs as:

1. The introduction of private ownership into state-owned businesses. This may include the sale of a majority or minority stake in these.
2. The Private Finance Initiative (PFI) is seen as a part of the PPP process. This involves PFIs and other arrangements where the public sector contracts to purchase services on a long-term basis 'so as to take advantage of private sector skills incentivized by having

private finance at risk. This includes concessions and franchises' where a private sector partner takes on the responsibility for providing a public service, 'including maintaining, enhancing or constructing the necessary infrastructure' (HM Treasury, 2000: 10).
3. Selling government services into wider markets and other partnership arrangements where private sector expertise and finance are used to exploit the commercial potential of government assets (HM Treasury, 2000: 10; Massey, 2002: 34).

By the end of 2002 a substantial number of projects were operating under the PPP scheme. The Chancellor of the Exchequer was moved to write:

> 40 hospitals, 150 new schools and scores of road and rail investments are being built right across Britain with the help of private finance – private finance providing additional investment in public services, not replacing public investment as in the past ... working in partnership, the public and private sectors can deliver complex infrastructure projects on time and on budget, with the private sector remaining responsible for the maintenance of the project for the long-term. In place of the old, sterile battle for territory between the public and private sectors, we now have public and private working together. Our demand for better value for money for public sector investments is resulting in a new and more responsible partnership, helping to deliver better public services for the people of Britain. (HM Treasury, 2003, Preface)

Not surprisingly the public body charged with auditing the nation's finances on behalf of Parliament, the National Audit Office (NAO) headed by Her Majesty's Comptroller and Auditor General, has taken a keen interest in the PFI. Whereas the rhetoric of a ministerial preface to a department's White Paper is there to put the *party*-political gloss on policy, the NAO is charged with investigating the concrete realities of delivery. It is worth exploring some of the more recent observations made by the NAO in detail as they illustrate many of the issues and difficulties inherent to the PFI process.

From its first report in 1997 on the Skye Bridge, it produced (up to early 2003) 29 reports concerned with aspects of PFI. These reflect the breadth of PFI projects across the public sector. There has been a critical emphasis on projects that are perceived to have gone wrong (Passport Agency reform in 1999, or the Immigration and Nationality Directorate's casework in 1999) or that have taken place in areas with a tradition of cost overrun. Over many decades these have often been most spectacularly apparent in the Ministry of Defence and there has been a range of reports in this field, for example on procurement and building (1999, 2000, 2002). Other critical areas have included public sector construction projects (2003) and the controversial London Underground PFI (2000). Some reports have been critical of the work undertaken under the PFI, while others (for example, Coleman, 2000) have taken a more sanguine approach. All have been conducted from the dispassionate accountant's perspective of measuring costs, performance and returns on investment that are the core of the NAO's methodology and of much new public management.

The NAO reports bear careful reading and there have been a mix of findings – some critical, some less so. Although earlier National Audit Office Reports on PFIs had sometimes been critical, or at least less than fulsome, some more recent publications have not been as tardy in their praise. The NAO's preamble to the report on public sector construction projects notes that the PFI 'is being used to procure many projects involving construction of assets which are needed to deliver public services' (2003, *Executive Summary*). Up to December 2002 PFI contracts in this field across the United Kingdom had been let for:

- Twenty five major hospital schemes;
- Seven prisons;
- Nine roads and a number of other projects such as;
- Departmental office accommodation and training facilities.

The Office of Government Commerce (OGC) has central responsibility for promoting good practice in public sector construction projects. It is also responsible for the central development of PFI policy. These two areas overlap in those projects where a service procured under the PFI requires the construction of an asset, such as a road or building (NAO, 2003, *Executive Summary*).

For its report on construction performance, the NAO carried out a census of all English PFI construction projects let by central government completed by summer 2002. It tested the hypothesis that 'PFI will deliver price certainty for departments and timely delivery of good quality assets' (2003, *Executive Summary*).

In general, the report states that the evidence gathered 'supported the hypothesis, though it is not possible to judge whether these projects could have achieved these results using a different procurement route' (2003, *Executive Summary*).

The NAO explains that:

Under a PFI contract the same private sector party, usually a consortium of companies, is responsible for delivering the required service over the whole life of the contract. In PFI accommodation projects, such as hospitals or prisons, the construction element typically represents around 25 to 30 per cent of the total value of the contract. But other project costs, such as maintenance, will be influenced by the quality of the construction work. (NAO, 2003, *Executive Summary*)

To summarise the NAO, in large public sector building projects, PFI 'incentivises' the consortium to:

1. Estimate the full cost of constructing and maintaining built assets when pricing the contract, as the consortium will not be able to recover unforeseen increases later by claiming them back from the department;
2. Complete the construction element as soon as possible because the consortium does not begin to receive payments until the asset is ready for use and the service is being delivered;
3. Achieve good quality construction as the consortium is obliged to maintain the building to agreed standards throughout the life of the contract. Failure to do so can result in payment deductions or financial damages. This encourages a 'whole life' approach to construction as longer-term costs can be reduced by building to higher standards. This differs from traditionally procured assets, where the companies responsible for construction have no interests in the long-term performance of the assets. (NAO, 2003, *Executive Summary*)

Furthermore, the evidence for the report:

showed that most PFI projects were delivering price certainty to departments with 29 out of the 37 projects surveyed reporting no construction related price increase after contract award. Where there had been a price increase it had been due to changes led not by the contractor but by the department or other parties. (NAO, 2003, *Executive Summary*)

These results demonstrate an improvement in performance in pure accountancy and auditing terms. They:

Compare well with historical experience of construction contracts in the public sector. In our 2001 report 'Modernising Construction'

(HC87, Session 2000–01) we reported that some 73 per cent of departments' and agencies' construction projects had run over budget for the public sector. (NAO, 2003, *Executive Summary*)

It should be noted, however, that:

> there have been a number of changes and initiatives in the construction industry in recent years which aim to improve construction results regardless of the form of procurement. These include encouraging closer working between clients and consortia, and setting targets for improvements in construction performance. There is also the Achieving Excellence Programme, which aims to improve departments' performance as procurers of construction. Finally, there are different procurement routes, other than PFI, such as design and build and prime contracting, which also aim to improve value for money in construction. (NAO, 2003, *Executive Summary*)

In other words, it is too early or too difficult to tell if the improvements are as a result of the PFI successfully modernising government, or of the construction industry effectively modernising itself to meet demanding customer requirements. But the NAO argues:

> There is strong evidence that the PFI approach is bringing significant benefits to central government in terms of delivering built assets on time and for the price expected by the public sector. In future projects departments need to weigh the prospect of such benefits in the balance with the other advantages and disadvantages of using the PFI or alternative forms of procurement. (NAO, 2003, *Executive Summary*)

PPPs, then, are a key element in the Labour government's strategy for modernising public services in the UK. They range across business structures and partnership arrangements from the PFI to the sale of equity stakes in state-owned businesses.

These include:

- A PPP for London Underground in which private sector partners will be granted long-term concessions to upgrade and modernise the tube infrastructure, including some £8 billion of new investment in the first 15 years;
- The introduction of private sector strategic partner into National Air Traffic Services (NATS) to fund and manage the company's large, modernising investment projects.

But as with earlier forms of privatisation, it is not clear whether the technique itself has produced the changes observed, or whether there have been other factors involved – for example, a more flexible and modern approach to customer demands of the kind alluded to by the NAO in its report on construction. What is clear, is that once in government New Labour remained committed to the kind of managerialist techniques pioneered by its Conservative predecessors. The reason for this was not to induce a culture change in the wider society, although it remained committed to modernising public services, but rather a determination to ensure that it was able to meet its promises to *deliver* better services in a coherent way. In order to do this it adopted NPM techniques and further refined them. Part of the process involved in this was a continuing commitment to the enfranchisement of citizens as consumers.

Contracts

Yet these managerialist techniques are concomitant to the increased use of contracts – indeed, CCT, Market Testing, PFIs and the whole panoply of NPM depends upon the increased use of contracts. Even the Next Steps agencies, discussed in a foregoing chapter, use pseudo-contracts in the form of a Framework Document setting out the rights and responsibilities of the Chief Executive with regard to her or his sponsoring department. The reason for these and the later introduction of Public Service Agreements (PSAs) is because of the constitutional principle that the Crown, being indivisible, cannot contract with itself, therefore the different institutions that comprise the Crown must establish an alternative to the formal notion of contracts. Yet the increased contractualism detracts from the principles of openness and clear lines of accountability inherent to consumerism. It 'inserts additional organisations, in the form of contractors directly delivering the service or facility, directly into the accountability relationships' (Greenwood, Pyper and Wilson, 2002: 248). As a result:

> As well as the service-users and the public sector provider, there are issues surrounding the accountability of the first deliverer of the service, for example the company holding the contract for refuse collection within a local authority area, the firm responsible for the cleaning service within an NHS Trust, or the in-house team which has secured the catering contract for schools and colleges. The result has been the creation of situations wherein the bodies responsible for direct

delivery of services are formally accountable not to the service users, but to the contracting authorities. Service-users seeking redress for an inadequate level of service provision have to take their case to the contracting authority, which then seeks redress from the contractor. (Greenwood *et al.*, 2002: 248)

As a consequence of this, we can see again that the issues surrounding the shift towards a more consumerist and market-led public sector is more complex than first principle a priori perspectives would suggest. The work of Public Choice authors, such as Buchanan and Tullock, would have us believe that the old welfarist hierarchies of the state act in the producers' interest. That is the self-maximising propensities of officials will lead them to act against the interest of citizens, in ways discussed in Chapter 1. Yet, the insertion of contracts and private sector agents acting on behalf of the elected governments at central and local level, introduces a principal/agent relationship that actually removes the citizen as consumer one stage further away from holding providers to account. It is to these and related issues that we now turn.

Consumerism

Soon after its re-election in 2001, the Labour Party embarked upon another reorganisation of the machinery of government and, most notably, of the centre of government: the Cabinet Office, Number 10 Downing Street and HM Treasury. Given the frustration experienced by Labour during its first term at the seeming inability of the public sector to deliver on the promises for reform of the public sector, the prime minister determined to focus on delivery – delivery, moreover, that was wedded to the concept of citizens as consumers. In the summer of 2001, the Cabinet Office reorganisation brought into existence the Office of Public Services Reform (OPSR) to 'advise the Prime Minister and work with Government Departments on how reform of public services, including the Civil Service and local government, can be achieved' (Cabinet Office, 2002b).

An early paper from the OPSR sought ways of putting these consumerist principles into practice. It noted with approval the development of NHS Direct to provide 24-hour nurse-led advice and health information, as well as the establishment by some local authorities of similar call centres to give advice and information to local people (2002b: 9). OPSR summarised government intentions to re-focus service delivery around the needs of citizens as customers by stating:

> Customers want accessibility and reliability. Where appropriate, they also want a reasonable choice. They want to be treated with respect. They want flexibility so that they can work a normal day or access services more conveniently. Rightly, they will not tolerate failure or endure chronic under-performance. (Cabinet Office, 2002b: 9)

These aims require a re-focusing of the producer-dominated welfarist hierarchies beyond that already achieved so that public services are:

> Refocused round the needs of the patients, the pupils, the passengers and the general public rather than the problems of those who provide the services. Joining up public services is the key, reshaping them across traditional departmental boundaries, and targeting the delivery of the outcomes that citizens seek. (Cabinet Office, 2002b: 8)

One of the ways in which the government has sought to implement these goals is through the further development of Best Value reviews that have to take cognisance of stakeholder views.

Value for Money

At first glance, the Value for Money Initiative (VFM) (often simply called *Best Value* when applied to individual reviews) appears indistinguishable in practice from the PFI and PPPs. Indeed, they may be linked together as part of the same attempt to improve service delivery through some measure of privatisation (Massey, 2002: 34–5). Although there is a clear overlap, the two are aimed at different targets and have a slightly different reasoning behind their adoption, however much they are both rooted in NPM approaches to administration. VFM is increasingly operationalised and delivered via Best Value reviews. The Local Government Act of 1999 introduced these reviews in a formal and structured way into sub-national government. The Best Value process, however, was trailed in the 1997 manifesto and tentatively introduced after Labour's election. Successive White Papers and Acts have structured its subsequent evolution.

The 1999 Act, despite being labelled *local government*, also applies to police authorities, the magistrates' courts and a variety of other organisations that operate at sub-national level. The Act requires these organisations to seek to secure economy, efficiency and effectiveness in the way they carry out their functions, but in addition to this they are required to engage a wide participation of user groups in the review (Asenova, Beck, Akintoye, Hardcastle, and Chinyio, 2002: 5–6). This mandatory consultation takes the consumerist logic of the Citizen's Charter one stage further and builds it into a concern for the pursuit of quality improvements, efficiently achieved and effectively delivered, but done so from the perspective of the individual citizen as a consumer of those services. It may be seen, then, that VFM is a structured guide for local authorities to obtain improvements in delivery, while the PFI is 'the government's preferred procurement strategy, which, in practice, may or may not be compatible with VFM or Best Value' (Asenova, Beck, Akintoye, Hardcastle, and Chinyio, 2002: 6–7). The private sector has welcomed the new business opportunities provided by the PFI, but it is difficult to discover the level of consumer satisfaction (if any) regarding the processes of Best Value, even though the pursuit of this is inherent to each review (Asenova, Beck, Akintoye, Hardcastle, and Chinyio, 2002: 6–19).

The initial methodology for a Best Value review is a more sophisticated version of the *Prior Options* to which Next Steps agencies and executive non-departmental public bodies have been subjected for over a decade at their five-year reviews (Massey, 1995; Greenwood, Pyper and Wilson, 2002: 33). As noted in Chapter 4, during the *Prior Options* process a series of questions are posed and then answered. They may be summarised here as:

1. Should this activity be done at all? If not, abolish or discontinue the activity. If yes, proceed to the next stage.
2. If it should be done, does it need to be carried out in the public sector? If not, it is privatised or hived out to an NGO. If yes, then on to the next question.
3. Should this activity continue to be carried out in its present location or can some other structure be considered?
4. Can some of it be contracted out in terms of delivery?
5. In what way may this activity be delivered more efficiently, effectively and economically in its present location, if that is where it is to remain?

With regard to Best Value reviews, it may be argued that there is a common thread, a shared administrative DNA with Prior Options in their approach. Although each Best Value review is carried out in a way commensurate with the activity and organisation under scrutiny, there are common characteristics, of which the requirement to consult is embedded. Each review begins with some rather basic business school concepts (based on interviews with the authors). The first of which is the '5Cs':

1. Challenge: to challenge the current approach for the delivery of a service or the way in which an activity is carried out.
2. Comparison: to compare the way an organisation carries out its activities with comparable organisations in other areas, including private sector organisations.
3. Consultation: to consult widely with key stakeholders. These are to include members of the organisation at all levels as well as external organisations and those organisations representing members of the community. This last aspect is an absolute requirement.
4. Competition: to identify opportunities where competition and market testing are appropriate for the provision of the activity being reviewed and wherever possible, to use these to enhance provision.
5. Collaboration: to identify and exploit all opportunities for collaboration in the management and provision of the activity or service, both within the organisation and the wider pantheon of public and private sector providers.

The reviews are conducted by a 'Review Team' that must include not only members of the organisation being reviewed – including junior members – but also external members, including people chosen from outside the organisation and its immediate client groups to act in the specific role of 'challenge agents'. Further standard business techniques are often employed as part of the methodology: these include an initial 'brainstorming' stage to complete FAST diagrams (Function, Analysis, Systems, Technique) and SWOT (strengths, weaknesses, opportunities, threats) analyses to establish the issues under review.

A typical review will broadly take the following (much abridged) pattern (information given to authors):

•   Appointment of team, to include external members and representatives of stakeholder organisations. Total membership varies, but may be around twenty people, including a Review Manager and support officers.
•   Initial meetings to conduct FAST and SWOT analyses, identify priorities, and identify internal and external organisations for consultation, comparison, and possible collaboration.

- Identification of priorities and key issues under each of the five 'Cs'.
- Identification of key (and specific) areas for review, with these areas being ranked in terms of priority:

  – Allocation of tasks to team members (such as conduct interviews, construct questionnaires and so forth).
  – Establish methodology for consultation and meeting priorities in the areas to be reviewed; subsequent to this establishing questionnaire design, focus groups, interview schedules for individuals and panels, EFQM assessments; procedures and protocols for canvassing hard-to-reach groups (for example, travellers or vulnerable members of the community).
  – Regular briefing and updating meetings.
  – Report and recommendations written and refined over several stages and drafts.
  – Constant referral to challenge agents and competition issues.
  – Writing of final report and submission to appropriate body.
  – Time-scale 4–8 months.
  – The intention of the government is that new performance targets will flow from each review and these will be influenced by the principles of Best Value, including:
  – Performance plans should support local accountability.
  – Best value is about effectiveness and quality, not just economy and efficiency, the new regime will be underpinned by target setting.
  – What matters is what works, so there is no presumption in favour of privatisation.
  – But the regime will continue to be linked to the use of increased competition as a basic management tool.
  – National and local targets should be built on performance information.
  – Independent auditors will confirm the integrity and comparability of performance information and report publicly on whether Best Value has been achieved, proposing efficacious remedies where it has not.
  – Central government retains the right to intervene wherever it deems it necessary so to do. (Adapted from Greenwood, Pyper and Wilson, 2002: 144, quoting *Local Government Chronicle*, 6 June 1997).

It may be seen that these principles enshrine an attempt to address the arguments of those anxious to import a greater concern for consumers' rights into the public sector. It remains to be seen whether this will be successful. The need to ensure that providers meet their obligations usually means this can only be done through the enforcement of contracts, and this contract compliance is itself an expensive business, often employing lawyers skilled in the art, but charging accordingly. Readers will be aware, therefore, of a certain circulatory element creeping into the arguments, and it may be that both citizens and government will have to live with some of the paradoxes thrown up by the process of modernisation.

As noted above, the increased contractualism of previous years, although injecting added competition and limiting producer power in the public services, had failed to adequately take account of the requirements of citizens as consumers. John Major's Citizen's Charter had attempted to locate the individual citizen at the centre of the public service provider's concerns, but it was under-funded and somewhat un-focused. Nonetheless, it was the administrative foundation upon which Best Value came to be constructed (Cabinet Office, 2003a, b).

The Citizen's Charter, benchmarking and back to Best Value

Launched in 1991, the *Citizen's Charter* represents clear consumerist logic in public sector management reform. It takes the individualist notions inherent in much of NPM, especially that emanating from the Virginia School, and implements it in a structured form within the United Kingdom's public administration. By 1991 virtually every public sector organisation in central and sub-national government throughout the United Kingdom possessed a charter and, furthermore, they made strenuous efforts to publicise their charter, outlining customers' rights to those customers and other stakeholders. Greenwood, Pyper and Wilson (2002: 243) note:

> The *Charter* spawned numerous spin-offs, including the Charter mark scheme, which was designed to acknowledge high standards of service provision in the public sector by rewarding individuals and organisations annually.

The scheme was adopted and developed by the Blair government. It was re-launched as *Service First* in 1998 (Cabinet Office, 1998) and then repositioned again after the 2001 Election within the Centre for Management and Policy Studies (CMPS) of the Cabinet Office. This is a unit charged with encouraging the development of better public services that had been merged with the Modernising Public Services group. Many of their aims and objectives are also overseen by OPSR in the way noted earlier in this chapter.

The government's renaming of the Citizen's Charter Programme as 'Service First' in 1998 reflected the continuing emphasis on providing responsive public services, that is, on effective delivery aimed at meeting individual citizen's needs. For example, the newly formed Department for Food and Rural Affairs (DEFRA) claims:

- Charters, or equivalent documents play an important role in delivering better services to the public. As part of our commitment for the better delivery of our services, we have published ... codes and customer charters from our inspectorates. (DEFRA, 2003)

As part of this its complaints procedure assures citizens:

A complaint is any written or spoken expression of dissatisfaction with the service we provide. We aim to ensure that we:

- treat complaints seriously and deal with them properly;
- resolve complaints promptly and informally whenever possible; and
- learn from complaints and take action to improve our service. (DEFRA, 2003)

Such schemes are set within the Cabinet Office's *Nine Principles of Public Service Delivery*, which state that every public service should:

1. **Set Standards of Service:** Set clear standards of service that users can expect; monitor and review performance; and publish the results, following independent validation wherever possible.
2. **Be Open and Provide Full Information:** Be open and communicate clearly and effectively in plain language, to help people using public services: and provide full information about services, their cost and how well they perform.
3. **Consult and Involve:** Consult and involve present and potential users of public services, as well as those who work in them; and use their views to improve the service provided.
4. **Encourage Access and the Promotion of Choice:** Make services easily available to everyone who needs them, including using technology to the full, and offering choice wherever possible.

5. **Treat All Fairly:** Treat all people fairly; respect their privacy and dignity; be helpful and courteous; and pay particular attention to those with special needs.

6. **Put Things Right When They Go Wrong:** Put things right quickly and effectively; learn from complaints; and have a clear, well publicised, and easy-to-use complaints procedure, with independent review wherever possible.

7. **Use Resources Effectively:** Use resources effectively to provide best value for taxpayers and users.

8. **Innovate and Improve:** Always look for ways to improve the services and facilities offered.

9. **Work with Other Providers:** Work with other providers to ensure that services are simple to use, effective and co-ordinated, and deliver a better service to the user. (Cabinet Office, 2003c)

There are obvious attempts here to join up with other aspects of modernisation and it is clear that many of the elements of Best Value have both drawn from this and fed-back into it.

These consumerist links are even more apparent when we consider the criteria that have been set for the award of a *Charter Mark* to a public sector organisation. Refined and developed over the last ten years, these criteria now run to several pages of Cabinet Office guidance on what is sought and how it will be evaluated. There are six broad criteria and many sub-criteria – each is assessed in its own right. A greatly abridged outline is shown in Box 6.4.

As a concomitant to the drive to make public services more accountable to (and through) consumers, the government began a benchmarking project under the last Major administration, but continued, expanded and developed during Labour's first term of office (Samuels, 1998). It culminated in the establishment of a new organisation in 2002–03, the Public Sector Benchmarking Service, set up as a collaboration between the Cabinet Office and HM Customs and Excise (Cabinet Office, 2003a). The Cabinet Office's Public Sector Excellence Programme, as the benchmarking project was renamed, has been running since 1996 (Cabinet Office, 2003d). The first phase was a small pilot project to test whether the private sector Business Excellence Model (BEM) could be applied to the public sector as a useful tool for improving an organisation's performance.

Preliminary evaluation of the project deemed it a success and phase two began its extension more widely across central government, especially Next Steps agencies (Samuels, 1998). The third phase, a more

Box 6.4 **Criteria for the award of a Charter Mark**

Criterion 1: Set standards and perform well. Demonstrate the organisation sets clear service and performance standards by consulting customers. It meets those standards. It monitors and reviews performance against standards and publishes the results. It designs, puts into practice and monitors standards.

Sub-criterion: Set precise and measurable standards for the main elements of the service that reflect the needs, expectations and rights of customers and the general public.

What the assessor is looking for: Set precise, measurable and challenging standards for the main services which take account of responsibility for delivering national and statutory standards and targets, and deal with local priorities. Set precise, measurable and challenging standards for customer service and these measure quality as well as quantity.

What counts as evidence? Clear standards for the main business, this may include any internal documents or information for the public that includes the organisation's standards. Examples are legal requirements, Audit Commission standards, processing times, accuracy rates, product outputs and quality of care standards. The organisation should show how these standards reflect the needs, expectations and rights of people who use the service, including how they are consulted.

Examples of evidence are: service standards, for example standards for how quickly the organisation responds to phone calls, letters and personal callers; reliability and punctuality standards; and commitments and standards relating to how staff serve customers.

Criterion 2: Actively engage with customers, partners and staff. Show the organisation: actively works with (engages with) customers, partners and staff to make sure it delivers high-quality services; consults and involves present and potential customers of public services, partners and staff; is open, and communicates clearly and effectively in plain language and in a number of different ways; and provides full information about services, their cost and how well they perform.

Sub-criterion: Consulting customers, partners and staff is a central part of the organisation.

What the assessor is looking for: People are consulted in a variety of ways, and regularly review these to make sure that the results are effective and reliable.

What counts as evidence? This is listed.

There then follow much more in the same style; criteria and sub-criteria and what counts as evidence. It is a very detailed set of instructions that prescribe what to do and describe what the assessors are looking for, establishing normative criteria as to what counts as evidence.

Extracted/adapted from Cabinet Office (2003b).

general roll-out across the public sector, was launched on 7 April 1998. As seen from the section above, it has been incorporated into much of the Best Value initiative and agencies (both national and sub-national) are expected to build it into their approach to day-to-day responses to customer demands. The programme seeks to:

- bring the benefits of the Excellence Model to the notice of public bodies;
- encourage all parts of the UK public sector to conduct self-assessments against the Model;
- assess their current overall performance and the reasons for the level achieved;
- identify those areas of their internal operation where improvement will have the greatest impact on their ability to meet their targets;
- help them share best practice systematically with each other, with the private sector and with government bodies in other countries. (Cabinet Office, 2003d)

Ministers view it as 'a means by which particular aspects of performance can be identified where a large proportion of agencies are under-achieving and where a central initiative may be appropriate in order to improve the general level of service provided' (Cabinet Office, 2003d).

From April 1999, the model used has been the preferred adaptation of the BEM, known as EFQM, after the European Foundation for Quality Management that developed it. It is now used by private sector organisations in Europe as a technique which assists organisations to identify both their strengths and those areas in which they need to improve, with organisations conducting a self-assessment against the Model and then developing an action plan to make improvements (Massey, 1999). It may be argued, however, that the voluminous paperwork containing guidelines, principles, protocols, indicators, examples, and targets are the best indicators about the nature of this new-found concern for the consumer. It is not about citizen emancipation, it is more about control.

This is the control over public servants and their organisations, activities, budgets and performance by ministers and a small cadre of very senior civil servants (Dunleavy, 1985, 1986, 1989). By enlisting the consumerist logic of NPM, a de-professionalising and management-centred version of individualism, ministers and their advisors sought to control the producer-dominated welfarist hierarchies of old. But the irony here is that they have substituted one version of public sector organisation antithetical to consumer control for another. As was noted in a previous section regarding contracts, what the reforms actually achieve is to remove clear lines of command and control and substitute them with an altogether more amorphous situation – a process of governance, rather than a clear span of government. Some observers have noted that the Best Value approach is akin to, indeed conforms to, a Total Quality Management (TQM) approach (Boyne, Gould-Williams, Law and Walker, 2002). Such a situation does not facilitate the participation of 'citizen-consumers' in policy making. Indeed, there is no real attempt to define just who these consumers actually are in most circumstances, beyond a risible scramble to identify 'stakeholders'.

This is not to completely decry all the attempts to discover citizen preferences, concerns and requirements and where possible to build these into the process of policy formulation and service delivery. But it is a stunted form of participation. For example, the *People's Panel*, established in 1998, used a panel of 5,000 members of the public over the age of 16, randomly selected to represent the population of the UK in terms of gender, age, religion and a range of other demographic indicators, to assess 'what people want and consult and work with people rather than impose solutions' (March 2000, p. 4). By January 2002, when the panel was wound up, the government held the view that 'government departments and agencies have improved greatly in their efforts to consult their customers and to assess satisfaction with the services they provide' (*People's Panel*, 2002a). The examples given above regarding the requirement to consult in the Charter process and Best Value programme are evidence of this. But consultation and market research carried out by pollsters does not equate to participation or to a more popular form of governmental policy making. The findings in no way bound the government to any set of policies, or indeed did anything more than 'inform the ministers' collective mind'. The straightjacket imposed by other aspects of managerialism – targets, performance criteria, inspection and regulation regimes – all militate against a more free-ranging and devolved form of politics and public administration. These issues are returned to in more detail in the next chapter.

Conclusion

In the twentieth century, one of the reasons for establishing the old welfarist hierarchies was a perception of market failure in certain areas and the need for government to intervene. Their dismantling in recent decades was a result of the perception of government failure

(Jackson, 2001: 21). The difficulties of seeking to leaven both market failure and government failure with a move towards consumerism in the public sector is that consumerism, as defined through the Best Value process, is flawed. In that:

- value is subjective;
- value is perceived by individuals and will vary according to individuals' tastes;
- different individuals will experience different access costs;
- perceptions of value for money will be influenced by ability to pay (Jackson, 2001: 21).

Certainly local authorities prefer the Best Value approach to that of CCT, in that it is less centrally controlled in detail and allows more discretion to respond to local needs and demands (Martin, 2000: 224). As such, it has returned a measure of autonomy to sub-national government. But it is autonomy to officers and providers, not necessarily to consumers. As research in NHS primary care trusts has demonstrated, 'there is a dearth of information about what kinds of services users are demanding and what benefits they are seeking. Lay consultation and representation on committees appears to be a poor substitute for systematic consumer research' (Sheaff, Pickard and Smith, 2002: 450). The TQM approach to modernisation is imposed from the top down and attempts to include citizen/consumer participation severely restricted and constricted within closely defined boundaries. The issues for accountability this elicits are discussed in Chapter 8.

There is no evidence available to demonstrate that consumers are any more empowered under the new structures. There is no evidence to demonstrate that the new structures are necessarily more efficient, effective and dynamic. Indeed, as was noted above, it may be that the efficiencies perceived and detected by organisations such as the NAO are the result of technological and organisational changes that were in any case being implemented as a result of other dynamics. What has occurred is a move towards accountability through accountancy, the mechanistic imposition of an arid regime of 'bean-counting' performance measurement and government through regulation. It is to this we now turn.

7

Performance Measurement

Performance measurement lies at the heart of public sector management, especially with regard to new public management. Many aspects of public management, such as contracts, regulatory oversight and organisational review, depend upon a comprehensive performance measurement system being in place for all public sector organisations. It is the spinal cord along which NPM's values are transmitted. Prior to the establishment of a comprehensive performance measurement regime, the public sector frequently operated using inadequate accounting methodology. No one really knew how much government activities cost. Indeed, no one knew how much it cost to deliver individual public services or even how much it cost to build large public sector construction projects such as electricity-generating power stations (Massey, 1988: 93).

It is staggering to realise the depth of the ignorance within government regarding costs and outputs prior to the 1980s. For example, the Central Electricity Generating Board (CEGB) that was responsible for generating electricity in England and Wales was established under the 1958 Electricity Act that set up the structures of the UK's nationalised electricity industry. It was dominated by engineers; the members of the board and all senior managers were engineers, or people with an engineering background and they made decisions based solely upon intended (engineering) outputs and they outcomes. That is, the corporation operated, along with other nationalised industries, a rather crude 'cash-box' approach to costs.

Throughout the 1960s, when there was a concerted effort by the CEGB to develop generating capacity based on coal, oil and nuclear power stations, the true costs of building each type were not known, and neither was there any attempt to control construction costs. Construction companies, who took it in turns to 'win' contracts, operated a 'costs plus' policy in that they were paid whatever the power station cost to build plus a level of profit (Massey, 1988). Given there was no incentive to build efficiently, effectively and to time, the budget and time overruns were excessive and wasted public funds. This pattern of behaviour was repeated throughout the public sector. It was not until the late 1970s that any effort was made to assert the kind of financial and accounting regimes common to the private sector (Massey, 1988). This was not an isolated phenomenon limited to construction and large-scale projects. Sir Derek Rayner, Mrs Thatcher's efficiency adviser, was shocked to discover upon his appointment, that not only were the costs of individual services unknown, but until the 1980s no one had thought it important enough to investigate how much it cost to run departments of state (Massey, 1993; Carter, Klein and Day, 1992). The true costs of government were not known and there was no existing methodology to calculate them accurately. The incremental approach to budgeting had hardly progressed since the days of Gladstone, consequently planning and audit operated in a fog of ignorance.

All this was to change and the method employed to enforce that change was the imposition of a regime of performance measurement. In this chapter we revisit some of the questions raised by Carter, Klein and Day (1992) to explore: What is performance measurement? How do we locate it in context? What is its purpose and who uses it? Are performance indicators (PIs) tools to control managers or tools of control for managers? First, we explore the nature of performance measurement, discussing the models used and the background and context of its development. We then discuss the developments that have occurred under the *Modernising Government* agenda of the Labour governments elected since 1997, before making the links between performance measurement and the new regulatory regime imposed upon the public sector in recent years.

What is performance measurement?

Background

Like so many of the initiatives, projects and programmes that have been discussed in this book, the use of PIs was announced in the Financial Management Initiative (FMI), circulated to government departments on 17 May 1982. The subsequent chronology is as follows (adapted from NAO, 2001: 57):

- **1982**, *the Financial Management Initiative*. The Initiative introduced the monitoring of objectives and performance indicators covering efficiency and productivity for all government departments.

- **1988**, *the Next Steps Initiative*. Executive Agencies required to report their performance against ministerially set targets covering the volume and quality of services, financial performance and efficiency.
- **1991**, *the Citizen's Charter Programme*. This required those parts of central government that deal with the public to publish, monitor and report against quantifiable standards of service.
- **1998**, *the White Paper, Modern Public Services – Investing in Reform* (Cm 4011). This set out the results of the Comprehensive Spending Review and contained a restatement of departmental objectives in line with governmental priorities.
- **1998**, *the White Paper, Public Services for the Future: Modernisation, Reform and Accountability* (Cm 4181), set out Public Service Agreements (PSAs) for each department and some cross-cutting areas, showing their aims and objectives and the progress they are expected to make.
- **1998**, *the Charter Programme is re-named Service First* and given a new emphasis to promote quality, effectiveness and responsiveness and the need for service providers to adapt in order to deliver services across sectors and different tiers of government.
- **1999**, *the Modernising Government White Paper* (Cm 4310) is published and reinforces the role of Public Service Agreements. It emphasises the shift to outcome measures and encourages the link between organisational and individual objectives.
- **2000**, *the Wiring it Up, Cabinet Office report* recommends the extended use of performance indicators to tackle the weaknesses in the handling of issues that cross departmental boundaries.
- **2000**, *the Spending Review* again reiterates the use of PSAs and makes PIs inherent to them.
- **2000**, *the Statistics Commission is established as an independent body*. Part of its remit is to measure progress against PSA targets.

The impact of the FMI's announcement of 'a general and co-ordinated drive to improve financial management in government departments' has been likened by some commentators to the storming of the Bastille (Carter, Klein and Day, 1992: 5). The FMI's authors announced it would seek to achieve its goals for each department through 'a clear view of their objectives; and assess, and wherever possible measure, outputs or performance in relation to these objectives' (Carter, Klein and Day, 1992: 5). With this dry statement was launched a regime that has annually gathered momentum, generating projects and initiatives in abundance.

There had been earlier initiatives, or attempts to introduce performance measurement and some element of planning into the public sector. Nearly all of these were American in origin and borrowed heavily from US business schools. The first- and in many ways most successful – of these was Planning Programming Budgeting (PPB), taken from the Rand Corporation via the US Department of Defense (Carter, Klein and Day, 1992: 7–10; Dunsire, 1972). This system was replete with objective setting and evaluation systems, grounded in a Taylorist belief in rational or scientific management. It encouraged departments to produce an explicit examination of outcomes. The British Ministry of Defence used it in a modest way in the late 1960s for planning, as did the Treasury, but in the form of output budgeting. It reappeared as an attempt at rational policy making across government in 1970 and was renamed Programme Analysis and Review by the Heath Government. It was retained, albeit in a diminished form by the Labour administrations of Wilson and Callaghan, being killed off by the imposition of cash-limited budgeting by the Treasury in the economic crisis of the late 1970s (Parsons, 1995).

Although PPB did not survive on either side of the Atlantic beyond the mid-1970s, it functioned as a trial run for NPM and as a training programme for those involved with recommending and shaping the new reform agenda. Britain's Fulton committee, which made a comprehensive set of recommendations to reform the civil service, was clearly influenced by the need to set objectives and measure performance, as set out in PPB manuals (Carter, Klein and Day, 1992: 10–15). At the time it was felt that the Fulton Report had been neutered by the civil service and sidelined by the government of the day, as it wrestled with yet another economic crisis. It became obvious through the 1980s, however, that many of its recommendations, albeit in an incremental way, were contained within and implemented by NPM (Massey, 1993). The FMI in particular owes much to the concepts underpinning PPB and the belief in a strong rational management of organisations, responsive to its customers.

As noted in the previous chapter, there was a growing realisation that if government costs were to be controlled and policy outputs properly targeted in terms of citizen/consumers, then the performance of government organisations needed to be measured. Carter, Klein and Day (1992: 20) observed:

> Following the Financial Management Initiative, performance indicators did indeed multiply. In 1985 the annual Public Expenditure White Paper contained 500 output and performance measures. In the two succeeding years, the figures rose first to 1200 and then to 1800. And by the time that the 1988 White Paper was published, the PI explosion had been such that no one was counting any more.

Early attempts to establish and evaluate PIs had been deemed a success by the Treasury and by 1987 their onward expansion and progress was assured (Durham, 1987). But there were evolving models, or types of PI each with a different emphasis and purpose. It is to these we now turn.

Models

Performance measurement is replete with difficulties. There are problems of quantifying qualitative data such as that pertaining to quality issues and public satisfaction. There are other problems in attempting to compare dissimilar services, and outputs, or to compare inputs with outputs, efficiency with effectiveness and so on (Carter, Klein and Day, 1992: 25–34; Flynn, 1990: 98–113). These issues need to be addressed by policy makers before they establish a performance measurement regime in either the public or private sectors, central or local government (Rogers, 1990; Rashid, 1999). In particular, there needs to be an awareness that what is measured and for whom it is measured, may change – indeed, *will* change – over time. For example, early PIs were developed purely as management (or Treasury tools). Later PIs, especially those developed under the Labour governments that have been elected since 1997, have switched emphasis emphatically towards populist indicators, such as league tables of schools, universities and hospitals, that are aimed at the public in their role as citizens/consumers. In other words, they are used to measure (and report on) the delivery of services and use quality indicators to indicate whether the intended outcomes of policy decisions have been achieved.

Terms and concerns

The notion of performance measure has been developed from the practice and profession of accountancy, which is itself often more akin to art than science (Carter, Klein and Day, 1992: 28). In borrowing terms and usage from the private sector, first attempts to reconcile private sector motivation with maintaining profit levels with public sector efficiency gains were misleading. It may be argued that:

> Even at the level of the firm in the market sector, the common belief that profit is a satisfactory PI presents a misleading picture. The accounts raise questions but do not answer them. (Vickers, 1965)

> To imagine that profit figures are a mechanical product is to ignore the fact that accountancy is one of the creative arts. (Carter, Klein and Day, 1992: 28)

Issues of profitability require comparisons with competitors and return on capital as well as planning for future growth and market share, for example short-term profit may be boosted at the expense of quality and result in long-term decline (Carter, Klein and Day, 1992: 28).

PIs must reflect the ownership and role of the organisation being measured and also its size and composition. For example, the simple, even crude notions of public or private ownership, trading or non-trading status previously used are of limited use. The PIs also need to take account the nature of the staff employed – for example, whether they are professionals used to exercising a degree of discretion and operating within bounded autonomy, such as lawyers and doctors. Or whether they are lower-grade clerical or administrative officers trained to follow rules and regulations of the kind found in traditional welfare hierarchies. Very complex organisations, such as the NHS, consist of large numbers of both kinds of employees. In this way the performance measurement takes account of an organisation's complexity and heterogeneity (Carter, Klein and Day, 1992: 33). With the development of the PFI and PPPs, the privatisation of monopolies and the delivery of public services through NGOs, the sheer complexity of governance within the differentiated polity means that measurements of performance have to reflect this plurality (Rhodes, Carmichael, McMillan and Massey, 2002). This makes it even more important to discover the costs of different inputs and the value of outputs. Proper – or at least informed – budgetary planning cannot progress without it and this has an impact across the public sector; from calculating GDP and the proportions allocated to the public sector, through to individual programme and project planning. But the complexity of modern governance, combined with the requirement to understand its costs, does not necessarily mean that performance indicators have to replicate that complexity. They can reflect it without replicating it and adding to the burden of delivery. Sophistication of measurement may be obtained through an elegance of simplicity, a point that we will return to later.

Some organisations operate within a competitive environment, some do not, but PIs must increasingly benchmark against best practice elsewhere, while reflecting the different kinds of accountability encountered throughout the public sector. Public services are accountable to ministers and through ministers to Parliament, but they are also legally accountable to the courts and also increasingly accountable to their customers, as discussed in the preceding chapter. Herein lay some problems for those measuring performance. Take the example of the Prison Service. In measuring its performance, there is a need to take account of the consumers, but just who constitute the consumers: the prisoners? The staff? the victims of crime, or society generally? Or are the customers all of these groups, each with their contradictory claims upon the service? Furthermore, an organisation's local environment often has an impact on its performance, one that is beyond its control. An obvious example is the impact of his or her social background on a child's performance at school. A school's catchment area is therefore crucial in how it performs within its area's league tables, with middle-class areas often (but not always) starting with a built-in environmental advantage (Carter, Klein and Day, 1992: 32). Therein lies the paradox of performance measurement and the need for creative accounting.

The terms used in performance measurement reflect these and other concerns. They illustrate the effort made to measure different aspects of performance and demonstrate that measurement to different audiences, comprising ministers, Parliament, consumers/citizens, the media, managers, the members of staff, and so forth. In this respect we can simplify the dynamics of performance measurement to just four questions:

1. Why do we want to measure these things – that is, what is the purpose?
2. Who are the measures for – that is, who is meant to use them?
3. What is it that we want to measure – what characteristics of performance are important?
4. How are we going to measure – what is our methodology for collecting, analysing and presenting data and is it robust and trustworthy? (Rogers, 1990: 45)

In this context, therefore, performance management may be seen as:

A means whereby accountability for contributing to the organization's strategic and/or operational objectives is allocated to employees and where these contributions are measured objectively. The outcomes are thus used to inform decisions about further objectives and needs of the organization and its employees. The outcomes must match what members want, introduce or reintroduce a performance culture and improve quality of service to customers. (Rashid, 1999: 19)

The terms used in performance management ascribe a special meaning to certain words. These are explained in more detail in Box 7.1. A key challenge faced by the performance measurement regime in the United Kingdom as it has developed has been to reconcile organisational goals

---

Box 7.1   Performance measurement concepts and terms

1. *Aims*. General outcomes to be achieved through actions or activities.
2. *Objectives*. The specific overall impact that is to be achieved by undertaking specific actions or activities.
3. *Targets*. Special tasks that need to be achieved over and above routine work.
4. *Inputs*. These are the resources used to deliver a service and may include money, staff time, buildings, equipment and consumables (like paper and photocopying, or more expensive items such as medicine and laboratory materials).
5. *Outputs*. These are the activities of the service or the benefits provided and may include things like patients treated, pupils taught, university degrees awarded and so forth.
6. *Outcome*. This refers to the impact of the service, 'healthier or more knowledgeable individuals, a safer society and so on' (Carter, Klein and Day (1992: 36)).
7. *Prescriptive PIs* are those that are linked to objectives or targets and are used to monitor progress towards their achievement (Carter, Klein and Day (1992: 49)).
8. *Descriptive PIs* simply record change, they provide a map rather than a prescribed route to the targets (Carter, Klein and Day (1992: 49)).
9. *Proscriptive PIs* specify things that should not occur in a well-run organisation, these are often found within those institutions dominated by a 'quality' regime.
10. *Economy* is the relationship of an outcome to a base using comparisons, for example standards, estimates, and forecasts.
11. *Economy* is the relationship between inputs and outputs with the goal of minimising inputs and maximising outputs.
12. *Benchmarking* is the process of measuring an organisation's performance against others that may be recognised as excellent or 'best in class'.
13. *Performance indicators* then are yardsticks, or guides used to assess the achievements of the results, they should cover both objective and subjective aspects.
14. *Performance measures* are used to quantify objectives and to assess achievement. They give an 'index of achievement and act as a judgement aid to consistency and fairness' (Rashid (1999: 20)).
15. *Social value* is the impact an activity or service has in terms of its contribution to qualitative aspects of society such as equity, opportunity for all and environmental issues. It is, as the preceding chapter showed, inherent to Best Value reviews.

Adapted from Rashid (1999: 19–20); Carter *et al.* (1992: 34–9).

with those of citizens, especially where the latter's aims have been inchoate or contradictory.

Often, of course, this is an attempt to reconcile the irreconcilable, nonetheless, governments have persevered in their efforts. The use of popular, or populist, consumer PIs such as through the use of league tables – especially time-series tables showing improvement or recidivist tendencies – have been attempts to achieve this. Records of targets achieved or missed often fit into these tables or are published separately. An example in 2001 was the setting by the Scottish Executive of maximum waiting times for NHS patients in priority areas such as heart disease and cancer to be treated (www. Scotland.gov.uk/news/2001/08). In the NHS, education and local government, league tables comparing like with like across the nation are now as eagerly awaited as the first cuckoo in spring, albeit with contradictory amounts of loathing and pride, depending upon the perspective of the observer. When it came to power with a modernising agenda in 1997, New Labour sought to build upon the performance measurement regime and to incorporate it into its approach to reforming the public sector. It is to these recent developments we now turn.

Further developments within the 'modernising government' agenda: public service agreements and service delivery agreements

As was discussed in the preceding chapters, there was a seamless transfer from the Conservative government to Labour so far as NPM was concerned. Labour took control of the levers of power and quickly realised that of those that were actually connected to the machinery of government, rather than performing a more ceremonial or ritual function, the performance measurement regime was among the most effective. In part this also reflected the conversion of the higher ranks of the civil service to an acceptance of the utility of NPM for exercising control over the federal sprawl of Whitehall, it especially reflected the efficacy and adaptability of performance measure as a managerial tool of control (Dunleavy, 1997). This section will explore in more detail the practical ways in which that has been developed, especially in the guidance given by the NAO, as it moved to assess the government's reform programme, an assessment moreover in its own NPM image.

The NAO took as its lead the government's own position regarding PIs and public service agreements within each department and agency.

It argued:

> Performance measurement is an integral part of modern government.
> It stands behind the creation of targets, contracts and agreements that
> control service delivery. Good performance information can help
> Departments to develop policy, to manage their resources effectively,
> to improve Departmental and programme effectiveness and to report
> their performance to Parliament and the general public, so promoting
> accountability for public resources. (NAO, 2001: 1)

Public Service Agreements (PSAs) were to become the mechanism for
achieving this. Introduced by Chancellor Gordon Brown in the
Comprehensive Spending Review of 1998, PSAs are a 'clearly stated
commitment to the public (and specific stakeholders) on what they can
expect, and each agreement sets out explicitly which Minister is accountable for delivery of targets underpinning that commitment' (Massey,
2002: 37). Furthermore:

> Public Service Agreement targets should flow from the Government's
> overarching themes and Departmental objectives. A good target not
> only demonstrates the achievement of a Departmental objective, but
> also encourages appropriate behaviour by staff in the organisations
> delivering the relevant services. (NAO: 2001: 2)

In other words, the government was now looking to establish 'intelligent' targets – that is, those aimed not only at achieving goals, but
intended to actually change the way in which people behave in order to
positively influence outcomes. Part of this process includes a regular
audit that assesses whether each organisation meets those targets. Each
PSA is supposed to contain:

1. A statement of who is accountable for its delivery.
2. The department's main aim, providing an overarching summary
   of objectives.
3. The department's objectives, the 'bold aspirations of what it hopes
   to achieve'.
4. Performance targets for each objective. 'These should be SMART –
   Specific, Measurable, Achievable, Relevant and Timed'. (NAO,
   2001: 1)

From this base, performance measurement is set to proceed.

Since the Comprehensive Spending Review of 2000, PSAs have been underpinned by new Service Delivery Agreements that begin with an accountability statement making clear who is responsible for delivering targets. It explains:

- How high-level targets will be achieved.
- How performance will be improved.
- How stakeholders' and consumers' needs will be met.
- How human and IT resources will be managed to achieve change. (Massey, 2002: 37)

The NAO's 2001 document, *Measuring the Performance of Departments*, goes into some detail as to how departments may go about this business, after noting that despite years of increasing numbers, an attempt to reduce the burden of audit has at last resulted in a reduction in the number of PSAs (NAO, 2001: 1). More recent PSAs have been reoriented away from the specification of outputs for public services, such as the number of operations carried out within a particular hospital, towards desired outcomes, such as improved life expectancy (NAO, 2001: 1). The use of SMART and 'intelligent' targets is one way this has been attempted.

To this end recent performance indicators have been established that fall into three main groups (NAO, 2001: 3):

1. The specification by government of overarching objectives that apply across all departments, such as that for the promotion of sustainable development. An example is provided by the (then) Department of the Environment, Transport and the Regions which created a set of sustainable development performance indicators on which all departments could draw – and which have been reflected in 12 of the 17 departmental PSAs.
2. Key government priorities such as reducing drugs misuse, unemployment, poverty and crime led to the creation of cross-cutting PSAs which provided shared objectives and targets for these policy areas. This approach facilitated the articulation of priorities through a few shared targets and encouraged joint working.
3. Where different targets overlap there is the opportunity for a shared target. An example is debt reduction for heavily indebted poor countries shared between the Treasury and the Department for International Development.

In setting these targets public sector organisations need to have a good understanding of the link between their activity and outcomes in order to minimise unintended effects or perverse behaviour and the unwanted skewing of performance as officials strive to meet targets and neglect other important areas of their work.

The performance indicators and benchmarking activities imposed upon the public sector have sometimes resulted not in improved performance, necessarily, but in an improved ability of public servants to play the game. In other words they alter their behaviour to score points under the new system. Loveday (2000: 215–37), illustrates this with regard to the history of performance measurement by police forces, in particular the use of crime data as an indicator of police effectiveness. He shows that in the 1960s and earlier many crimes were simply not recorded, as there was no way they could be solved. Officers found it was simpler to 'go through the motions' of taking a statement and then ignoring it when a safe period of time had elapsed. By the mid-1970s, however, public perceptions and fear of rising crime led the police to seek more resources. One way of galvanising the politicians into providing more resources was to emphasise the rise in crime:

> As a result, all crime was now logged and quite rightly much of it then logged as unsolved. Minor vandalism that used to be ignored now entered the crime statistics as a tidal wave of criminal damage. Saturday night fights, always a common feature of the English way of life and for most of history tolerated as some kind of youthful rite of passage, were logged as an unstoppable flow of assaults and crimes of violence. It worked, as by the 1980s the police were the recipients of massive investments across the UK. With the funding, however, came the requirement to illustrate efficient performance, especially after the miners were defeated and the Conservative Government felt strong enough to apply the NPM treatment to the criminal justice system. The police were expected to demonstrate all this money had led to improved detection rates. (Massey, 2001: 17–19)

One entrepreneurial way to achieve this, according to Loveday (2000), was to persuade criminals in jail to confess to a large number of crimes in return for favours of one kind or another. The more enterprising police forces had dedicated teams that spent a large amount of time in prison getting prisoners to confess to crimes. They confessed on occasion moreover to crimes that it is alleged they did not commit, or indeed were wholly fictitious; sometimes this resulted in detection rates that exceeded 100 per cent (Loveday, 2000: 226–9).

There is a greater irony than the obvious one to be seen here, in that research in the United Kingdom and the United States:

Demonstrates that police forces have very little impact on crime levels, except for public order offences. In (the UK) we have made the reduction of crime itself one of the performance indicators for our police forces yet it is abundantly clear that the police themselves have hardly any impact on this. Indeed most senior officers recognise this and have done so for very many years. It is social issues like employment, culture, family breakdown and the number of young men between the ages of fifteen and twenty-five that make the difference, not police on the beat or even higher detection rates, however they may be calculated. (Loveday, 2000: 215–37).

As in education, health-care and other parts of the public sector, we not only have an example in policing of performance indicators giving rise to unfortunate behaviour, they are often the wrong indicators in the first place. But instead of realising there are problems and seeking to assess ways to go forward with the co-operation and active participation of the professionals involved, those who set the performance indicators often behave like amateur cooks who have discovered spicy food. That is, if a little is good, but ineffective, then the answer must be to ladle in more and more. (Massey, 2001: 17–19)

A further problem for governments that produce a cornucopia of targets is that when those targets are not met critics may argue it is the government, not the public sector organisations that have failed.

By some estimates the key performance targets set by the government had grown to over 400 by 2003 (*The Independent*, 16 December 2002). Yet this obscured the many hundreds of PSAs and SDAs, which raised the number of individual PIs to well over a thousand. Each major area of government found itself constrained to operate within the performance regime. For example:

1. The Courts were set conviction rates that were unreachable and have had to be extended.
2. The NHS was set the target of cutting waiting lists by 100,000, and although met (with some interesting manipulation of the lists in some areas) the numbers began to rise again almost immediately.
3. Primary schools were set attainment targets that were clearly too high especially in those areas where it was hard to recruit teachers or there were serious problems of social deprivation.

4. Secondary schools; as with primaries, but with the added problem of truancy.
5. Higher Education was set the interesting set of targets that aim to increase participation to 50% of 18–30 year olds, while introducing a fee system, and seeking to maintain high standards with no substantive increase in central government funding. The more cynical observers may suggest these are incompatible targets. By the end of 2002 other areas with unmet targets included;
6. Street crime.
7. Fires in the home (reduction of).
8. Suicide (reduction of).
9. The Arts, targets to increase popular participation.
10. Sport; as with the arts.
11. Adoption; targets to increase the number of children adopted out of local authority care.
12. Child poverty (reduction of).
13. Treating offenders; targets to rehabilitate offenders, with the aim of turning them into ex-offenders.
14. Light rail use, targets to increase the number of passengers who use trams.
15. Car use (reduction of).
16. Animal disease (to prevent outbreaks of).
17. Voter apathy (reduction of).
18. Armed forces (increase in).
19. Third World Hunger (reduction of).
20. Global warming (measures to reduce). (Based on a list in *The Independent*, 5 December 2002)

On observing the above list one minister is reported to have admitted that in some cases setting targets 'was a substitute for having a proper policy', while the head of the prime minister's Strategy Unit conversely noted, 'It is very important that we understand that they are tools to support judgement: they are not substitutes for judgement' (*The Independent*, 5 December 2002). The NAO's view is that 'the format of targets can be varied so that they closely address the policy objective' (2001: 4). Yet this presupposes that the policy objective is clearly set. Where this is not the case there is the concern that 'targets may unintentionally create incentives for perverse or unwanted activity, or that they may create so tight a focus on targeted areas that no attention is paid to important but untargeted areas' (NAO, 2001: 4).

In order to assist departments and other public sector organisations in this task, the NAO has produced (as part of Annex 1 to the 2001 report) a list of 12 questions with a total of 42 subsidiary questions. The NAO believes this list is something 'Departments may wish to consider as they develop and implement their Public Service Agreement targets and measures' (2001: Annex 1, 10–12). There is not the room here to reproduce the entire list, but a small portion gives a hint of the full flavour:

Main question 1: Are performance measures underpinned by a clear understanding of how programmes and activities impact on desired outcomes?

Sub-question 1: Have the main influences on the desired outcome been clearly identified?

Sub-question 2 with three sub-sub-questions: Have departmental activities and performance measures been chosen with regard to:

   a.   The main influences on outcomes?

   b.   The motivations of people involved in delivering and receiving services?

   c.   The results of relevant research and programme evaluations? (2001, 10)

And so on over several pages of Annex 1. *Measuring the Performance of Government Departments* is a useful document not only because it provides such a useful guide to 'how to do performance measurement', but also because it provides a clear indication of the perspectives underpinning the performance measurement regime. The regime is a natural concomitant to NPM and is a manifestation of the policy makers' concern to oversee the public sector through a managerialist regime of comprehensive reach and influence; it is a ubiquitous tool of command and control. It is linked inexorably with a regulatory regime, designed to inspect and report upon the performance and quality of the public sector.

Regulation, regulation, regulation

The idea of a host of inspectors is not new: in 1920 the Fabians argued the British civil service should be divided into two, with half acting as inspectors and overseers and the other half as 'doers' engaged in executive work (Hood *et al.*, 1999: 19). Few took this idea seriously at the time, but for many contemporary public servants it has a certain resonance. Hood and his colleagues' mapping exercise for the period 1994–95 alone counted over 135 regulators employing over 15,000 people directly and spending between £700 million to £1 billion of their own budget (1999: 23). For those who are interested, the appendices of the report list these bodies and their functions. These are just the regulators that exist within the UK – if EU regulatory bodies are added, such the Court of Auditors, the sums multiply again. These figures, however, are simply the beginning of the process, in that most of the costs are not incurred by the regulators themselves; rather, they are incurred by those subjected to the regulation through compliance costs. These are notoriously hard to calculate, as they raise important counter questions as to what organisations would do in the event there was no regulation.

Costs of compliance are not routinely logged. Hood's study made an attempt to calculate the compliance costs for one inner London borough in 1995 in dealing with central government departments, inspectorates, ombudsmen, and local audit bodies. It came to no less than £1.8m per year (in 1995 figures). If that figure is extrapolated to all local authorities in England, taking account of their different sizes and functions, it produces a figure for 1996 alone of £173 million, or about 30p in every £100 spent by English local government. Further examples include OFSTED inspections of secondary schools, which, as far back as 1996, cost each school around £20,000 in expenses directly connected to each visit (not counting the mock inspections often launched by the local education authority in advance of a visit) (1999: 21; quoted in Massey, 2001).

It should also be remembered that in addition to the direct costs and the compliance costs there are lost opportunity costs. All the time public sector professionals are complying with the demands of the regulators they are not doing their proper jobs: the doctors and nurses are not on the wards, teachers are not in the classrooms, police officers are not preventing and detecting crime (Massey, 2001). Furthermore, regulatory agencies often insist on the construction of expensive and time-consuming quality or auditing structures within the organisations they are overseeing. Within higher education the Quality Assurance Agency has become adept at this kind of imposition, but similar examples exist throughout the public sector. The costs are borne by the taxpayer and the citizens as consumers.

Critics of NPM and regulation have focused on these costs, with Parsons (2000) being particularly scathing. In regard to the performance regime imposed upon British higher education, he has wryly commented that:

> Instead of giving rise to diversity and quality teaching and research the application of NPM in higher education will have produced uniformity, and the McDonaldisation of higher education; instead of facilitating experimentation and innovation it will have produced a mentality of compliance and playing safe and the covering of corporate backsides and copying what is deemed to be 'best practice'. History will record, I fear, that our benchmark in the British University system was not to be the plucky resistance of a Norway, but the systematic collaboration worthy of a Vichy.

And even more scathingly he has argued that:

> NPM is the nearest we have come in this country, for a few hundred years at least, to a kind of state religion. To question or deny its essential doctrines is to place oneself beyond the pale. To shout as it parades past that it is stark naked – that the emperor has no clothes – is to risk being bundled away or injected with a tranquilliser or sent to a gulag. (Parsons, 2000: 12)

Parsons' perspective expressed here is that of many of the professionals operating within the performance measurement regime demanded by NPM. It is clearly not the view taken by the NAO or policy makers intent upon ensuring their manifesto commitments are delivered within a 'modern' public sector.

For example, Grace argues that regulation is 'the modern idiom' and good regulation, such as that advocated by the NAO, seeks to actually minimise regulation per se and the concomitant 'bureaucracy' (2003: 74). Its aim, as manifested in the NAO and the Audit Commission, is to strengthen user focus through involving them in the process of audit and Value for Money (2003: 74–5). This perspective is not accepted by Cope and Goodship (2002), however, who argue their research on regulators, especially the Audit Commission, suggests that despite the intentions of regulators and policy makers the public, 'represents the excluded and forgotten dimension of public service delivery' (2002: 38). As with many of the PIs themselves, these perspectives are often irreconcilable and represent the opposing viewpoints regarding the implementation of the performance measurement regime within the UK's public sector.

Conclusion

We have argued elsewhere that many of the attempts at enforcing change and modernisation in the public sector have resulted in a kind of 'accountability through accountancy' (Massey, 2002). In this chapter we have shown how techniques developed within the profession of accountancy have been applied to the British public sector as part of NPM. This has led to the implementation of a performance measurement regime, a sub-set of which has been a new regulatory regime, overseeing the modernisation of government. The practice and process, although meeting with the support of both the Labour and Conservative governments responsible for its implementation as well as other elites within the political and administrative system, is not without controversy and remains deeply problematic. This reflects the fact that although often presented as an attempt to run services efficiently under the guise of neutral ideology-free managers, the approach is itself rooted in a Taylorist view of management and of human nature. Its attempt to make services accountable to citizens as consumers and to equip them, through the use of performance measures, with the ability to make informed choices also remains controversial. In the next chapter we discuss the issues of accountability arising from these reforms and attempts at modernisation.

8

Accountability

The concept of accountability lies at the heart of good government and public administration. Openness, transparency and effectively functioning systems of accountability are positive attributes of a healthy polity, while governing systems which are deemed to be unaccountable or lacking in accountability fail their citizens in important respects. Indeed, as Kenneth Kernaghan and John Langford pointed out in their classic study of the subject, accountability is 'an enduring value, not only in government but in society generally', in the sense that all people have a vested interest in ensuring that those who exercise power over them, or on their behalf, are held properly accountable (Kernaghan and Langford, 1990: 160).

In this chapter, we shall attempt to view accountability through the prism of modernisation and the new public management. Having set out some of the main themes and issues associated with the concept of accountability, the impact of these developments in this sphere will be assessed. We shall see that, although in some respects the new public management appears to have weakened the functioning of systems of accountability, and perhaps even created accountability 'gaps', in other senses the advent of new accountability regimes, under the mantle of modernisation and NPM, seems to have improved matters. It is certainly the case that the map of accountability has become increasingly complex in recent years. For the purposes of this chapter, regulation shall be considered as the use of a particular set of mechanisms, or agents, through the work of which accountability is to be secured.

Defining a concept: layers of accountability

On the surface, the concept of accountability is deceptively simple. However, closer examination reveals some of the complexities, facets and features of this key component of good government and public administration. From a process of simple analysis, multiple layers emerge: 'Accountability is a complex, fragmented and evolving concept within the British state' (Flinders, 2001: 16).

From the outset, we should be clear about what we mean when we use the term 'accountability'. There would seem to be some merit in drawing a distinction between 'responsibility' and 'accountability', although not all analysts take this view. For example, Woodhouse (1994) utilises the concepts of accountability and responsibility in an interchangeable fashion. However, this can lead to a certain degree of imprecision and even confusion, and an element of differentiation can be helpful. As we shall see, 'responsibilities' can be taken to refer to matters for which politicians and officials are to be held accountable.

Beyond this, the difference between 'answerability' and 'accountability' should be clarified. While some social scientists (see, for example, Hart, 1968: 264–5 and Leiserson, 1964) have been prepared to argue that the concepts are virtually interchangeable, others have countered by drawing a meaningful distinction between the two. Butler (1973) and Marshall (1986) see accountability as fundamentally stronger than mere answerability. According to these interpretations, answerability involves a commitment, on the part of office-holders (political or official), to provide answers to questions, and nothing more. Answerability, or, in the terminology used by Marshall, 'explanatory accountability', carries with it no liability for matters which may have gone wrong. Accountability, on the other hand, involves a commitment to provide answers to questions, and much more besides. Full accountability encompasses explanatory accountability or answerability plus a preparedness to amend the systems, processes or policies which have caused problems. Woodhouse (1994: 31) exemplifies this with reference to 'the installation of new procedures to prevent a repeat of the incident' (although she goes on to introduce an unnecessary complication by citing the disciplining of officials as a possible element of amendatory action – this properly belongs in the real of sanctions, discussed below).

Beyond amendatory accountability and mere answerability, the fuller version of accountability would also encompass a willingness to deliver redress of grievances in cases of proven error, plus the possibility of exposure to sanctions. The existence of sanctions, or negative consequences for the office-holder, is intrinsic to a full and meaningful concept of accountability. Woodhouse uses the concept of 'sacrificial responsibility' in place of sanctions, but this is misleading on a number of counts. First, she merges the meanings of 'responsibility' and 'accountability' in the manner we have already criticised as unhelpful. Secondly, the concept of 'sacrifice' implies a judgement about the innocence of the 'victim'. Finally, she discusses only one type of sanction, the most drastic – ministerial resignation.

Once the idea of sanctions is accepted as a facet of full accountability, we must take into account the role of the controlling agent or sanctions-holder. Importantly, not all agents or agencies of accountability are sanctions-holders. For example, although central government ministers are accountable to Parliament, and may face the prospect of sanctions being imposed upon them if they fail properly to discharge their responsibilities to Parliament, this does not mean that Parliament will normally be in a position to invoke sanctions. For these ministers, the effective sanctions-holder is the prime minister, who holds the power to displace, demote or dismiss ministers who have failed in regard of their responsibilities. In the same light, although civil servants are ultimately accountable to ministers, the effective sanctions-holders are their civil service superiors in whose power it lies to impose formal reprimands, financial penalties, demotion or dismissal.

To summarise, we can say that accountability has several layers, the first and weakest of which is answerability, or explanatory accountability. The stronger and more complete version of accountability adds to answerability the layers of amendatory accountability, redress of grievances and sanctions. These layers are set out in Box 8.1.

Modes of accountability

As we have already seen, academic analysts have adopted a range of different approaches in the attempt to come to terms with the concept of accountability. Here, we offer some comments on stewardship models, catalogues, the differentiation between internal and external accountability, a directional model, and accountability typologies.

Box 8.1 **Layers of accountability**

Answerability or explanatory accountability
Amendatory accountability
Redress of grievances
Sanctions

For some commentators, the meaning of accountability is closely associated with the idea of stewardship. Thus, Gray and Jenkins (1985: 138) see accountability as involving a liability to

> present an account of, and answer for, the execution of responsibilities to those entrusting those responsibilities. Thus accountability in intrinsically linked to *stewardship* ... Stewardship is established when one party trusts another party with resources and/or responsibilities.

These 'resources' and 'responsibilities' may be defined very broadly, to encompass 'the public interest' (Oliver, 1991: 23), or, more specifically, to refer to the duties and expected standards of conduct associated with posts or offices ('role' and 'personal' responsibilities, as discussed in Pyper (1996: 3–5)).

Other approaches to understanding accountability place less emphasis on the matters *for which* politicians and officials are said to be accountable, and instead stress the importance of the sources *to which*, and the mechanisms *through which* accountability can be achieved. At a very simple level, this can involve the production of catalogues of basic information. For example, ministers in central government are:

- Accountable for a series of both 'role' and 'personal' responsibilities.
- Accountable to Parliament, their ministerial colleagues collectively, and the prime minister in particular.
- Accountable through a wide array of mechanisms, including Parliamentary Questions, debates, select committees, standing committees, ombudsmen, external auditors (the National Audit Office), the courts, inquiries of various types, and party bodies of different descriptions.

In addition to central government ministers, it is possible to use similar catalogues to chart the accountability of civil servants, local government officers and members, or NHS managers and executives. Public sector managers, officials and office-holders of every type might have the key features of their accountability set out in this way.

Accountability catalogues are useful, up to a point. However, they are rather descriptive and raise additional questions. Consequently, analysts have tried to go further. One basic method adopted involves the identification of dual lines of accountability, external and internal, attached to each of which are specific mechanisms or devices.

Thus, external accountability can be seen to operate when politicians, managers or officials have to account for their roles to individuals or bodies beyond the confines of their own organisation or institution. This can be seen when, for example, ministers are held accountable for their departmental responsibilities to Parliament via a range of mechanisms including Questions, debates and select committees. In local government and the National Health Service, financial accountability should be achieved externally through the scrutiny brought to bear by the Audit Commission and Audit Scotland. External accountability might have the work of politicians as its major focus, and only touch upon the roles of officials in a secondary fashion, as is the case with the parliamentary mechanisms mentioned above. Alternatively, while the focus might be upon the ultimate accountability of elected office-holders, detailed scrutiny could be brought to bear on the roles of officials. This form of external accountability can be seen in action through the work of, for example, the ombudsmen (parliamentary, health service and local government), the agencies of external financial audit (Audit Commission and Audit Scotland), and the regulatory agencies which examine the functioning of public utilities.

Conversely, internal accountability operates within organisations or institutions and, at the level of central government, it can be illustrated with reference to a civil servant's accountability to departmental or agency line managers, up to the permanent secretary and/or the agency chief executive, and ultimately – beyond all of these – to ministers. A very wide range of devices and mechanisms are designed to bring about internal accountability, including systems of performance appraisal and review which deploy indicators, against which the efficiency and effectiveness of work can be judged. Internal financial accountability is almost a world of its own, within which we can see, for example, delegated budget and resource allocation systems which impose reporting and control procedures to cost centres which have delegated financial management powers.

Our knowledge and understanding of accountability can be taken beyond the use of these basic catalogues and broad classifications by making reference to the ideas of some key analysts. A directional model of accountability was posited by Elcock (1991). In this, accountability flows upwards, outwards and downwards. Officials or managers may therefore be 'simultaneously accountable *upwards*, ultimately to politicians, *outwards* to professional colleagues and *downwards* to citizens' (Elcock, 1991: 162). At one level, this would appear to be a fairly good way of looking at accountability. However, Elcock's approach is limited in important respects. He omits elected office-holders from his model, and makes it clear that he intends it to apply primarily to officials. This serves to minimise some problems of application, but only at the price of clarity. One illustration of this can be seen with reference to the accountability of central government ministers to Parliament. Should this best be described as *upward, outward or downward*? A rationale could be constructed for the application of any of these terms. The directional model's applicability to the position of managers and officials is also open to some questioning. Elcock argues that officials are accountable '*downwards* to citizens', but this is rather misleading because a strict interpretation of the constitutional position of civil servants must acknowledge that they are not accountable to the people and are accountable the people's representatives in Parliament only in certain clearly specified circumstances.

The more conventional approach taken by Lawton and Rose provides an alternative way of examining accountability. They categorise accountability by type: political, managerial, legal, consumer, and professional (1991: 23). Within this approach political accountability is viewed through the prism of the traditional concept of parliamentary accountability, which encapsulates both individual and collective ministerial responsibility. Although offering some interesting insights into the meaning and application of accountability, this type of analysis leads to two significant problems. Typologies of accountability have a tendency to make light of the tensions, contradictions and overlaps between the various 'types'. One illustration of this can be seen in local government, where a manager might be subject to conflicting strains of accountability – to senior managers and officers eager to secure tight budgetary control, and to the local authority's customers and clients for the speedy and efficient delivery of a service. Tensions and conflicts of this sort could be missed if we considered two of Lawton and Rose's types of accountability ('consumer' and 'managerial') on their own merits and in isolation. We shall return to this theme when examining the impact of the new public management on accountability. The same problem arises in relation to other configurations of this typology. Another deficiency of the typology approach to understanding accountability stems from limitations of scope. Regardless of the number of 'types' identified, it is usually possible to cite other types of accountability, which have been omitted. Lawton and Rose fail to 'type' popular accountability (see McConnell, 1996) and their neglect of ethical or moral aspects of accountability has also been identified (see Hinton and Wilson, 1993: 129).

The impact of modernisation and the new public management

Having established the importance of accountability as a feature of sound governance, defined the concept with reference to layers of importance, and discussed some of the issues and debates surrounding modes of accountability, we can now turn our attention to the specific impact which modernisation and the new public management has had on the notions and functioning of accountability in Britain.

New emphases

Accountability tended to feature in the developing literature of the new public management rather as an afterthought. However, as time passed, the proponents of NPM would occasionally attempt to attach a retrospective importance to accountability and, in effect, claim that enhanced accountability was a prime object of the exercise right from the start. A typical example of this can be found in the work of Hughes (1998).

To his credit, Hughes is much more attuned to the fundamentally political basis of public management than many other NPM commentators. He makes a simple but important point with admirable force:

> Whatever it is called – public administration or public management – the business of government is embedded in politics ... The political basis of the public sector is sometimes forgotten. (Hughes, 1998: p.225)

However, although Hughes stands apart from many other proponents of the new public management by virtue of his emphasis on the primacy of politics, he shares their tendency to oversimplify (to the point of distortion) the operation of pre-NPM accountability systems. In this chapter we have already seen that accountability is, and has always been, a multi-faceted concept. The subtleties and complexities of accountability, even within the so-called 'traditional' systems of government and public administration (note that even the use of language tends to exaggerate the all-embracing novelty of the new public management), are minimised. A rough caricature of accountability is sketched out, wherein ministerial responsibility is portrayed as almost the sole component of the system, and is seen to be a limited and flawed charade. From this, it is but one easy step to the conclusion that 'the perceived failure of the system of accountability under the traditional model of public administration' was 'a major reason for the adoption of managerialism' (Hughes, 1988: 234). The drive to enhance accountability was, according to this view of the world, 'a major factor' in the managerial reforms introduced by the Thatcher governments.

Even discounting the simplistic approach taken towards 'traditional' accountability, a detached observer would perceive two fundamental difficulties with all of this. In the first place, as we have seen in the preceding chapters of this book, matters of accountability featured dimly, at best, in the visions of those who led the charge towards the new public management. Instead, the major foci were on the achievement of 'value for money', 'quality' improvements to services and the adoption of micro-management techniques and processes derived from private sector practice. Even a cursory examination of the Thatcherite managerial reforms, epitomised by the Next Steps initiative which brought about a basic reordering of the civil service, shows how little thought was given to issues of accountability. In fact, the relative neglect of these issues led to some serious problems as the agencification programme was implemented. The problems and challenges created by NPM led some observers (see, for example, Flinders, 2001: chapter 1) to call for a refor-mulation, or 'reinvention' of accountability. Secondly, the evangelists for the new public management tended to be interested in quite specific but narrowly focused brands of accountability, often at the cost of neglecting other more potent forms of accountability.

If we accept that the general effect of the new public management and modernisation was to give increased emphasis to specific features of accountability, such as internal managerial and external 'consumerist', what were the relative advantages and disadvantages of this?

Positive features

The positive features of the types and forms of accountability empha-sised and encouraged by the new public management can be summarised with reference to four developments.

The first of these requires some detailed consideration. This was the enhancement of official accountability to Parliament through a series of changes which effectively led to the creation of a broader and, arguably, more meaningful concept of ministerial responsibility. It is important to recognise that these changes cannot be attributed solely to the emergence of the new public management. Indeed, it has been argued elsewhere (see, for example, Pyper, 1996: chapter 2) that the 'new regime' of parliamentary accountability which developed in the period from the mid-1960s owed its origins to a combination of key contributory factors. In simple terms, this 'new regime' saw the traditional mechanisms of parliamentary scrutiny (informal contacts, Parliamentary Questions, debates, standing committees, the Public Accounts Committee and the array of unco-ordinated and rather disjointed select committees) supplemented by the new, more systematic select committees (from 1966 onwards) and the Parliamentary Commissioner for Administration (from 1967). As they developed, these mechanisms came to offer a much wider range of parliamentary scrutiny over the executive than had ever existed before (Drewry, 1988; Gregory and Pearson, 1992). Although the new mechanisms were not flawless, the scrutiny was of a higher calibre and greater depth than that provided by the more traditional mechanisms in the past. However, undoubtedly the most significant contribution made by the select committees and the Parliamentary Commissioner for Administration (the Parliamentary 'Ombudsman') to the system of accountability was the enhancement of civil service accountability to Parliament. It was now possible to argue that, de facto, if not de jure, civil servants were becoming directly accountable to Parliament. What this meant was that although governments, and indeed constitutional purists, would not formally recognise that a constitutional change had taken place, in practice, in the real world, the functioning of the select committees and the Parliamentary Ombudsman had altered the relationship of accountability between civil servants and Parliament to the point where a much clearer and more direct line existed.

The investigations of the Parliamentary Ombudsman into cases of alleged maladministration set in motion a process of internal scrutiny within the affected government departments and agencies. This brought the attention of ministers and senior civil servants to the work being carried out by middle- to low-ranking officials. However, as well as strengthening the lines of internal accountability, the investigations brought about a limited but definite move towards the creation of external accountability of civil servants to Parliament. The Parliamentary Ombudsman acts as an agent of Parliament, and this meant that civil servants answering questions before him were effectively answering to Parliament. Similarly, the work of the select committees provided both improved functioning of internal lines of accountability (by ensuring that ministers and senior civil servants supervised the collection of evidence for the committees and the performance of their staff before the committees) and external accountability to Parliament. In spite of the restrictions of the 'Osmotherly Memorandum', which set out the rules governing appearances of civil servants before the committees and was a firm statement of constitutional orthodoxy, the practical involvement of officials with the select committees over the years was to have the general effect of enhancing their accountability to Parliament.

It might be argued, with some justification, that all of this predated the emergence of the new public management. However, one would not need to strain too much in order to perceive the influence of managerial approaches and perspectives behind, for example, the concept of the Parliamentary Ombudsman, with its prime emphasis on accountability for matters administrative and managerial. Nonetheless, to reiterate, the most important point to emerge from the establishment of the 'new regime' of parliamentary accountability concerned the creation of an increasingly meaningful civil service accountability to Parliament, even in the face of denial by successive governments and constitutional pundits. This de facto civil service accountability was to be further extended as a by-product of the reform which epitomised a key element of the new public management in British central government: the Next Steps initiative.

At an earlier point in this chapter we noted that a clearly developed understanding of accountability did not lie at the heart of Next Steps. Fundamentally, Next Steps was an attempt to bring about improvements to the management and delivery of services by means of structural change and the application of new managerial methods. The failure to think through the implications of this reform for accountability was to produce some serious problems, as we shall see. Notwithstanding this, it seems clear that the creation of a plethora of executive agencies under the Next Steps initiative was to have important implications for the accountability of civil servants (Pyper, 1995). The executive agency concept was designed to emphasis an explicit distinction between the policy-making and policy-execution functions of government (this is, of course, one of the lodestars of the new public management). However, in the real world these functions are simply not amenable to such clear-cut differentiation. In any case, it became clear right at the outset that ministers were not prepared to follow through to the logical consequence of such a policy-management dichotomy and make the civil servants who were to be based in the new executive agencies constitutionally accountable to Parliament for the management and operation of their agencies. Instead, the primacy of ministerial accountability was restated. Notwithstanding this, from its inception in 1988, Next Steps served to underline the significance of the developments in civil service accountability within the 'new regime' alluded to above (by emphasising that officials working in the new agencies would be subject to scrutiny by the Parliamentary

Ombudsman and the select committees) and also expanding the reality of official accountability to Parliament in an important respect. This expansion came in the realm of arguably the most traditional mechanism of scrutiny, Parliamentary Questions.

The Thatcher government, which had introduced the Next Steps executive agencies, was forced in stages to move away from its initial position that there were no consequences for parliamentary accountability and the doctrine of ministerial responsibility. The first move came when the agencies were actually established, and it was decided that Questions relating to matters of agency management or administration would be answered, not as in the past by means of ministerial replies published in Hansard, but by letters from agency chief executives to the MPs who had asked the Questions. The clear dissatisfaction of MPs with this arrangement led to a decision that all replies by chief executives would be placed in the library of the House of Commons. Continued concern on the part of MPs, who argued that even this arrangement was a poor replacement for the old system, led to the final concession by that government. This allowed for the publication of all chief executives' replies in Hansard – a clear break with the precedent that only government ministers could formally answer Parliamentary Questions in the official record of proceedings, and an obvious illustration of the emerging concept of direct civil service accountability to Parliament (despite the government disclaimers to the effect that only ministers were formally and constitutionally accountable).

The second positive development concerns the enhancement of internal lines of accountability, particularly in the realm of finance, to senior managers and ultimately to politicians. As we saw in Chapter 4, initially this was epitomised within central government by an array of developments, including devolved budgeting, later encompassed by the Financial Management Initiative. A further development of this brand of internal accountability would be seen in the growth of resource accounting and budgeting. This produced somewhat clearer and more open lines of accountability linking middle managers with senior officials and ministers. These trends were given further emphasis within central government under the Next Steps initiative. The internal accountability relationships between executive agencies and their parent departments were published in the Framework Documents, which established the basic rules of operation for the new agencies.

The third important development concerning the types and forms of accountability given emphasis by the new public management and modernisation saw an increasing stress placed upon grassroots accountability, to 'clients' 'customers' or 'consumers'. This was epitomised by the emergence of Charterism and the *Service First* programme, which we discussed in Chapter 6. The positive aspects of this development were related to its supplementation of more remote and attenuated types of accountability. However, concerns arose regarding the potency of the accountability systems produced by Charters, as well as the operational strains and constitutional contradictions produced by the emergence of direct official accountability to service users. Nonetheless, it can be argued that, ostensibly at least, the impact of Charterism (the flagship of which survived the change of government in 1997 and emerged in relaunched form as 'Service First') was positive. It obliged the providers of public services 'to engage directly with the question of service standard and service quality' (Falconer, 1996: 197) and created a system wherein public service managers are obliged to answer to service users for the performance of their organisations and for the use they have made of public resources. Other supplements to the traditional forms of accountability available through the mechanisms of representative democracy became particularly prevalent in local government. Stoker (2004: 16) notes that:

> Post-war local government rested on the overhead democracy model. That model relied on two linkages: citizens control elected politicians (electoral accountability) and politicians control bureaucrats (bureaucratic accountability).

Waves of new public management and modernisation led to a plethora of supplementary, citizen (or client/customer/consumer) based modes of accountability:

> accountability to service users through panels, committees, boards and discussion of forms of direct participation through citizen-initiated ballots or local authority or central government endorsed referendums. More broadly, there is a considerable emphasis on and growth in schemes for public participation and consultation that potentially cut across the simplistic linkages of the overhead democracy model ... Accountability directly to stakeholders involved in using services based in local communities of interest or geography is a much more accepted, indeed expected, part of local politics at the beginning of the twenty-first century than it was in the late 1960s and 1970s. (Stoker, 2004: 18)

The fourth important positive development was the emergence of new regulatory regimes in areas of public service which had, heretofore, experienced problematic forms of accountability, characterised by remoteness and imprecision. This could be seen most clearly in the public utilities – those charged with the provision of gas, water and electricity supplies and telecommunications facilitites (Pyper, 1996: chapter 5). The regulatory agency model was, however, extended beyond these spheres, eventually encompassing rail services and a myriad of public services and organisations.

It was in the realm of the public utilities that the most obvious improvements to accountability would be discerned – although it should be noted that the move away from the exiting accountability frameworks in these areas of the public sector was not uncontroversial. It is not our purpose here to examine the rationale for and specific manifestations of, the ownership changes introduced in the public utilities. It is sufficient to say that privatisation, that keystone of the managerialist approach to the problem of governance, swept though the utility sphere during the 1980s, resulting in the end of public ownership in the gas, electricity and telecommunications industries throughout the United Kingdom, and the advent of private ownership in water supply for England and Wales. While in the public sector, these utilities had been subjected to different regimes of accountability.

In Scotland, the water and sewerage authorities were closely integrated with local government. These services were administered and delivered through departments of local authorities. The accountability arrangements saw internal lines run from officers to members, with the elected politicians ultimately accountable externally to the electorate and central government through the normal range of popular and financial organs of accountability, including elections, the local ombudsman and the Accounts Commission. Privatisation of the water utility did not extend to Scotland. However, a restructuring exercise in 1996 saw the establishment of three new regionally based authorities. These quangos were accountable to the centre (initially the Scottish Office, then, from 1999 the Scottish Executive). This replaced one form of accountability, which had at least an element of localism, with another, avowedly based on centralism.

It might be argued, nonetheless, that in the other public utilities the post-privatisation systems of accountability, produced by a particular new public management and modernisation drive, represented an improvement on the former system.

The regional water authorities in England and Wales were composed of local authority nominees plus ministerial appointees. This led to an accountability hybrid, involving both local and central government. In the other major utilities, gas, electricity and telecommunication, the regime of accountability was framed around the nationalised industry or public corporation model. Within this, ministers accounted to Parliament for the work of their departments, and, in the case of a 'sponsoring department' for a public corporation, the minister's accountability included the work of the industry or public corporation. This theory was sensible enough, but, in practice, Parliament was unable to secure detailed accountability for the operations of the public corporations. Ministers would dodge scrutiny by refusing to provide Parliament with specific answers or data on grounds of 'commercial sensitivity'. Ministers would argue that managerial issues were none of their business, and they would often deflect questions in the direction of the boards on these grounds. At the same time, however, MPs found it virtually impossible to bring the board members to account, as they in turn were usually keen to argue that it was ministers who had ultimate responsibility. The key parliamentary mechanisms of scrutiny, Questions, debates, and the Public Accounts Committee, were not adequate for the function of bringing about ministerial accountability for these organisations. The sole dedicated organ of scrutiny, the Select Committee on the Nationalised Industries, could not cope with the challenge of securing detailed scrutiny of all of the public corporations. As a result, there were significant gaps in the accountability regime.

In this light, it seems sensible to conclude that the new accountability arrangements which were put in place when the utilities were privatised, although problematic in some respects, resulted in a net improvement. The legislation which privatised the utilities established new regulatory agencies which issued the operating licences to the commercial participants in the developing markets (or 'quasi-markets' where privatisation had not brought immediate competition), negotiated and then enforced the pricing formulae, obtained and published information helpful to the service users, and oversaw the systems for resolving consumer complaints. The regulatory agencies were non-ministerial government departments, headed by directors-general. Thus, the Offices of Telecommunications (OFTEL), Gas Supply (OFGAS), Electricity Regulation (OFFER) and Water Services (OFWAT) were established. OFGAS and OFFER were subsequently merged into a single energy regulator, OFGEM. Privatisation was therefore accompanied by the retention of a form of public accountability. While the locus of accountability had shifted away from Parliament, and the records of the regulators were variable (influenced by such factors as the approach of the director general, the scale of the utility being regulated, and the prevailing style of the utility's board of directors), the existence of these dedicated and specialised agencies in the sphere of each utility marked a clear improvement in the quantity and quality of accountability. Moreover, one of the key characteristics of a sound regime of accountability, transparency, was brought about through the work of the new regulators:

> the creation of the regulators has resulted in considerably greater openness than was the case under nationalisation, through imposing a form of external supervision which … did not exist previously … individual regulators have been, by the standards of British public bodies, exceptionally open in reaching some of their decisions. (Prosser, 1994: 255)

Negative features

The positive contributions made towards enhancing aspects of the system of accountability by NPM-inspired developments must be placed in context. It is clear that some negative effects were also felt. As one of the academic proponents of modernisation notes, 'complicated divisions of labour, the consuming impact of specific expertise, and the sheer scale and variety of government intervention make accountability a considerable challenge' (Stoker, 2004: 209).

Insofar as NPM led to the emergence of supplementary mechanisms and processes of accountability it deserves credit. However, in some senses at least, it appeared that NPM developments promoted certain types of accountability at the expense of others. In general, less importance was attached to certain traditional forms of popular accountability while increasing emphasis was given to accountability upwards to central government and to particular, and quite narrow, strains of accountability to 'consumers'.

One illustration of this came in the realm of the water and sewerage service in Scotland. As already noted, these were removed from the ambit of local authorities and reestablished as quangos accountable to central government. A more remote form of accountability was substituted for a localised one, and this was not adequately compensated for by the establishment of fairly toothless consumer councils. While there seemed to be perfectly sound managerial reasons for this reorganisation, it undoubtedly diluted a specific form of accountability. Curiously, although this was the single public utiltity to remain within the public sector (as we noted above, the others were privatised) the resulting framework of accountability was weaker than that which emerged through the use of regulatory agencies in water in England and Wales, gas, electricity and telecommunications.

Recourse to the use of quangos was not intrinsic to the new public management and modernisation. The use of appointed rather than elected bodies for a range of public functions was a well-established practice even as early as the 1970s. However, despite their rhetoric (which was replete with quango-bashing phraseology), the managerialist and modernising administrations of the 1980s and 1990s tended to create at least as many quangos as they abolished (see, for example, Skelcher, 1998; Flinders and Cole, 1999; Flinders and Smith, 1999). In part, this stemmed from the NPM penchant for pursuing divisions between matters of policy and administration or management – many quangos fitted quite neatly within this dichotomy. As we noted above in relation to the public utility regulators, the use of appointed rather than elected bodies does not invariably signify a dilution in accountability. Nonetheless, critics of the 'quangocracy' argue that even if detailed financial, managerial and other forms of accountability are strengthened through the use of appointed bodies, 'the key point (is) that these other forms of accountability (cannot) replace the need for collective accountability for the policy and resource allocations of these bodies' (Stoker, 2004: 43).

As we have seen, a clear trend within new public management approaches to accountability is the differentiation between forms and types of accountability, in order to give particular emphasis to such concepts as managerial and consumer accountability. To some extent, this stems from the predisposition of managerialists to compartmentalise public sector functions and operations into 'policy' and 'management'. As we argued earlier in this chapter, the attempt to make the concept of accountability divisible, through giving emphasis to supposedly distinct strands of political, managerial, consumer, and other brands of accountability, is inherently flawed and runs the risk of creating accountability gaps and vacuums. This is a general weakness inherent within the new public management approach to accountability.

Perhaps the clearest illustrations of the sort of problem this can cause came in the sphere of the executive agencies established under the Next Steps initiative. We have noted some of the positive aspects of Next Steps as far as accountability is concerned. However, there was also a downside. At the heart of the Next Steps approach there was an underlying assumption that there exists a reasonably clear dichotomy between matters of policy, which are largely the preserve of ministers, and matters of administration and management, which lie in the domain of the civil service. This implied a further clear distinction in the realm of accountability. In the main, the functioning of the executive agencies has not been problematic in this regard. In two high-profile agencies, however, these supposedly clear distinctions broke down and were shown to be severely problematic in terms of accountability. In the cases of both the Child Support Agency and the Prison Service Agency the chief executives struggled to maintain the distinction between matters of policy and matters of management.

Ros Hepplewhite, the first chief executive of the CSA, pursued the logic of Next Steps to its conclusion as she attempted to differentiate between her responsibility to account for the management and operation of the agency, and the accountability of ministers for the policy and legal framework within which the agency operated. To observers, however, the fundamental problem of the CSA was obvious. This agency had been created solely and specifically to implement a particular policy, framed under the Child Support Act, but this policy and the Act were both fundamentally flawed. The policy failings of ministers then became translated into the managerial failings of the agency, as it generated massive backlogs of work, repeatedly missed its performance targets and produced huge numbers of 'customer' complaints. Finally, as it became clear that the CSA had failed to meet even its revised targets and news broke that a team of management consultants was being sent in to review the agency, Hepplewhite resigned in 1994. This case provided a clear demonstration of the close interaction between matters of policy and management, and the serious consequences which can arise, in this case for a senior civil servant, when this is not fully recognised by ministers.

The themes were similar in the case of the Prison Service Agency, where running disputes broke out between the minister at the parent department (Michael Howard, the Home Secretary) and the agency chief executive (Derek Lewis, Director General of the Prison Service). Howard blamed Lewis for overall management failings which led to a series of high-profile escapes by prisoners from top security establishments, while Lewis attributed at least some of the managerial problems to ministerial policy and interference. In the end, Lewis was dismissed by his ministerial superior, although he successfully challenged this in court and won substantial compensation.

The Labour government which took office in 1997 attempted to redress the accountability problems arising in these cases (see Chapter 5). A medium- to long-term review process was put in place in the Child Support Agency, and its activities were more closely monitored by ministers. As a result of the review process, new internal reporting systems and a new formula for the calculation of CSA awards were introduced. Nevertheless, serious problems remained, and another CSA chief executive resigned in November 2004. Accountability arrangements for the Prison Service were immediately changed with the arrival of the new government in 1997. Home Office ministers reassumed full responsibility for accounting to Parliament for this prisons policy and management.

As Flinders (2001: 16) notes:

> the core tenets of new public management sit uneasily with ministerial responsibility. Despite the subtle reinterpretation of several aspects of the convention the attempt to reconcile devolved management with constitutional theory has proved problematic. Officials have been placed in a particularly invidious position, as their traditional anonymity has been weakened and responsibility deflected onto them, while their duty not to criticize their minister remains in place.

Structural changes such as agencification can have the effect of spawning complex accountability relationships. This phenomenon can also be seen in the local context, where the 'partnership revolution', a key feature of local government modernisation, has resulted in the emergence of an increasingly complex set of multiple interdependencies, which have hugely complicated the lines and processes of accountability:

> Partnerships are at the heart of local governance. These can be relatively informal, taking the form of networks. alternatively, they might be formalised contractual arrangements involving, for example, central government, local government and the voluntary and private sectors. Such partnerships help to overcome problems associated with the fragmentation of service delivery in localities; ideally, they integrate disparate services in the best interests of the consumer. Yet despite their advantages, there are frequently problems of coordination. Inter-agency networks are also seen by some as a threat to formal political accountability as appointed bodies gain influence at the expense of elected members. (Greenwood *et al.*, 2002: 135)

Partnerships proliferated under New Labour. It was estimated that by 2002 over 5,000 individual partnership bodies with a collective spending responsibility of over £4 billion had emerged at local and regional levels in the UK (Sullivan and Skelcher, 2002: 26–7). Over 300 multi-agency partnerships were set up in the policy sphere of crime and disorder, 500 as part of the 'Sure Start' scheme designed to aid the development of children from deprived families, 900 within the 'Single Regeneration Budget' programme aimed to revive deprived communities, and around 400 in the 'Local Strategic Partnerships' initiative which sought to develop and oversee a long-term vision of development for specified areas (Stoker, 2004: 161–2). Taken as a whole, these new bodies represented a major supplement to the traditional structures and processes of the public sector, particularly at local level, yet there seemed to be relatively limited knowledge and information regarding the bases and functioning of the partnerships, and the complex accountability relationships which resulted did not lend themselves to easy understanding or scrutiny.

We noted above that new public management's tendency to spawn many and varied strands of accountability, such as consumer accountability, managerial accountability, and so on, is not without some benefits. However, it is worth reiterating the point that these brands of accountability can become devalued simply because the new public management has created a set of overriding imperatives, including 'value for money' and 'efficiency', which have a tendency to relegate matters of accountability to a secondary order of consideration.

We must take care to offer a balanced perspective even in those spheres where it appears that the impact of NPM and modernisation upon accountability has been generally positive. One instance of this can be seen in the move towards enhanced accountability to customers, clients and service users within the Charterist and consumerist initiatives. As we saw in Chapter 6, charterism and *Service First* offers service users the chance to receive more information about the forms and standards of service they have the right to expect from should expect from public sector organisations. These initiatives also champion the production of straightforward and accessible complaints systems. The promotion of answerability or explanatory accountability is therefore intrinsic to these schemes. 'Putting things right' is a key principle which is built into the Charters. This symbolises a focus on redressing grievances and taking amendatory actions to ensure systems failures are not repeated. Despite all of this, however, it is clear that there are significant variations in the forms of redress available, and the weakest Charters fail to promise financial compensation to service users. The Charter commitments do not have legal force, and this means that service users who remain dissatisfied with the level of redress offered after successfully pursuing a complaint, have not further options available to them. Beyond this, the scope and extent of amendatory actions taken in order to avoid future recurrence of the same failing can also vary quite significantly, and these actions are not subject to any form of enforcement. To conclude, therefore, the Charters have had the effect of improving some weaker forms of accountability (answerability and the milder forms of redress) but they have been less impressive with respect to the stronger and more meaningful strains of accountability, including sanctions.

Within the developing 'consumerist' ethos, the concept of contractualism came to be closely associated with that of Charterism. Again, this was discussed in some depth in Chapter 6. Here, it is appropriate for us to note the general implications for accountability of initiatives such as compulsory competitive tendering, market testing, internal markets, purchaser–provider splits, and the Private Finance Initiative. Contractualism has had the effect of introducing additional organisations (the contractors directly delivering the service or facility) into the public service accountability relationships. This means that issues and questions arise concerning the accountability of those charged with direct delivery of the service, as well as that of the public sector provider – for example, a company holding the contract for a local council's refuse collection service, a firm responsible for an NHS trust's cleaning operations, or an in-house team holding the catering contract for local schools and colleges. The net impact is that an organisation charged with direct delivery of the service is not formally accountable to the service users, but to the contracting authority. In these circumstances, customers or clients who seek to secure redress for a deficient service have to approach the contracting body, which in turn will try to achieve redress from the contractor. While such arrangements might have the merit of keeping service costs under control and facilitating managerial modernisation, they are clearly less likely to secure the transparency, openness and efficient redress of grievances which are inherent to fully functioning and effective regimes of accountability.

In conclusion, it can be said that the impact of the new public management and modernisation on accountability has been mixed. In some respects, there would seem to have been a definite weakening of systems of accountability, largely caused by the creation of new imperatives (especially financial) which have come to override the importance of accountability. However, in other respects matters are not quite so clear, and the broad effect of the new public management in some spheres would seem to have been to enhance the functioning of systems of accountability. This can be seen especially in the advent of new and improved regimes of accountability in the realm of the former public utilities and the strengthening of civil service accountability (in some respects at least) brought about by the executive agencies and associated developments. As we tried to emphasise in the early part of this chapter, however, when dealing with questions of accountability much depends upon the use of specific terms, and the definitions of key concepts.

9

Conclusion: Recurring Issues in Public Management

In Chapter 2 we noted that the study of government, especially when it engages in asking fundamental questions, has historically involved some personal risk to the analyst. It remains true that in many parts of the world the life and liberty of political dissidents are often endangered. The precedence for this is an ancient one, for example in 399BC the Athenians put Socrates to death for asking fundamental political questions (Stone, 1989). Colonel Sidney, whose death in the defence of republican liberty we retold in Chapter 2, was one of those who paved the way for the eventual triumph of liberal democracy. But democracy is fallible because it is dependent upon the actions and intentions of citizens and their leaders for its continuing success. It is also dependent upon proper functioning institutions and the trust people place in those institutions; the rituals of governance and the rationality of policy making all play a part (Wynne, 1982). Policies often fail and citizens become disenchanted; voter apathy is seemingly *de rigueur* in many countries. Yet the alternatives, however they may be adorned by those who advocate them, are hardly attractive.

These are not trite observations to be shrugged off lightly. The kind of society that allows books of this nature to be written, that allows free citizens to question the role of the state and encourages those same citizens to exercise their right to the redress of their grievances is relatively new in historical terms and far from being universal. The study of public administration, public management, government and governance is the study of those institutions and procedures that nurture and protect citizens and their liberty. Conversely, it is also the study of institutions and procedures that may be used to deny that protective shield to individual and collective rights and in some states may be used to suppress the cultivation of a free and civilised society. It is the study, therefore, of the 'seamy side of politics' (Price, 1983).

171

It is so much more than a simplistic debate regarding the nature of the delivery of services, or whether markets are preferable to bureaucracies for implementing public policy. The study of public management is about fundamental notions of the role of the state and the place of the citizen in relation to the state. In this book we have attempted to ensure that we have explored the seismic changes imposed upon the public sector, while showing the reader some of the multiplicity of historical, theoretical, economic, cultural and political factors involved in those changes. Without an understanding of the broader context of the restructuring of institutions and procedures, the rules of the game, we cannot understand how and why things are the way they are, much less why some reforms and policies fail, while others succeed. Indeed, it is the context within which these things are located that defines 'success' and 'failure' and explains why some policies may be successfully transported to some polities and not to others.

In Chapter 2 we explored the different theories and perspectives regarding the role of government, governance and public administration. The discussion provided the academic, political, historical and cultural context in which the analysis of the succeeding chapters is located. Change in contemporary Europe, the United Kingdom and the United States, is situated within a milieu of organisational, constitutional and political complexity. This is the situation whether that change is formed from a drive for 'modernisation' or as a response to political expediency. In the United Kingdom, public sector management and governance are more easily implemented because of the non-statutory nature of much of the public sector, but even this constitutional anomaly, dating back to the feudal position of the civil service as an appendage of the Crown, does not guarantee the success of the policies once implemented. Indeed the hollowing out of the state and the differentiated nature of the polity ensures that many government policies are doomed to failure. This situation arises not because of a lack of commitment on the part of public servants, but because with power and authority ebbing away from London to Brussels, the devolved countries and amorphous power-brokers within the internationalised (or globalised) economy, the UK national government has lost the ability to impose its will through the hierarchical institutions of command and control. The modern world is immune to several of the techniques that an old-style national government may use to modernise itself. Much change therefore is imposed from outside, or rather, as we have shown, it is the result of external triggers forcing governments and institutions to respond to change elsewhere by changing themselves (Massey, 2003).

These events and the dynamics that propel them are understood and indeed motivated by different perspectives (or a priori views) regarding the nature of society and the proper relationship between the state and individuals. Many of these perspectives possess within themselves both a normative and an explanatory motive. By this we mean, they seek to explain how and why government works in the way it does, but they also seek to demonstrate the way in which government *ought* to work. The impact of these perspectives, and of the disputes between those who hold them, has formed the basis of much that has been discussed in this book. The English-speaking world has traditionally taken a more minimalist view of the role of the state, considering it to be a collectivity of institutions fashioned to deliver policies and services. From this perspective has grown the marketisation of state services and the managerialist reforms we have explored. It is a view rooted in a common law approach to government, one that includes an individualistic, but not necessarily egalitarian vision of society. Other approaches overlay or rest uneasily beside this perspective within the broader European tradition and they include a Weberian, hierarchical view; statist perspectives; Marxist perspectives; and egalitarian and communitarian perspectives. We have touched upon these where appropriate, and have sought to demonstrate the rich historical and political context within which modernisation and change are located.

In part, the struggle to modernise, change, review and remodel the public sector over such a long period – seemingly unceasingly – is a response by policy makers to the issues raised by the internationalisation of the policy process and the conflicts engendered by (amongst others), post-Fordist, post-bureaucratic principles of organising state and social institutions, technological advance and social exclusion. Often these problems are seemingly intractable, being the paradox of progress where professional and managerial interests clash with each other and with those of citizen consumers (Willis, 1995; McCourt and Minogue, 2001; Haynes, 2003). The search for 'stakeholder interests', 'citizen preferences' and responsive 'joined-up government' are reflective of this. It is not clear when these managerialist processes will be played out – indeed, Self plaintively asked at the end of his exploration of the politics of public choice: 'Can faith be restored in the capacity of democratic societies to solve their economic and social problems? Is better and more constructive government possible?' (1993: 262).

He concludes that:

Any measures to improve the performance of government will be fruitless without the reinvigoration of democracy itself ... The basic need is to affirm the importance of and increase the opportunities for responsible citizenship, not just through voting but through active participation in parties, local governments and interest groups ... The political process should be as open and transparent as possible. Civics should be rediscovered in a more realistic but positive way ... These reforms are quite practicable, but it is a tough task to rescue politics from its opposite tendencies towards apathy or extremism. The capacity of democratic societies to take charge of their affairs and to find more effective and equitable answers to their urgent problems remains very doubtful. (1993: 280)

Self's gloomy prognosis reflects his realisation of the problems and paradoxes of modern governance. Richards and Smith (2002: 285) partly echo this view about complexity (but without the obvious pessimism) with their comment that, 'During the last thirty years, policy-making has become much more difficult and complex'.

This appreciation of complexity led first Prime Minister Major's government and then more particularly the Blair governments to address the problems inherent to this by a 'two-pronged' approach:

First, it has rejected the 'corporatist solution' adopted by Labour governments of the 1960s and has instead embarked upon a strategy aimed at binding together different elements of society – government, the private sector, the voluntary sector, etc. ... Such a strategy is tactically astute, as Government can enjoy the plaudits where such initiatives are successful, and where they fail responsibility is shared. Second, the Blair Government has pursued a strategy of joined-up government. This is an attempt to resolve one of the problems of the governance era – fragmentation – by wiring the system back up together again. ... The future of public policy-making in Britain appears to be conditioned by the core executive attempting to resolve a dilemma: on the one hand it needs to meet the ever more disparate needs of an increasingly complex and diverse society while at the same time it wishes to maintain its status as the most powerful actor in the policy process. Resolving this dilemma will not be easy. (2002: 285)

This understated observation perfectly captures the difficulties of governance in an age of complexity, super-pluralism and a bewildering diversity of interests and mechanisms of service provision. This book has charted the ways in which different attempts to realise these ambitions have impacted upon public sector management.

Continuing trends and issues

A process of rolling reforms and 'modernisation' has beset the public sector for nearly three decades. Terry (2003: 1) has characterised the 1980s as:

> a decade of massive upheaval in the structures for delivering public services, with the creation of executive agencies in central government, privatisation of utilities, contractorization in local government and a renewed emphasis on better financial management and accountability. These reforms, subsequently characterised as the 'New Public Management', were essentially driven by beliefs about the importance of means rather than ends.

In other words, the argument ran that once the market mechanisms were effectively established there would be a trickle-down effect of benefits accruing to ordinary citizens. But it may be argued that such a view is overly simplistic and that competition proved to be short-lived in areas such as utility privatisation, whilst in other areas, such as the privately-run railways, debilitating market failures soon became readily apparent (Terry, 2003: 1–2).

The restrictive practices that were swept away by these reforms led to awareness, therefore, that the market required other types of interventions in order to protect against the natural tendencies of monopolists and other powerful actors to exploit their positions of strength. Accordingly, the 1990s became:

> The era of the rise of inspectorates and audit bodies, as many commentators have noted, and trial by media. In a public service culture that had become increasingly contract-driven, inspectorates were an appealing device. They provided a reassurance that those in government were still in control of the standards that mattered most to citizens and consumers. But they have proved a blunt instrument for improvement, and they represent a permanent bureaucratic overhead that can easily proliferate. Witness the experience of the Audit Commission: its budget has doubled since 1997 and there has been a near five-fold increase in staff since it was founded. (Terry, 2003: 1)

These costs are only part of the overhead ultimately borne by the taxpayer, in that every hour spent dealing with the often excessive demands of regulators and quality assurance agencies means an hour of lost opportunity to develop and deliver better services and meet the needs of citizens.

A concomitant to the regulatory and managerialist state is the downgrading of professional power and autonomy. Certainly, the government is dependent upon the knowledge and compliance of professional groups to deliver its policies; education and health policy cannot be delivered if teachers, doctors and nurses decide not to implement it. Indeed, the reluctance of sufficient numbers of people to come forward to train for some of these occupations and then having trained to remain in post is a continuing problem for policy makers. Quite simply, the power of managers over professionals, the loss of autonomy, poor pay and the burdens of bureaucracy have conspired to de-motivate many public sector professionals and thereby frustrate the enthusiastic implementation of 'modernising' policies (Terry, 2003: 2–3; Massey, 2002).

The years of reform and modernisation have been rooted in two principal instruments, or levers. Government traditionally uses its power over money and structure to implement change. But:

> Over-reliance on the first of these in achieving policy leads to the risk of waste and inefficiency. Over-reliance on the second runs the risk of creating a sense of turbulence and inconsistency, leading to further waste and inefficiency. (Terry, 2003: 2)

The emphasis of all recent governments on inputs and threats of reform continue to reflect this and may prove as futile in achieving real change. Terry argues that the way forward to secure 'real' modernisation is to engage with the professional groups and explore how things actually work in the public sector, alongside an initiative to promote training, career development and leadership in public management (Terry, 2003: 3). The lessons of this book suggest that there certainly needs to be a reorientation away from inputs (official boasts about how many new doctors, teachers, police officers there are) and targets (official boasts about meeting officially set targets), towards an exploration of ways of delivering real improvements in outputs. The impact of regionalisation and devolution within the framework of a federalising European Union underscore the need to understand multi-level governance, within a differentiated polity (Rhodes *et al.*, 2003; Burch, Gomez and Hogwood, 2003; Doig, 2003). Society and governance have never been so complex and it has never been so difficult for policy makers to actually achieve their goals or to satisfy (frequently contradictory and conflicting) citizen demands.

In addition to the aforementioned continuing trends and issues, there is an underlying concern by some policy makers and observers with the notions of accountability and trust. We explored many of the attempts to make public officials and organisations accountable in a variety of ways and by using a variety of means throughout this book, but with an especial emphasis on the subject in Chapter 8. New forms of accountability will need to be linked to the need to increase citizens' trust in those officials. In addition to issues surrounding citizen and stakeholder preferences, contracts, best value, and the plethora of other reforms, one issue that will loom large in coming years regarding 'trust' will be the role of the central civil service. We have discussed many of the arguments elsewhere (Greenwood *et al.*, 2002; Rhodes *et al.*, 2003), but in the new devolved constitutional settlement, with the delivery of most services located in the devolved countries, local government, non-departmental public bodies and the private sector, the role and purpose of the central civil service is increasingly under scrutiny. The delivery, or executive functions of central government are largely agencified and marketised, while its role as a neutral policy adviser to ministers is under threat from a large increase in the number of special advisers (party-political apparatchiks and 'whiz-kids') drafted in to advise ministers and increasingly to oversee career officials (Wicks, 2003).

For some informed observers, the need to increase citizens' trust in the honesty and integrity of government is linked to the need to draw clearer boundaries between the career civil service, appointed advisers and ministers. One way of achieving this is to place the civil service onto a statutory basis – in other words to enact a Civil Service Act (Wicks, 2003). The reason for this is that with the perceived increase in the politicisation of the civil service it needs to be made clear that:

> The civil service is the principal instrument of central government for formulating and for ensuring the delivery of its programme. Yet while the institution of the civil service is the property of government – 'the transferable human technology' of government as it has been called – it is not the property of 'the government' of the day. (Wicks, 2003)

Wicks, amongst others, argues the need to remove the civil service from its feudal background as an appendage of the Crown and to give it a statutory basis in order to:

- Formally establish the civil service;
- Set out, in broad terms, the conditions on which the government of the day can maintain and use the civil service to formulate and implement its programme;
- Provide for the maintenance of codes of conduct regulating the conduct of civil servants and special advisers;

- Establish an independent Civil Service Commission with powers to assure the effective implementation of the provisions of the legislation. (Wicks, 2003: 2–3)

Such a solution is obviously not universally shared, but it has the benefit of ensuring clarity of structure and procedure, allowing citizens to locate the duties and functions of officials and ensure they are observably separate from those of ministers and party political appointees.

We began this book by asking a series of questions: What is public administration? What is public management? And we located those questions within the broader debate regarding the role and function of government and its relationship to individuals and civil society. The journey we have taken in this book, as with many quests, has provided us not with answers, but with more questions for the future. Increasingly, policy makers and citizens alike will be asking the basic questions:

- What is the purpose of government in the internationalised age of globalisation and (in the UK's position) Europeanisation?
- What is the proper relation of government and the private sphere of civil society to each other?
- How can we ensure proper accountability of government institutions to individual citizens in this internationalised age?

We have discussed aspects of these issues in terms of basic theoretical approaches, the new public management, regulatory regimes and so forth. As mentioned earlier, many of these issues are traceable back to ancient times and Plato's quest for 'justice'. We cannot give the answers, except to note that the imposition of one 'right' way is not the way forward.

Public administration will need to engage with a plurality of citizen perspectives, and a plurality of groups, including those who do not accept the notion of liberal democracy; militant groups, groups seeking to control and prevent environmental degradation and those with opposing views and interests and many others. We will need to wrestle with the role of supra-national government and notions of national sovereignty, balanced against a multiplicity of interests. Amid all of these debates we suggest that two principles will remain: the need to ensure that the authority of those in positions of power must rest upon the consent of those governed and that this must be an active participatory consent, not a grudging acceptance mired in apathy. Secondly, modernisation, as currently understood, will fail if it seeks to continue on its path of 'one best way' and the unseemly 'McDonaldisation' of the public sector.

References

Aberbach, J., and Rockman, B. (2000) *In the Web of Politics: Three Decades of the U.S. Federal Executive* (Washington, DC: Brookings Institute).

Aberbach, Joel D. and Rockman, Bert A. (2001) 'Reinventing Government, Or Reinventing Politics?', in B. Guy Peters and Jon Pierre (eds), *Politicians, Bureaucrats and Administrative Reform* (London: Routledge).

Adonis, Andrew (1994) 'The Transformation of the Conservative Party in the 1980s', in Andrew Adonis and Tim Hames (eds), *A Conservative Revolution? The Thatcher–Reagan Decade in Perspective* (Manchester: Manchester University Press).

Adonis, Andrew and Hames, Tim (eds) (1994) *A Conservative Revolution? The Thatcher–Reagan Decade in Perspective* (Manchester: Manchester University Press).

Ascher, K. (1987) *The Politics of Privatisation: Contracting Out Public Services* (Basingstoke: Macmillan).

Asenova, D., Beck, M., Akintoye, A., Hardcastle, C. and Chinyio, E. (2002) 'Partnership, Value For Money and Best Value in PFI Projects: Obstacles and Opportunities', *Public Policy and Administration*, 17(4), 5–19.

Baber, W.F. (1987) 'Privatizing Public Management: The Grace Commission and Its Critics', in S.H. Hanke (ed.) (1987), *Prospects for Privatization*, Proceedings of the Academy of Political Science, vol. 36, no. 3 (New York: APS).

Baggott, Rob (1998) *Health and Health Care in Britain* (Basingstoke: Macmillan, 2nd edition).

Barnekov, T., Boyle, R. and Rich, D. (1989) *Privatisation and Urban Policy in Britain and the United States* (Oxford: Oxford University Press).

Bellamy, C. and Taylor, J. (1998) *Governing in the Information Age* (Buckingham: Open University Press).

Bernstein, S. (2001) *The Compromise of Liberal Environmentalism* (New York: Columbia University Press).

Bloch, M. (ed.) (2004) *Marxist Analyses and Social Anthropology* (London: Routledge).

Borins, Sandford (2002) 'New Public Management, North American Style', in Kate McLaughlin, Stephen P. Osborne and Ewan Ferlie (eds), *New Public Management: Current Trends and Future Prospects* (London: Routledge).

Boyne, G., Gould-Williams, J., Law, J. and Walker, R. (2002) 'Best Value – Total Quality Management for Local Government', *Public Money and Management*, 22(3), 9–16.

Brack, Duncan (1996) 'Liberal Democrat Policy', in Don MacIver (ed.), *The Liberal Democrats* (Hemel Hempstead: Prentice Hall/Harvester Wheatsheaf).

Brereton, Don (1992) 'From Scrutinies to Market Testing: The Work of the Efficiency Unit', *Public Policy and Administration*, 7(3), 71–74.

Bruce, Allan (1997) 'Competitive Markets in the National Health Service', *Talking Politics*, 9(3), 184–88.

Bruce, Allan and Jonsson, Ernst (1996) *Competition in the Provision of Health Care: the Experience of the US, Sweden and Britain* (Aldershot: Arena).

Buchanan, J. (1999) *The Logical Foundations of Constitutional Liberty*, (Indianapolis: Liberty Fund).

Burch, M., Gomez, R. and Hogwood, P. (2003) 'Devolution and the EU', *Review*, 23, November, 3–7.

Butler, David (1973) 'Ministerial Responsibility in Australia and Britain', *Parliamentary Affairs*, 26(4), 403–14.

Butler, Sir Robin (1993) 'The Evolution of the Civil Service – a Progress Report', *Public Administration*, 71(3), 395–406.

Cabinet Office (1998) *Service First: the New Charter Programme* (London: Cabinet Office).

Cabinet Office (2000) *People's Panel: Newsletter*, No. 5 (London: Cabinet Office).

Cabinet Office (2001) *People's Panel: Newsletter*, No. 8 (London: Cabinet Office).

Cabinet Office (2002a) *People's Panel: Newsletter*, March (London: Cabinet Office).

Cabinet Office (2002b) *Reforming our Public Services: Principles into Practice*, Office of Public Service Reform (London: Cabinet Office).

Cabinet Office (2003a) *The Public Sector Benchmarking Service*, at http://www.benchmarking.gov.uk/default1.asp.

Cabinet Office (2003b) *The Charter Mark: Guide for Applicants*, London, Cabinet Office, also at http://www.chartermark.gov.uk/.

Cabinet Office (2003c) *The Nine Principles of Public Service Delivery*, at http://www.servicefirst.gov.uk/1998/introduc/nine.htm.

Cabinet Office (2003d) *Public Sector Excellence Programme*, at http://www.cabinet-office.gov.uk/eeg/1999/benchmarking.htm.

Caiden, G.E., Lover, R., Sipe, L.F. and Wong, M.M. (eds) (1983) *American Public Administration: A Biographical Guide to the Literature* (New York: Garland Publishing).

Campbell, John (1994) *Edward Heath: A Biography* (London: Pimlico).

Carroll, Peter and Steane, Peter (2002) 'Australia, the New Public Management and the New Millennium', in Kate McLaughlin, Stephen P. Osborne and Ewan Ferlie (eds), *New Public Management: Current Trends and Future Prospects* (London: Routledge).

Carter, N., Klein, R. and Day, P. (1992) *How Organisations Measure Success: the Use of Performance Indicators in Government* (London: Routledge).

Chancellor of the Exchequer (2002) *Opportunity and Security for All: Investing in an Enterprising, Fairer Britain: New Public Spending Plans 2003–2006* Cm 5570 (London: HMSO).

Chang, J. (1991) *Wild Swans: Three Daughters of China* (London: Flamingo).

Chapman, Richard (1992) 'The End of the Civil Service?', *Teaching Public Administration*, 12(2), 1–5.

Chapman, Richard (1997) 'The End of the Civil Service', in Peter Barberis (ed.), *The Civil Service in an Era of Change* (Aldershot: Dartmouth).

Clark, Alan (1998) *The Tories: Conservatives and the Nation State 1922–1997* (London: Weidenfeld and Nicolson).

Coleman, J. (2000) 'Examining the Value for Money of Deals Under the Private Finance Initiative/Public Private Partnership', *Public Policy and Administration*, 15(4), 71–81.

Considine, M. and Painter, M. (eds) (1997) *Managerialism: the Great Debate* (Melbourne: Melbourne University Press).

Cook, Chris (1998) *A Short History of the Liberal Party 1900–1997* (Basingstoke: Macmillan, 5th edition).

Cope, S. and Goodship, J. (2002) 'The Audit Commission and Public Services: Delivering for Whom?', *Public Money and Management*, 22(4), 33–40.

Cory, D. (2003) 'Could Do Better', *Public Finance*, 31 January–6 February, 22–23.

Crosland, Anthony (1956) *The Future of Socialism* (London: Jonathan Cape).

Dahl, Robert A. (1956) *Preface to Democratic Theory* (Chicago: University of Chicago Press).

DEFRA (2003) *Service First (Citizen's Charter and Complaints Procedures)*, at http://www.defra.gov.uk/corporate/opengov/servicefirst.htm.

Denham, A. (1996) *Think Tanks of the New Right* (Aldershot: Dartmouth).

Denny, Charlotte (2002) 'Britain Takes Steeper Dive into the Red', *The Guardian*, 28 November.

Department of Health (1991) *Working for Patients*, Cm 555 (London: HMSO).

Department of Health (2000) *The NHS Plan – A Plan for Investment: A Plan for Reform*, Cm 4818 (London: The Stationery Office).

Doig, I. (2003) 'Devolution in Scotland – a Progress Report', *Review*, 23, November, 14–16.

Draper, Derek (1997) *Blair's Hundred Days* (London: Faber & Faber).

Drewry, Gavin (1988) 'Forward from FMI: "The Next Steps" ', *Public Law*, Winter, 505–15.

Drewry, Gavin (ed.) (1988) *The New Select Committees: a Study of the 1979 Reforms* (Oxford: Clarendon Press, 2nd edition).

Dunleavy, P. (1985) 'Bureaucrats, Budgets and the Growth of the State: Reconstructing an Incremental Model', *British Journal of Political Science*, 15(3).

Dunleavy, P. (1986) 'Explaining the Privatisation Boom: Public Choice versus Radical Approaches', *Public Administration*, 64(2), 13–34.

Dunleavy, P. (1989) 'The Architecture of the British Central State: Parts 1 and 2', *Public Administration*, 67(3 and 4), 249–75 and 391–417.

Dunleavy, P. (1991) *Democracy, Bureaucracy and Public Choice: Economic Explanations in Political Science* (Hemel Hempstead: Harvester Wheatsheaf).

Dunleavy, P. and O'Leary, B. (1987) *Theories of the State: the Politics of Liberal Democracy* (Basingstoke: Macmillan).

Dunsire, A. (1973) *Administration: the Word and the Science* (London: Martin Robertson).

Durham, P. (1987) *Output and Performance Measurement in Central Government: Some Practical Achievements* (London: HM Treasury).

Efficiency Unit (1988) *Improving Management in Government: the Next Steps* (London: HMSO).

Efficiency Unit (1991) *Making the Most of Next Steps: the Management of Minister's Departments and Their Executive Agencies* (London: HMSO).

Elcock, Howard (1991) *Change and Decay? Public Administration in the 1990s* (Harlow: Longman).

Elcock, Howard and Jordan, Grant (1987) *Learning from Local Authority Budgeting* (Aldershot: Avebury).

Elcock, Howard, Jordan, Grant, Midwinter, Arthur, with Boyne, George (1989) *Budgeting in Local Government: Managing the Margins* (Harlow: Longman).

Elliot, Larry and MacAskill, Ewen (1998) 'Brown's £12 Billion Sale', *The Guardian*, 12 June.

Ellis, J. (2000) *Founding Brothers: the Revolutionary Generation* (New York: Vintage Books).

Etzioni, A. (1993) *The Spirit of Community: Rights, Responsibilities and the Communitarian Agenda* (New York: Crown Publishers).

Etzioni, A. (1994) 'Who Should Pay for Care?', *The Sunday Times*, 3 July, quoted in Parsons, 1995.

Falconer, Peter (1996) 'Consumerism and Charterism', in Robert Pyper (ed.), *Aspects of Accountability in the British System of Government* (Eastham: Tudor).

Farnham, D. and Horton, S. (eds) (1999) *Public Management in Britain* (Basingstoke: Palgrave).

Ferlie, E. and Fitzgerald, L. (2002) 'The Sustainability of the New Public Management', in McLaughlin et al., *New Public Management: Current Trends and Future Prospects* (London: Routledge).

Flinders, Matthew (2001) *The Politics of Accountability in the Modern State* (Aldershot: Ashgate).

Flinders, Matthew and Cole, M. (1999) 'Opening Pandora's Box? New Labour and the Quango State', *Talking Politics*, 12(1).

Flinders, Matthew and Smith, Martin (eds) (1999) *Quangos, Accountability and Reform* (Basingstoke: Macmillan).

Flynn, N. (1990) *Public Sector Management* (London: Harvester Wheatsheaf).

Flynn, Norman (1997) *Public Sector Management* (Hemel Hempstead: Prentice Hall/Harvester Wheatsheaf, 3rd edition).

Foote, Geoffrey (1997) *The Labour Party's Political Thought: a History* (Basingstoke: Macmillan, 3rd edition).

Friedman, M. (1962) *Capitalism and Freedom* (Chicago: University of Chicago Press).

Friedman, M. (1980) *Free to Choose* (Harmondsworth: Pelican Books).

Fulton Report (1968) *The Civil Service* Cmnd 3638 (London: HMSO).

Garrett, John (1980) *Managing the Civil Service* (London: Heinemann).

Giddens, Anthony (1998) *The Third Way: the Renewal of Social Democracy* (Cambridge: Polity Press).

Giddens, Anthony (2000) *The Third Way and Its Critics* (Cambridge: Polity Press).

Giddens, Anthony (2002) *Where Now for New Labour?* (Cambridge: Polity Press).

Gillie, Alan (1994) 'The Unified Budget: Expenditure Plans and Taxation', in P. Jackson and M. Lavender (eds), *The Public Services Yearbook 1994* (London: Chapman & Hall).

Grace, C. (2003) 'Regulation: the Modern Idiom', *Public Money and Management,* 22(2), 73–4.

Gray, Andrew and Jenkins, William I. (1985) *Administrative Politics in British Government* (Brighton: Wheatsheaf).

Gray, J. (2004) *Al Qaeda and What It Means to Be Modern* (London: Faber & Faber).

Greenwood, John, Pyper, Robert and Wilson, David (2002) *New Public Administration in Britain* (London: Routledge).

Greer, Patricia (1992) 'The Next Steps Initiative: the Transformation of Britain's Civil Service', *The Political Quarterly,* 63(2), 222–27.

Greer, Patricia (1994) *Transforming Central Government: the Next Steps Initiative* (Buckingham: Open University Press).

Gregory, Roy and Pearson, Jane (1992) 'The Parliamentary Ombudsman After Twenty Five Years', *Public Administration,* 70(4), 469–98.

Halligan, John (2001) 'Politicians, Bureaucrats and Public Sector Reform in Australia and New Zealand', in B. Guy Peters and Jon Pierre (eds), *Politicians, Bureaucrats and Administrative Reform* (London: Routledge).

Hart, H.L.A. (1968) *Punishment and Responsibility* (Oxford: Clarendon Press).

Hassan, Gerry (1999) *A Guide to the Scottish Parliament: the Shape of Things to Come* (Edinburgh: The Stationery Office).

Hassan, Gerry and Warhurst, Chris (eds) (2000) *The New Scottish Politics: the First Year of the Scottish Parliament and Beyond* (Edinburgh: The Stationery Office).

Hassan, Gerry and Warhurst, Chris (eds) (2002) *Anatomy of the New Scotland* (Edinburgh: Mainstream).

Haynes, P. (2003) *Managing Complexity in the Public Services* (Milton Keynes: Open University Press).

Hennessy, Peter (1990) *Cabinet* (London: Fontana).

Hennessy, Peter (1989) *Whitehall* (London: Secker & Warburg).

Hennessy, Peter (1993) 'Questions of Ethics for Government', *FDA News,* 13(1).

Herman, Arthur (2002) *The Scottish Enlightenment: The Scots' Invention of the Modern World* (London: Fourth Estate).

Hickie, Des (1995) 'Conservatism, Theory and Public Service Management', in John Wilson (ed.), *Managing Public Services: Dealing With Dogma* (Eastham: Tudor).

Hinton, Peter and Wilson, Elisabeth (1993) 'Accountability', in John Wilson and Peter Hinton (eds), *Public Services in the 1990s* (Eastham: Tudor).

Hirschman, A. (1970) *Exit, Voice, and Loyalty* (Cambridge, Mass.: Harvard University Press).

HM Government (1994) *Better Accounting for the Taxpayer's Money: The Government's Proposals,* Cm 2626 (London: HMSO).

HM Government (1995) *Better Accounting for the Taxpayer's Money: The Government's Proposals,* Cm 2929 (London: HMSO).

HM Government (1998) *Modern Public Services Reform for Britain: Investing in Reform,* Cm 4011 (London: HMSO).

HM Treasury (1992) *Public Expenditure Analyses to 1994–95: Statistical Supplement to the 1991 Autumn Statement* (London: HMSO).

HM Treasury (1997) *Resource Accounting Manual* (London: HMSO).

HM Treasury (2000) *Public–Private Partnerships: the Government's Approach* (London: HM Treasury).

HM Treasury (2002) *Budget Report, 2002* (London: HM Treasury).

HM Treasury (2003) *Public–Private Partnerships: Helping to Deliver a Better Britain* (London: HM Treasury). See also www.hm-treasury.gov.uk.

Hogwood, Brian W., Judge, David and McVicar, Murray (2001) 'Agencies, Ministers and Civil Servants in Britain', in B. Guy Peters and Jon Pierre (eds), *Politicians, Bureaucrats and Administrative Reform* (London: Routledge).

Holland, P.F. (1988) 'Efficiency and Effectiveness in the Civil Service: the Rayner Scrutinies', *CIGPA Paper Number 2* (Sheffield: Sheffield City Polytechnic).

Holliday, I. (2000) 'Executives and Administrations', in P. Dunleavy, A. Gamble, I. Holliday and G. Peele (eds), *Developments in British Politics* (London: Macmillan).

Hood, C. (1990) *Beyond the Public Bureaucracy State? Public Administration in the 1990s*, Inaugural lecture, London, LSE.

Hood, C. (1998) *The Art of the State: Culture, Rhetoric and Public Management* (Oxford: Oxford University Press).

Hood, C., Scott, C., James, O., Jones, G. and Travers, T. (1999) *Regulation Inside Government: Waste-Watchers, Quality Police, and Sleaze Busters* (Oxford: Oxford University Press).

Horton, Sylvia and Farnham, David (eds) (1999) *Public Management in Britain* (Basingstoke: Macmillan).

Hughes, Owen E. (1998) *Public Management and Administration: an Introduction* (Basingstoke: Macmillan, 2nd edition).

Hulme, Geoffrey (1994) 'Social Security', in P. Jackson and M. Lavender (eds), *The Public Services Yearbook 1994* (London: Chapman & Hall).

Hutton, Will (1996) *The State We're In* (London: Vintage, revised edition).

Jackson, P. (2001) 'Public Sector Added Value: Can Bureaucracy Deliver?', *Public Administration*, 79(1), 5–28.

Jackson, Peter (1988) 'Foreword', in Public Finance and Accountancy, *The Financial Management Initiative* (London: CIPFA).

Jackson, Peter M. and Price, Catherine M. (eds) (1994) *Privatisation and Regulation: a Review of the Issues* (Harlow: Longman).

James, Oliver (2003) *The Executive Agency Revolution in Whitehall: Public Interest versus Bureau-Shaping Perspectives* (Basingstoke: Palgrave Macmillan).

Jordan, G. (1997) 'Recycling or Reinventing? The Search for Governmental Efficiency', in A. Massey (ed.), *Globalization and Marketization of Government Services: Comparing Contemporary Public Sector Developments* (Basingstoke: Macmillan).

Jordan, Grant (1987) 'Introduction: Budgeting – Changing Expectations', in H. Elcock and G. Jordan (eds), *Learning From Local Authority Budgeting* (Aldershot: Avebury).

Keegan, William (1985) *Mrs Thatcher's Economic Experiment* (Harmondsworth: Penguin).

Kendall, Ian, Moon, Graham, North, Nancy and Horton, Sylvia (1996) 'The National Health Service', in David Farnham and Sylvia Horton (eds), *Managing the New Public Services* (Basingstoke: Macmillan, 2nd edition).

Kernaghan, Kenneth and Langford, John (1990) *The Responsible Public Servant* (Halifax, Nova Scotia: The Institute for Research on Public Policy and the Institute of Public Administration of Canada).

Klein, Rudolf (1995) *The New Politics of the NHS* (London: Longman, 3rd edition).

Kooiman, J. (2003) *Governing as Governance* (London: Sage).

Kuhn, T. (1970) (first published 1962) *The Structure of Scientific Revolutions* (Chicago: Chicago University Press).

Labour Party (1997) *New Labour: Because Britain Deserves Better* (London: Labour Party).

Labour Research (1993) *Privatising the Government* (London: Labour Research).

Laffin, M. and Thomas, A. (2000) 'Designing the National Assembly for Wales', *Parliamentary Affairs*, 53(3), 557–76.

Lawton, Alan and Rose, Aidan (1991) *Organisation and Management in the Public Sector* (London: Pitman).

Leach, S. (1995) 'The Strange Case of the Local Government Review', in John Stewart and Gerry Stoker (eds), *Local Government in the 1990s* (Basingstoke: Macmillan).

Lee, S. (2000) 'New Labour, New Centralism: the Centralisation of Policy and the Devolution of Administration in England and its Regions', *Public Policy and Administration*, 15(2), 96–109.

Leiserson, Avery (1964) 'Responsibility', in J. Gould and W.L. Kolb (eds) *A Dictionary of the Social Sciences* (London: Tavistock).

Liberal Democrats (1997) *Make the Difference* (London: Liberal Democrats).

Liberal Democrats (2001) *A Real Chance for Real Change* (London: Liberal Democrats).

Likierman, Andrew (1988) *Public Expenditure* (Harmondsworth: Penguin).

Likierman, Andrew (1998) 'Resource Accounting and Budgeting – Where Are We Now?', *Public Money and Management*, 18(2), 17–20.

Lindblom, Charles E. (1965) *The Intelligence of Democracy* (New York: Free Press).

Local Government Chronicle, 6 June 1997.

Lodge, M. (2002) 'Varieties of Europeanisation and the National Regulatory State', *Public Policy and Administration*, 17(2), 43–67.

Loveday, B. (2000) 'Managing Crime: Police Use of Crime Data as an Indicator of Effectiveness', *International Journal of the Sociology of Law*, 28, 215–37.

Ludlum, Steve and Smith, Martin J. (eds) (1996) *Contemporary British Conservatism* (Houndmills: Macmillan).

Lynch, Peter (2001) *Scottish Government and Politics* (Edinburgh: Edinburgh University Press).

MacIver, Don (ed.) (1996) *The Liberal Democrats* (Hemel Hempstead: Prentice Hall/Harvester Wheatsheaf).

Mandelson, P. and Liddle, R. (1996) *The Blair Revolution: Can New Labour Deliver?* (London: Faber & Faber).

Margetts, H. (1997) 'The Automated State', in A. Massey (ed.), *Globalization and Marketization of Government Services: Comparing Contemporary Public Sector Developments* (Basingstoke: Macmillan).

Marquand, D. (1988) *The Unprincipled Society* (London: Jonathan Cape).

Marsh, David (1991) 'Privatisation Under Mrs. Thatcher: a Review of the Literature', *Public Administration*, 69(1) Winter.

Marshall, Geoffrey (1986) *Constitutional Conventions: the Rules and Forms of Political Accountability* (Oxford: Clarendon Press).

Martin, S. (2000) 'Implementing "Best Value": Local Public Services in Transition', *Public Administration*, 78(1), 209–27.

Massey, A. (1988) *Technocrats and Nuclear Politics* (Aldershot: Avebury).

Massey, A. (1993) *Managing the Public Sector: a Comparative Analysis of the United Kingdom and the United States* (Aldershot: Edward Elgar).

Massey, A. (1993) *Managing the Public Sector: a Comparative Analysis of the United Kingdom and the United States* (Cheltenham: Edward Elgar).

Massey, A. (1995) *After Next Steps* (London: Cabinet Office).

Massey, A. (1997) 'In Search of the State: Markets Myths and Paradigms', in *Globalization and Marketization of Government Services: Comparing Contemporary Public Sector Developments* (Basingstoke: Macmillan).

Massey, A. (1999) 'Quality Issues in the Public Sector', *Public Policy and Administration*, 14(3), 1–5.

Massey, A. (2001) *Governance in the Age of Government*, Inaugural Lecture, (Portsmouth: University of Portsmouth).

Massey, A. (2002) *The State of Britain: a Guide to the UK Public Sector* (London: Public Management and Policy Association).

Massey, A. (2003) 'Europeanization as Modernization', in Butcher, T. and A. Massey (eds), *Modernizing Civil Services* (Cheltenham: Edward Elgar).

Massey, A. (2004) *Report on an ESRC Funded Workshop: Mapping the Future: Research into Public Policy, Administration and Management in Britain* (Swindon: ESRC).

McConnell, Allan (1996) 'Popular Accountability', in Pyper (ed.), *Aspects of Accountability in the British System of Government* (Eastham: Tudor).

McConnell, Allan (2000) 'Governance in Scotland, Wales and Northern Ireland', in R. Pyper and L. Robins (eds), *United Kingdom Governance* (London: Macmillan).

McCourt, W. and Minogue, M. (eds) (2001) *The Internationalization of Public Management: Reinventing the Third World State* (Cheltenham: Edward Elgar).

McLaughlin, Kate, Osborne, Stephen P. and Ferlie, Ewan (eds) (2002) *New Public Management: Current Trends and Future Prospects* (London: Routledge).

Meehan, E. (1999) 'The Belfast Agreement: Distinctiveness and Cross-Fertilisation in the UK's Devolution Programme', *Parliamentary Affairs*, 52(1), 19–31.

Mellett, Howard (1998) 'Editorial: Resource Accounting and Budgeting in the Public Sector', *Public Money and Management*, 18(2), 3–4.

Metcalf, Les and Richards, Sue (1990) *Improving Public Management* (London: Sage, 2nd edition).

Middlemas, K. (1979) *Politics in Industrial Society* (London: Deutsch).

Midwinter, Arthur and Monaghan, Claire (1993) *From Rates to the Poll Tax* (Edinburgh: Edinburgh University Press).

Minogue, M., Polidano, C. and Hulme, D. (eds) (1988) *Beyond the New Public Management: Changing Ideas and Practices in Governance* (Cheltenham: Edward Elgar).

Mosley, Paul (1988) 'Economic Policy', in H. Drucker, P. Dunleavy, A. Gamble and G. Peele (eds), *Developments in British Politics 2* (Houndmills: Macmillan, revised edition).

Mullard, Maurice (1993) *The Politics of Public Expenditure* (London: Routledge, 2nd edition).

National Audit Office (1997) *The Skye Bridge* (London: The Stationery Office).

National Audit Office (1997) *The Contributions Agency: the Contract to Develop and Operate the Replacement National Insurance Recording System* (London: The Stationery Office).

National Audit Office (1999a) *The Home Office: the Immigration and Nationality Directorate's Casework Programme* (London: The Stationery Office).

National Audit Office (1999b) *Examining the Value for Money of Deals under the Private Finance Initiative* (London: The Stationery Office).

National Audit Office (1999c) *Ministry of Defence: the Procurement of Non-Combat Vehicles for the Royal Air Force* (London: The Stationery Office).

National Audit Office (1999d) *The United Kingdom Passport Agency: the Passport Delays of Summer 1999* (London: The Stationery Office).

National Audit Office (2000a) *The Private Finance Initiative: the Contract for the Defence Fixed Telecommunications System* (London: The Stationery Office).

National Audit Office (2000b) *The Financial Analysis for the London Underground Public Private Partnerships* (London: The Stationery Office).

National Audit Office (2001) *Measuring the Performance of Government Departments* (London: NAO).

National Audit Office (2002) *Ministry of Defence: Redevelopment of MOD Main Building* (London: The Stationery Office).

National Audit Office (2003) *PFI: Construction Performance* (London: The Stationery Office).

Newman, Janet (2001) *Modernising Governance: New Labour, Policy and Society* (London: Sage).

Newman, Janet (2002) 'The New Public Management, Modernisation and Institutional Change: Disruptions, Disjunctures and Dilemmas', in Kate, McLaughlin, Stephen, P. Osborne and Ewan, Ferlie (eds), *New Public Management: Current Trends and Future Prospects* (London: Routledge).

Next Steps Team (1998) *Next Steps Briefing Note September 1998* (London: Cabinet Office).

Oates, Graham (1988) 'The FMI in Central Government', in Public Finance and Accountancy, *The Financial Management Initiative* (London: CIPFA).

O'Connor, J. (1973) *The Fiscal Crisis of the State* (New York: St Martin's Press).

Office of Public Services Reform (2002) *Better Government Services: Executive Agencies in the 21st Century* (London: Stationery Office).

Oliver, Dawn (1991) *Government in the United Kingdom: The Search for Accountability, Effectiveness and Citizenship* (Buckingham: Open University Press).

Olson, M. (1971) *The Logic of Collective Action* (New York: Schocken Books).

Osborne, David and Gaebler, Ted (1992) *Reinventing Government: How the Entrepreneurial Spirit is Transforming the Public Sector* (New York: Plume).

Osmond, J. (ed.) (1998) *The National Assembly Agenda* (Cardiff: The Institute of Welsh Affairs).

Osmond, J. (1999) *The Civil Service and the National Assembly* (Cardiff: The Institute of Welsh Affairs).

Ott, A.F. and Hartley, K. (1991) *Privatization and Economic Efficiency* (Aldershot: Edward Elgar).

Page, E. (1985) *Political Authority and Bureaucratic Power: a Comparative Analysis* (Brighton: Harvester Wheatsheaf).

Painter, Chris (1999) 'Public Service Reform from Thatcher to Blair: A Third Way', *Parliamentary Affairs*, 52(1), 94–112.

Parry, Richard (2001) 'Devolution, Integration and Modernisation in the United Kingdom Civil Service', *Public Policy and Administration*, 16(3), 53–67.

Parry, Richard and Jones, Amy (2000) 'The Transition from the Scottish Office to the Scottish Executive', *Public Policy and Administration*, 15(2), 53–66.

Parry, Richard, Hood, Christopher and James, Oliver (1997) 'Reinventing the Treasury: Economic Rationalism or an Econocrat's Fallacy of Control?', *Public Administration*, 75(3), 395–415.

Parsons, D.W. (1995) *Public Policy: an Introduction to the Theory and Practice of Policy Analysis* (Cheltenham: Edward Elgar).

Parsons, D.W. (2000) *Public Policy as Public Learning: an Inaugural Lecture*, London, Queen Mary, University of London.

Peters, B. Guy and Pierre, Jon (2001) *Politicians, Bureaucrats and Administrative Reform* (London: Routledge).

Pimlott, Ben and Rao, Nirmala (2002) *Governing London* (Oxford: Oxford University Press).

Plowden Report (1961) *Control of Public Expenditure* Cmnd 1432.

Pollitt, C. (1990) *Managerialism and the Public Services: the Anglo-American Experience* (Oxford: Basil Blackwell).

Price Waterhouse (1991) *Executive Agencies: Facts and Trends Edition 3* (London: Price Waterhouse).

Price Waterhouse (1992) *Executive Agencies: Facts and Trends Edition 4* (London: Price Waterhouse).

Price, D.K. (1983) *America's Unwritten Constitution* (Baton Rouge: Louisiana State University Press).

Prime Minister (1994) *The Civil Service: Continuity and Change* Command Paper 2627 Session 1993–94.

Prime Minister (1999) *Modernising Government* Command Paper 4310 Session 1998–99.

Prosser, Tony (1994) 'Regulation, Markets and Legitimacy', in Jeffrey Jowell and Dawn Oliver (eds), *The Changing Constitution* (Oxford: Clarendon Press).

Pyper, Robert (1991) 'The Politics of the Public Purse', *Politics Review*, 1(2), November, 13–18.

Pyper, Robert (1995a) *The British Civil Service* (Hemel Hempstead: Prentice Hall/Harvester Wheatsheaf).

Pyper, Robert (1995b) 'Ministerial Responsibility and Next Steps Agencies', in Philip Giddings (ed.), *Parliamentary Accountability: a Study of Parliament and Executive Agencies* (Basingstoke: Macmillan).

Pyper, Robert (ed.) (1996) *Aspects of Accountability in the British System of Government* (Eastham: Tudor).

Pyper, Robert (1999) 'The Civil Service: a Neglected Dimension of Devolution', *Public Money and Management*, 19(2), 45–9.

Pyper, Robert and Kirkpatrick, Iris (2001) 'The Early Impact of Devolution on Civil Service Accountability in Scotland', *Public Policy and Administration*, 16(3), 68–84.

Ranade, Wendy (1997) *A Future for the NHS? Health Care for the Millennium* (Harlow: Longman, 2nd edition).

Rashid, N. (1999) *Managing Performance in Local Government* (London: Kogan Page).

Rhodes, R.A.W. (1994) 'The Hollowing out of the State', *Political Quarterly*, 65(2), 138–51.

Rhodes, R.A.W. (1997) *Understanding Governance. Policy Networks, Governance: Reflexivity and Accountability* (Buckingham: Open University Press).

Rhodes, R.A.W., Carmichael, P., McMillan, J. and Massey, A. (2003) *Decentralizing the Civil Service: From Unitary State to Differentiated Polity in the United Kingdom* (Buckingham: Open University Press).

Richards, Sue (1987) 'The Financial Management Initiative', in J. Gretton and A. Harrision (eds), *Reshaping Central Government* (Hermitage: Policy Journals).

Richards, D. and Smith M. (2002) *Governance and Public Policy in the UK* (Oxford: Oxford University Press).

Riddell, Peter (1994) 'Ideology in Practice', in Andrew Adonis and Tim Hames (eds), *A Conservative Revolution? The Thatcher–Reagan Decade in Perspective* (Manchester: Manchester University Press).

Rogers, S. (1990) *Performance Management in Local Government* (Harlow: Longman).

Rourke, F. (ed.) (1986) *Bureaucratic Power in National Policy Making* (Boston: Little, Brown & Company, 4th edition).

Samuels, M. (1998) *Towards Best Practice: an Evaluation of the First Two Years of the Public Sector Benchmarking Project 1996–98* (London: Cabinet Office).

Sandholtz, W. and Stone Smith, A. (1998) *European Integration and Supranational Governance* (Oxford: Oxford University Press).

Saunders, P., and Harris, C. (1994) *Privatization and Popular Capitalism* (Buckingham: Open University Press).

Savage, S. and Atkinson, R. (eds) (2001) *Public Policy Under Blair* (Basingstoke: Palgrave).

Savas, E.S. (1987) *Privatisation: the Key to Better Government* (Chatham, NJ: Chatham House Publishers).

Schimmelfennig, F. (2000) 'International Socialisation', *European Journal of International Relations*, 6(1), 109–39.

Self, P. (1977) *Administrative Theories and Politics* (London: George Allen & Unwin, 2nd edition).

Self, P. (1993) *Government by the Market: The Politics of Public Choice* (Basingstoke: Palgrave Macmillan).

Shaw, Eric (1994) *The Labour Party Since 1979: Crisis and Transformation* (London: Routledge).

Sheaff, R., Pickard, S. and Smith, K. (2002) 'Public Service Responsiveness to Users' Demands and Needs: Theory, Practice and Primary Healthcare in England', *Public Administration*, 80(3), 435–54.

Shils, E. (1997) *The Virtue of Civility* (Indianapolis: Liberty Fund).

Sidney, A. (1996) *Discourses Concerning Government* (edited by Thomas West) (Indianapolis: Liberty Fund).

Simon, Herbert (1957) *Administrative Behaviour* (New York: Free Press).

Sisson, C.H. (1976) 'The Civil Service After Fulton', in W.J. Stankiewicz (ed.), *British Government in an Era of Reform* (London: Collier/Macmillan).

Skelcher, Chris (1998) *The Appointed State* (Buckingham: Open University Press).

Smith, M. (1999) *The Core Executive in Britain* (Basingstoke: Palgrave).

Smith, Martin J. (1996) 'Reforming the State', in Steve Ludlum and Martin J. Smith (eds), *Contemporary British Conservatism* (Basingstoke: Macmillan).

Smith, T. (1979) *The Politics of the Corporate Economy* (London: Martin Robertson).

Stillman, R. (1999) 'Conclusion: American versus European Public Administration', in J.M. Kickert and R. Stillman (eds), *The Modern State and its Study: New Administrative Sciences in a Changing Europe and United States* (Cheltenham: Edward Elgar).

Stivers, C. (1993) *Gender Images in Public Administration: Legitimacy and the Administrative State* (New York: Sage).

Stoker, Gerry (2004) *Transforming Local Governance: From Thatcherism to New Labour* (Basingstoke: Palgrave Macmillan).

Stone, I. (1987) *The Trial of Socrates* (Boston: Little, Brown & Company).

Sullivan, Helen and Skelcher, Chris (2002) *Working Across Boundaries* (Basingtoke: Palgrave Macmillan).

Swann, D. (1988) *The Retreat of the State: Deregulation and Privatisation in the UK and US* (London: Harvester Wheatsheaf).

Terry, F. (2003) 'Public Management – Time for a Re-Launch', *Review*, 23, November, 1–3.

Thain, Colin and Wright, Maurice (1992) 'Planning and Controlling Public Expenditure in the UK, Part 1: the Treasury's Public Expenditure Survey', *Public Administration*, 70(1), Spring, 3–24.

Thain, Colin and Wright, Maurice (1996) 'The Private Government of Public Money Revisited', in P. Barberis (ed.), *The Whitehall Reader* (Buckingham: Open University Press).

Theakston, Kevin (1995) *The Civil Service Since 1945* (Oxford: Blackwell).

Thomas, Richard (1997) 'Mr Balls Beams at Dream Come True', *The Guardian*, 7 May.

Tomalin, C. (2002) *Samuel Pepys: the Unequalled Self* (London: Penguin).

Travers, Tony (2003) *The Politics of London: Governing an Ungovernable City* (Basingstoke: Palgrave Macmillan).

Veljanovski, C. (1987) *Selling the State: Privatisation in Britain* (London: Weidenfeld & Nicolson).

Vickers, G. (1965) *The Art of Judgement* (London, Chapman & Hall).

Weber, M. (1946) 'Essay on Bureaucracy', in F. Rourke (1986), *Bureaucratic Power in National Policy Making* (Boston: Little, Brown & Company, 4th edition).

White Paper (1970) *The Reorganisation of Central Government* Cmnd 450, (London: HMSO).

White Paper (1982) *Efficiency and Effectiveness in the Civil Service* Cmnd 8616, (London: HMSO).

White, Michael (1998) 'Turning the Treasury Screw', *The Guardian*, 26 May.

Wholey, Joseph S. (1978) *Zero-Base Budgeting and Program Evaluation* (Lexington, Mass.: D.C. Heath & Company).

Wicks, N. (2002) *Defining the Boundaries within the Executive: Ministers, Special Advisers and the Permanent Civil Service: Issues and Questions Paper* (London: Committee on Standards in Public Life).

Wicks, N. (2003) *Why the Government Needs to Define the Boundaries Between Ministers, Civil Servants and Special Advisers*, PASC Conference, www.parliament.uk/parliamentary_committees/public../pasc_conference_wi cks.cf.

Wildavsky, Aaron (1964) *The Politics of the Budgetary Process* (Boston: Little, Brown & Company).

Wildavsky, Aaron (1975) *Budgeting: Comparative Theory of Budgetary Process* (Boston: Little, Brown & Company).

Wilding, P. (1982) *Professional Power and Social Welfare* (London: Routledge & Kegan Paul).

Willis, J. (1995) *The Paradox of Progress* (London: Radcliffe Medical Press).

Wilson, David and Game, Chris (1998) *Local Government in the United Kingdom* (Basingstoke: Macmillan, 2nd edition).

Woodhouse, Diana (1994) *Ministers and Parliament: Accountability in Theory and Practice* (Oxford: Oxford University Press).

Wynne, B. (1982) *Rationality and Ritual* (London: British Society for the History of Science).

Young, Ken and Rao, Nirmala (1997) *Local Government Since 1945* (Oxford: Blackwell).

Index